Italian
in 30 Days

Course Book

Italian
in 30 Days

**by Paola Frattola
and
Roberta Costantino**

Course Book

Berlitz Publishing
New York   Munich   Singapore

Contacting the Editors
Every effort has been made to provide accurate information in this publication, but changes are inevitable. The publisher cannot be responsible for any resulting loss, inconvenience or injury. We would appreciate it if readers would call our attention to any errors or outdated information by contacting Berlitz Publishing. email: comments@berlitzpublishing.com

Original edition: 2001 by Langenscheidt KG, Berlin and Munich

Berlitz Trademark Reg. U.S. Patent Office and other countries. Marca Registrada. Used under license from Berlitz Investment Corporation

Printed in China by CTPS, September 2010

Cover photo © photodisc/age fotostock

Cover design: Claudia Petrilli
Interior art: Ulf Marckwort, Kassel
Editorial: Emily Bernath, Gabrielle Docherty, Christopher Gross, Markus Kreiklem, Juergen Lorenz, Lorraine Sova

Contents

Introduction **11**

The Italian Language **12**

Italian Pronunciation **14**

Lesson 1   **Alla stazione**   **17**
At the station

Grammar: Present tense of **essere** *(to be)* ■ Gender of nouns and adjectives ■ Negation
Country and culture: Making friends

Lesson 2   **Finalmente a casa**   **23**
At home at last

Grammar: Present tense of **stare** (to stay, to remain) and **avere** (to have) ■ How are you? ■ Types of adjectives ■ Questions (I) ■ Cardinal numbers 0–10
Country and culture: Visiting people

Lesson 3   **L'appartamento**   **31**
The apartment

Grammar: Gender and number of nouns ■ The definite article ■ The indefinite article ■ **c'è – ci sono** ■ Cardinal numbers 11–20
Country and culture: Hospitality

Lesson 4   **Che tipo è Alessandra?**   **39**
What type of person is Alexandra?

Grammar: Present indicative of the 1st conjugation (verbs ending in **-are**) ■ Present tense of **fare** (to do) ■ Cardinal numbers 21–100
Country and culture: The Italian family

Lesson 5   **A tavola!**   45
            Dinner is ready!

Grammar: Present indicative of the 2nd and 3rd conjugation
(verbs ending in **-ere** and **-ire**) ▪ Cardinal numbers from 101
onwards
Country and culture: Buon appetito!

Test 1   52

Lesson 6   **Una telefonata**   54
            A telephone call

Grammar: Present tense of **dare, dire, scegliere, tenere, salire** ▪
Present tense of verbs ending in **-care** and **-gare**
▪ Special nouns
Country and culture: "Pronto"!

Lesson 7   **La famiglia Simoni**   63
            The Simoni family

Grammar: Questions (II) ▪ "How often?" ▪ Times of the day
Country and culture: One child ... "e basta!"

Lesson 8   **A Milano in giro per negozi**   71
            A stroll through downtown Milan

Grammar: Present tense of **andare** and **venire** ▪ The prepositions
in, a, di, da ▪ Ordinal numbers
Country and culture: Shopping in Italy

Lesson 9   **Primo giorno in ufficio**   79
            The first day at the office

Grammar: Reflexive verbs ▪ Days of the week ▪ Telling the time
Country and culture: Commuting in Italy

Lesson 10   **La sera, in un locale**   87
            An evening at a restaurant

Grammar: Present tense of **bere** ▪ Possessive pronouns
Country and culture: Who pays?

Test 2   **96**

Lesson 11   **Un fine settimana al mare**   **98**
A weekend by the sea

Grammar: Present tense of **sapere** ■ Modal verbs **potere, volere, dovere** ■ Prepositions + definite article
Country and culture: Holidays "all'italiana"

Lesson 12   **Il lunedì in ufficio**   **105**
Monday at the office

Grammar: Perfect tense (I)
Country and culture: "Tifosi" - everywhere!

Lesson 13   **Lo zio d'America**   **113**
The uncle from America

Grammar: Perfect tense (II) ■ Expressions of time
■ Months and seasons ■ Dates ■ Preposition **da**
Country and culture: Immigration in Italy

Lesson 14   **Al mercato rionale**   **121**
At the local market

Grammar: Partitive article ■ The pronoun **ne** ■ Indirect object pronouns ■ The verb **piacere** ■ Quantities
Country and culture: A buon mercato!

Lesson 15   **Dove andiamo stasera?**   **129**
Where're we going tonight?

Grammar: Direct object pronouns ■ Infinitive constructions
Country and culture: Going to the movies

Test 3   **136**

Lesson 16   **In macchina in città**   **138**
Driving in the city

Grammar: Imperative ■ Prepositions defining location
Country and culture: Driving in Italy

Lesson 17 **Una gita a Firenze** **147**
A trip to Florence

Grammar: Double pronouns ▪ Infinitive and pronoun
▪ **ecco! – eccolo!**
Country and culture: Tourist information

Lesson 18 **Una telefonata di lavoro** **155**
A business call

Grammar: Pronouns in the Imperative ▪ Spelling words
Country and culture: On the phone

Lesson 19 **Davanti al televisore** **163**
Watching TV

Grammar: The present progressive with **stare** + gerund
▪ Present tense of **uscire** ▪ Double negatives ▪ Preposition **di**
Country and culture: Television in Italy

Lesson 20 **Un giorno di festa** **171**
A holiday

Grammar: Perfect tense and pronouns ▪ Prepositions **a** and **in**
Country and culture: Italian holidays

Test 4 **180**

Lesson 21 **La nonna racconta** **182**
Grandmother remembers

Grammar: Imperfect ▪ **mentre – durante** (while/during)
▪ Prepositions relating to time
Country and culture: Birthdays and name days

Lesson 22 **Sfilata di moda** **189**
The fashion show

Grammar: Comparative and superlative ▪ Other irregular
comparatives ▪ Comparative clauses ▪ Colour adjectives
▪ Irregular adjective forms
Country and culture: Italian fashion

Lesson 23 **Una lettera** **197**
A letter

Grammar: **si**-constructions ■ The weather
Country and culture: The weather

Lesson 24 **In farmacia** **205**
At the pharmacy

Grammar: Demonstrative pronouns ■ The body
Country and culture: The Italian health care system

Lesson 25 **Il corso di ginnastica** **213**
Gymnastics classes

Grammar: Personal pronouns
Country and culture: The Italian school system

Test 5 **220**

Lesson 26 **Un inconveniente** **222**
An inconvenience

Grammar: Conditional ■ **ci** ■ **credo di sì – credo di no**
Country and culture: Emergency services

Lesson 27 **Lezione di cucina** **231**
A cooking lesson

Grammar: **ci vuole – occorre – bisogna** ■ Prepositions defining
locations ■ **stare per** + infinitive
Country and culture: Sales receipts

Lesson 28 **Un invito** **239**
An invitation

Grammar: **qualche, qualcuno, qualcosa** ■ **nessuno, niente, nulla**
■ **ognuno, ogni** ■ **tutto** ■ Expressing feelings
Country and culture: Invitations

Lesson 29 **Valentina si sposa** 247
Valentina gets married

Grammar: Future tense ▪ Adverbs
Country and culture: Weddings

Lesson 30 **Progetti** 257
Plans for the future

Grammar: Relative clauses **che, cui, il quale, la quale**
Country and culture: Empty promises?

Key to exercises 262

Vocabulary 275

Introduction

Italian in 30 Days is a self-study course, which, in a very short time, will provide you with a basic knowledge of everyday Italian. This book is designed to familiarize you with the main grammatical structures of Italian and provide you with a good command of essential vocabulary. In 30 lessons you will acquire both an active and a passive understanding of the language, enabling you to function effectively in day-to-day life in Italian-speaking countries.

Each of the 30 lessons has the same pattern: first, there is a short text in Italian – generally a dialogue – then a grammar section, followed by a number of exercises to help you consolidate the knowledge already acquired. At the end of each lesson you will find a vocabulary list and short informative texts giving you an insight into everyday life in Italy. Each lesson is an episode in a story and focuses on typical day-to-day situations. The tests, together with the key to the exercises at the end of the book, will enable you to check the progress you are making.

The audio CD contains all the Italian dialogues from the book. Lessons 1-10 are spoken twice: the first time, quickly and fluently so that you get used to hearing everyday Italian and, the second time, slowly and more clearly. From lesson 11 onwards you'll be advanced enough to follow the Italian text, which will now be spoken only once, in the faster speech of everyday language.

The author and publishers wish you every success with the course and hope you enjoy using it.

Italian evolved from Latin, just as French, Spanish, Portuguese, and Romanian. What is known as standard Italian today dates back to when the great Italian novelist Alessandro Manzoni (1785-1873) gave Italy a national language by resolving that it should basically be Tuscan Italian with a heavy contribution from the Italian used in the other regions of Italy. The language spoken and written in Tuscany had taken precedence over the regional forms from the twelfth century to Manzoni's times because of the political, artistic and social prominence of Florence.

There are approximately 64 million speakers of Italian. These are the countries where you can expect to hear Italian spoken (figures are approximate):

Italy (**Italia**)

Italian is the national language, spoken by almost the entire population (59 million). Other languages: Sardinian in Sardinia (1.5 million); Rhaeto-Romanic in Friuli, near the border with Slovenia and Austria.

Switzerland (**Svizzera**)

Italian is one of the four official languages, spoken by about 800,000 people in the southern part, particularly the canton of Ticino. Other languages: German in the north (5 milllion); French in the west (1.3 million); Romansh in the east (50,000).

Italian is also spoken amongst large Italian immigrant communities, particularly in the United States (**Stati Uniti**), with almost 1.5 million speakers, and Canada (**Canada**), with over half a million speakers.

The Italian alphabet is the same as English, with the addition of accents which indicate stress only (see below). However, the letters j, k, w, x and y only appear in foreign words.

English has absorbed numerous Italian words, for example: balcony, studio, umbrella, volcano as well as terms in the fields of food (e.g. broccoli, macaroni, pizza, spaghetti) and music (e.g. concerto, piano, solo, trio, viola)

Italian Pronunciation

CONSONANTS

Letter	Approximate pronunciation	Example
c	1) before **e** and **i**, like *ch* in *chip*	**cerco**
	2) elsewhere, like *c* in *cat*	**conto**
ch	like *c* in *cat*	**che**
g	1) before *e* and **i**, like *j* in *jet*	**valigia**
	2) elsewhere, like *g* in *go*	**grande**
gh	like *g* in *go*	**ghiaccio**
gl	like *lli* in *million*	**gli**
gn	like *ni* in *onion*	**bagno**
h	always silent	**ha**
r	trilled like a Scottish *r*	**deriva**
s	1) generally like *s* in *sit*	**questo**
	2) sometimes like *z* in *zoo*	**viso**
sc	1) before e and i, like *sh* in *shut*	**uscita**
	2) elsewhere, like *sk* in *skin*	**scarpa**
z/zz	1) generally like *ts* in *hits*	**grazie**
	2) sometimes like *ds* in *roads*	**romanzo**

b, d, f, k, l, m, n, p, q, t and **v** are pronounced as in English.

VOWELS

a	1) short, like *a* in *cat*	**gatto**
	2) long, like *a* in *father*	**casa**
e	1) can always be pronounced like *ay* in *way*, but without moving tongue or lips	**sera**
	2) in correct speech, it is sometimes pronounced like *e* in *get* or, when long, more like *ai* in *hair*	**bello**

i	like *ee* in *meet*	**vini**
o	can always be pronounced like *o* in *go*	**sole**
u	1. like *oo* in *foot*	**fumo**
	2. like *w* in *well*	**buono**

In groups of vowels **a**, **e** and **o** are strong, and **i** and **u** are weak vowels. The following combinations occur:

two strong vowels	pronounced as two separate syllables	**beato**
a stong vowel and a weak vowel	1) the weak one is pronounced more quickly and with less stress than the strong one; such sounds are diphthongs and constitute only one syllable:	**piede**
	2) if the weak vowel is stressed, then it is pronounced as a separate syllable	**due**
two weak vowels	pronounced as a diphthong; it is generally the second one that is more strongly stressed	**guida**

STRESS

Generally, the vowel of the next to last syllable is stressed. When a final vowel is stressed, it has an accent written over it (**caffè**). Normally, when the stress falls on the syllable before the next to last one, it is not indicated by an accent.

A	ah	N	ehnneh
B	bee	O	o
C	chee	P	pee
D	dee	Q	koo
E	eh	R	ehrreh
F	ehffay	S	ehsseh
G	jee	T	tee
H	ahkah	U	oo
I	ee	V	voo
J	ee loonggah	W	voo doppeeah
K	kahppah	X	eeks
L	ehlleh	Y	ee grehkah
M	ehmmeh	Z	dzehtah

Alla stazione

Piera:	Scusi, Lei è Alessandra Jansen?
Persona:	No, mi dispiace, sono Silvia Lagosta.
Paolo:	Forse questa è Alessandra ...
Piera:	Ma no, Alessandra è bionda.
Valentina:	Mamma, ecco Alessandra, la ragazza con la valigia.
Piera:	Alessandra, Alessandra! Siamo qui! Ciao, cara!
Alexandra:	Buongiorno, signora Simoni.
Piera:	Benvenuta a Milano, cara, tutto bene?
Alexandra:	Sì, tutto bene, grazie, ma sono un po' stanca per il viaggio. Questo è Stefano, vero?
Piera:	No, questo non è Stefano, questo è Paolo, un amico di Valentina. Stefano è a casa, con la nonna.
Alexandra:	E questa è Valentina!
Valentina:	Giusto, io sono Valentina, piacere, Alessandra.
Alexandra:	Piacere.
Piera:	Ora andiamo, Alessandra è molto stanca, poverina, il viaggio è così lungo. Andiamo, andiamo!

At the station

Piera:	Excuse me, are you Alexandra Jansen?
Lady:	No, I'm sorry, I am Silvia Lagosta.
Paolo:	Maybe that is Alexandra …
Piera:	Surely not, Alexandra is blond.
Valentina:	Mum, there's Alexandra! The girl with the suitcase!
Piera:	Alexandra, Alexandra! Over here! Hello, dear!
Alexandra:	Hello, Mrs. Simoni.
Piera:	Welcome to Milan, dear, is everything OK?
Alexandra:	Yes, everything is fine, thank you. I am just a bit tired from the trip. That's Stefano, right?
Piera:	No, that's not Stefano, that's Paolo, a friend of Valentina's. Stefano is at home with grandma.
Alexandra:	And that is Valentina!
Valentina:	Right, I'm Valentina. Nice to meet you, Alexandra.
Alexandra:	Nice to meet you too.
Piera:	Let's go now. Alexandra is very tired, poor thing. The journey was very long. Let's go, let's go!

essere	*(to be)*	
io	**sono**	(I am)
tu	**sei**	(you are)
lui, lei, Lei	**è**	(he, she is; you [formal] are)
noi	**siamo**	(we are)
voi	**siete**	(you are)
loro	**sono**	(they are)

In Italian, verbs are often used without the subject pronoun (*io, tu, lui* etc.): Sono stanco (I am tired).

▪ *Lei* = "You" is the formal address used for women as well as men. The corresponding verb form is the third person singular: Lei è molto gentile. (You are very kind.)

Gender of nouns and adjectives

Italian has two grammatical genders: masculine and feminine. These are generally easily identifiable by their endings:

Questo è Paolo.   **ending with -o** = *masculine*   *plural* **-i**
Questa è Valentina.   **ending with -a** = *feminine*   *plural* **-e**

The same rule applies to many adjectives:
Alexandra è bionda.   *Alexandra e Valentina sono bionde.*
Stefano è biondo.   *Stefano e Paolo sono biondi.*

Negation

As a rule the negation **non** immediately precedes the verb.

*Questo **non** è Stefano.*

Can you separate these into individual words?	**1.** Valentinaèacasaconlanonna.	
	2. PaoloèunamicodiValentina.	*Exercise 1*
	3. NomidispiacenonsonoAlexandrasono Silvia.	
	4. Alexandraèlaragazzabiondaconlavaligia.	
	5. QuestononèPaoloquestoèStefano.	

Which parts belong together?	**1.** Questa è	**a** è stanca.	
	2. Il viaggio	**b** non è Stefano.	*Exercise 2*
	3. Piera non	**c** Lei è Silvia Lagosta?	
	4. Questo	**d** Alexandra.	
	5. Scusi,	**e** è lungo.	

Exercise 3

Arrange the various parts to form sentences.

1. Lei è – Scusi, – sono – mi dispiace, – Marina Valenti? – No, – Stefania De Vito

....
....

2. Stefano, – un amico – Questo – di – No – vero? – è – è – questo – Paolo, – Valentina

....
....

3. è – per il viaggio – Alexandra – un po' stanca

....
....

4. ragazza bionda – con – Alexandra – è – la – la valigia

....
....

5. ma a casa – non è alla – nonna – stazione – con la - Stefano

....
....

Exercise 4

Fill in the correct form of essere.

1. Questa .... Valentina.

2. La mamma .... stanca.

3. (Noi) .... alla stazione.

4. Paolo e Marco .... a scuola.

5. Il viaggio .... lungo.

6. Voi .... biondi.

7. Stefano e Paolo .... a casa.

Put the sentences
from exercise 4
into the negative.

1. ....

2. ....

3. ....

4. ....

5. ....

6. ....

7. ....

Exercise 5

Fill in the blanks.

Alexandra .... (1) la ragazza con .... (2)
valigia. Lei è .... (3) per il .... (4).

Valentina:	Ciao, Alexandra, ... (5) a Milano!
Alexandra:	(6)............. Valentina.
Valentina:	Tutto .... (7)?
Alexandra:	Sì, ... (8), tutto bene.
Valentina:	.... (9) un po' stanca?
Alexandra:	Sì, sono .... (10) stanca.
	.... (11) è Sandro?
Valentina:	No, questo non .... (12) Sandro,
	.... (13) .... (14) Stefano.
Alexandra:	.... (15)
Stefano:	.... (16).

Exercise 6

Vocabulary

a casa	at home	**mi dispiace**	I am sorry
alla stazione	at the station	**molto**	much, plenty
amico *m*	friend (male)	**no**	no
andiamo	let's go	**non**	not
benvenuto	welcome	**nonna** *f*	grandmother
biondo	blond	**ora**	now
buongiorno	good day, hello	**per il viaggio**	because of the journey
caro	dear	**piacere**	it's a pleasure to meet you
casa *f*	house, flat *Br* / apartment *Am*	**poverino**	poor thing
		questo/questa	this
ciao	hello, goodbye	**qui**	here
con	with	**ragazza** *f*	girl
così	so	**scuola** *f*	school
di	from	**scusi**	excuse me
ecco	here/there is	**sì**	yes
essere	to be	**signora** *f*	woman, lady
forse	maybe	**stanco**	tired
gentile	nice, friendly	**stazione** *f*	train station
giusto	correct, right	**tutto bene**	everything's OK
grazie	thank you		
lungo	long	**un po'**	a little
ma	but	**valigia** *f*	suitcase
mamma *f*	mum *Br* / mother *Am*	**vero**	true
		viaggio *m*	journey

Making friends   Italians change quickly from the formal you, *Lei* (singular) or *Loro* (plural), to the more informal *tu* (singular) or *voi* (plural). The latter are generally used when talking to close friends, relatives and children and among young people. It is customary to embrace as a form of greeting and to exchange a kiss on the cheek. With strangers it's polite to shake hands both when you meet and say goodbye.

Ciao! is an informal, universal expression meaning both hello and goodbye.

Finalmente a casa

Piera:	Finalmente a casa!
	Dov'è Stefano? Stefano, Stefano!
Stefano:	Sono qui, mamma. Ciao Alessandra.
Alexandra:	Ciao Stefano, come stai?
Stefano:	Bene, grazie, e tu?
Alexandra:	Non c'è male, grazie.
Carlotta:	Buongiorno.
Piera:	Questa è Carlotta, la nonna di
	Valentina e Stefano, e questa è Alessandra.

Carlotta:	Come?
Piera:	Questa è Alessandra
Alexandra:	Piacere, signora Carlotta.
Carlotta:	Piacere, Alessandra, e benvenuta. Come sta
	la mamma?
Alexandra:	Sta molto bene, grazie.
Piera :	La nonna è vecchia e un po' sorda.
(sottovoce)	Ha già 83 (ottantatré) anni ...
Carlotta:	Non ancora 83.
Piera:	Ah, sì, è vero. Per 5 (cinque) settimane
	ancora 82 (ottantadue).
Carlotta:	E non sono sorda.

At home at last

Piera:	At home at last! Where is Stefano?
	Stefano, Stefano!
Stefano:	I'm here, mum. Hello, Alexandra.
Alexandra:	Hello Stefano, how are you?
Stefano:	Fine, thanks, and you?
Alexandra:	Not bad, thank you.
Carlotta:	Hello.
Piera:	This is Carlotta, Valentina and Stefano's grandmother.
	And this is Alexandra.
Carlotta:	What's that?
Piera:	This is Alexandra.
Alexandra:	It's a pleasure to meet you, Mrs. Carlotta.
Carlotta:	It's nice to meet you too, Alexandra, welcome.
	How's your mother?
Alexandra:	She's fine, thank you.
Piera (aside):	Grandmother is old and can't hear very well.
	She is 83 ...
Carlotta:	Not 83 yet.
Piera:	Yes, you're right, you're still 82 for another five weeks.
Carlotta:	And I am not deaf.

stare	*(to stay, remain)*
io	*sto*
tu	*stai*
lui, lei, Lei	*sta*
noi	*stiamo*
voi	*state*
loro	*stanno*

How are you?

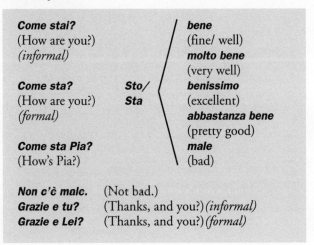

Come stai? (How are you?) *(informal)*		**bene** (fine/ well)
		molto bene (very well)
Come sta? (How are you?) *(formal)*	**Sto/ Sta**	**benissimo** (excellent)
		abbastanza bene (pretty good)
Come sta Pia? (How's Pia?)		**male** (bad)

Non c'è male. (Not bad.)
Grazie e tu? (Thanks, and you?) *(informal)*
Grazie e Lei? (Thanks, and you?) *(formal)*

---

avere	*(to have)*
io	*ho*
tu	*hai*
lui, lei, Lei	*ha*
noi	*abbiamo*
voi	*avete*
loro	*hanno*

■ **Idioms:** *avere* fame (to be hungry); *avere* sete (to be thirsty); *avere* nove anni (to be 9 years old).

Adjective

There are two types of adjectives in Italian:
1.

masculine:	**ending in** *singular* **-o**	*plural* **-i**
feminine:	**ending in** *singular* **-a**	*plural* **-e**

    *Marco è italian**o** – Marco e Sandro sono italian**i**.*

    *Maria è italian**a** – Maria e Sandra sono italian**e**.*

But: *Marco e Maria sono italian**i**.*

2.

Masculine and *feminine* adjectives in the *singular* **ending in -e** take the ending **-i** in the *plural*.

*Marc è frances**e**. Stephanie è frances**e**.*

*Marc e Pierre sono frances**i**.*

*Stephanie e Amelie sono frances**i**.*

Questions (I)

The statement is simply intonated differently, with the voice rising towards the end of the sentence:

Statement: *Valentina è italiana.* (Valentina is Italian.)

Question: *Valentina è italiana?* (Is Valentina Italian?)

Exercise 1

Fill in the correct form of *stare*.

1. Buongiorno, signora Lagosta, come
   ....?

2. Ciao Marco, come ....?

3. (Io) .... bene grazie, e tu?

4. Come .... Valentina?

5. La mamma .... bene, grazie.

6. Marco e Paolo .... molto bene. ▶

7. Come .... ? Stiamo bene, grazie.

8. Marco non .... molto bene oggi.

Which parts belong together?

1. Come sta	**a** stanno molto bene.
2. La nonna	**b** la nonna di Stefano.
3. Carlotta è	**c** stai?
4. Come	**d** Lei è Teresa Rossi?
5. Sandra e Guido	**e** Silvia?
6. Scusi,	**f** sta benissimo.

Which of these phrases are formal and which are informal?

1. Come stai?

2. E Lei?

3. Buonasera.

4. Ciao, Marco.

5. Come sta?

6. Sto bene, grazie, e tu?

7. Non c'è male, grazie, e Lei?

Formal: ....   Informal: ....

Fill in the correct form of *avere*.

1. Marco .... un amico a Berlino.

2. Ingrid .... una figlia.

3. La nonna .... 82 anni.

4. Marco e Paolo .... una casa a Roma.

5. (Tu) Non .... una valigia?

Exercise 5

Write out your answer to the questions using the words in brackets.

1. Come stai?

....

(bene)

2. Dov'è Stefano?

....

(casa – nonna)

3. Questo è Marco?

....

(No – Paolo)

4. Sei stanca?

....

(Sì – molto)

5. Valentina è tedesca?

....

(No)

Exercise 6

Which word doesn't belong?

1. buongiorno – ciao – come – buonasera

2. nonna – figlia – sorda – mamma

3. valigia – stazione – viaggio – anni

Exercise 7

Match each adjective to the respective country.

1. inglese	**a** Svizzera
2. francese	**b** Svezia
3. italiano	**c** Inghilterra
4. spagnolo	**d** Germania
5. tedesco	**e** Francia
6. svizzero	**f** Italia
7. giapponese	**g** Spagna
8. svedese	**h** Giappone

Insert the correct adjective. Pay special attention to the endings!

Marco è .... (1) (Italia). Lui ha molti amici:
John è .... (2) (Inghilterra), Bernhard è .... (3) (Svizzera), Valentina è .... (4) (Italia), Anna e Teresa sono .... (5)(Spagna), Hotohico è .... (6) (Giappone) e Simone, Pierre e Janine sono .... (7) (Francia).

Exercise 8

Cardinal numbers (0 – 10)

0 zero	3 tre	6 sei	9 nove
1 uno	4 quattro	7 sette	10 dieci
2 due	5 cinque	8 otto	

Vocabulary

abbastanza	enough, pretty much	**finalmente**	at last, finally
ancora	still, yet	**francese**	French
anno *m*	year	**già**	already
avanti	come in	**giapponese**	Japanese
avere	to have	**ha 83 anni**	he/she is 83 years old
bene	good, fine	**inglese**	English
benissimo	excellent	**italiano**	Italian
buonasera	good evening	**male**	bad
come	how	**non ancora**	not yet
Come stai/sta?	How are you? (informal/ formal)	**non c'è male**	not bad
		oggi	today
		Permesso?	May I?
dove	where	**sete** *f*	thirst
e	and	**settimana** *f*	week
fame *f*	hunger	**sordo**	deaf, hard of hearing
figlia *f*	daughter	**sottovoce**	quietly

spagnolo	Spanish, Spaniard	**svizzero**	Swiss
stare	to stay, remain	**tedesco**	German
svedese	Swedish, Swede	**vecchio**	old

Visiting people

On entering someone else's house or flat (apartment) you would first ask **Permesso** or **È permesso?** (May I?). Expect a friendly **Avanti** (Come in).

When visiting friends it is not common to take off one's shoes before entering. However, you should not open an umbrella in someone else's place. This is said to bring bad luck.

L'appartamento

Alexandra:	Complimenti! Avete una casa molto bella.
Piera:	Sì, è grande, ma c'è sempre molto lavoro.
Alexandra:	Questa è la camera di Valentina?
Piera:	Sì e qui, a destra, c'è la camera di Stefano.
Alexandra:	Dov'è la cucina?
Piera:	La cucina è qui in fondo. Hai fame, Alessandra?
Alexandra:	No, grazie, non ancora.
Piera:	Se hai sete, il frigorifero è sempre pieno: coca-cola, aranciata, tè freddo...

Alexandra:	Grazie, signora Simoni, Lei è davvero molto gentile.
Piera:	Poi qui a destra c'è il soggiorno, con la televisione. E qui a sinistra c'è la tua camera da letto, Alessandra.
Alexandra:	Oh, che carina!
Piera:	Poi ci sono due bagni e ...

The apartment

Alexandra:	My compliments! You have a wonderful flat (apartment).
Piera:	Yes, it is large, but it's always a lot of work.
Alexandra:	Is that Valentina's room?
Piera:	Yes, and here to the right is Stefano's room.
Alexandra:	Where is the kitchen?
Piera:	The kitchen is at the back. Are you hungry, Alexandra?
Alexandra:	No thanks, not yet.
Piera:	If you are thirsty, the fridge is always full: cola, orangeade, iced tea …
Alexandra:	Thank you, Mrs. Simoni, that's very kind of you.
Piera:	Here, to the right is the living room with the TV. And here, to the left is your room, Alexandra.
Alexandra:	Oh, how nice!
Piera:	Then there are two bathrooms and …

Nouns

As indicated before, most Italian nouns ending in -o are masculine and those ending in -a are feminine.
In addition, there is a third group of nouns ending in -e.
Those nouns can be either masculine or feminine.
Their plural form ends in -i. For example:

padre (father)   = ending in **-e** = *masculine*   *plural:* **padri**

madre (mother) = ending in **-e** = *feminine*   *plural:* **madri**

The definite article

masculine		feminine	
singular	*plural*	*singular*	*plural*
il	**i**	**la**	**le**
il tavolo	**i tavoli**	**la casa**	**le case**
(the table)	(the tables)	(the house)	(the houses)

▨ **Exceptions:**

Words starting with a **vowel** or **h** carry the article *l'*
(masculine and feminine), in the plural **gli** (masculine) and
le (feminine).

Words starting with **z**, **s+consonant**, **ps** or **gn** carry the
article **lo** (plural **gli**) for masculine, feminine **la** – **le**, e.g.

masculine		feminine	
singular	*plural*	*singular*	*plural*
l'appartamento	**gli appartamenti**	**l'idea**	**le idee**
lo spagnolo	**gli spagnoli**	**la spagnola**	**le spagnole**
lo zio	**gli zii**	**la zia**	**le zie**

The indefinite article

masculine	feminine
un	**una**
un tavolo	**una casa**
(a table)	(a house)

▨ **Exceptions:**
Feminine nouns starting with a **vowel** or **h** are preceded by
un', while masculine nouns retain *un*. Masculine nouns
starting with **z**, **s+consonant**, **ps** or **gn**, are preceded by *uno*,
female nouns by *una*, e.g.

**un appartamento, un'idea, uno spagnolo,
una spagnola, uno zio, una zia.**

c'è... / ci sono ... (there is, there are)

C'è	**un bagno**	**Ci sono**	**due bagni**
	una casa		**tre case**
	una signora		**due signore**

Exercise 1

Masculine or feminine?
Fill in the correct form of the definite article and form the plural.

	singular	*plural*
1.	.... porta	....
2.	.... letto	....
3.	.... quadro	....
4.	.... sedia	....
5.	.... poltrona	....
6.	.... tappeto	....
7.	.... tavola	....

Can you guess which of the above nouns means what? Match the Italian to the corresponding English term.

door – bed – armchair – carpet – picture – chair – table

This is a slightly trickier version of exercise 1. Consult the vocabulary section if you need any help.	*singular*	*plural*
	1. .... chiave	....
	2. .... bicchiere	....
	3. .... televisione	....
	4. .... giornale	....
	5. .... madre	....
	6. .... padre	....

TV – glass – father – newspaper – mother – key

Exercise 2

Fill in the correct article.

il, l' or *lo*?

1. .... armadio
2. .... bagno
3. .... hotel
4. .... treno
5. .... appartamento
6. .... svedese

la or *l*?

7. .... camera
8. .... amica
9. .... zia
10. .... stazione
11. .... anitra
12. .... fame

Exercise 3

Add the indefinite article.

1. .... bagno
2. .... camera
3. .... cucina
4. .... amico
5. .... spagnolo
6. .... zio

7. .... stazione
8. .... amica
9. .... hotel
10. .... aranciata
11. .... treno
12. .... frigorifero

Exercise 4

Exercise 5

Describe this room in your own words.

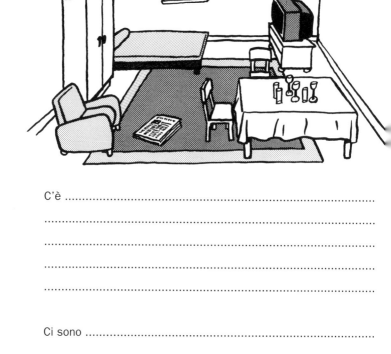

C'è ....

....

....

....

....

Ci sono ....

....

....

....

....

Form short sentences with the words listed in each line and the verb *essere*.

Pay particular attention to the endings of the adjectives.

1. frigorifero – pieno

....

2. camera – di Valentina – non – grande

....

3. casa – Simona – bello

....

4. Marco – gentile

....

5. zia – Valentina – gentile

....

6. Alexandra – tedesco – biondo

....

7. stazione – grande

....

8. appartamenti – grande

....

Cardinal numbers (11 – 20)

11 undici	**14** quattordici	**17** diciassette	**20** venti
12 dodici	**15** quindici	**18** diciotto	
13 tredici	**16** sedici	**19** diciannove	

a destra	right	**hotel** *m*	hotel
a sinistra	left	**idea** *f*	idea
amica *f*	friend (*female*)	**in fondo**	at the back,
appartamento *m*	flat *Br* /		at the end
	apartment *Am*	**lavoro** *m*	work
aranciata *f*	orangeade	**letto** *m*	bed
armadio *m*	wardrobe,	**madre** *f*	mother
	cabinet	**padre** *m*	father
bagno *m*	bathroom	**pieno**	full
bello	pretty, beautiful	**poi**	then
bicchiere *m*	glass	**poltrona** *f*	armchair
c'è/ci sono	there is/are	**porta** *f*	door
camera *f*	room	**quadro** *m*	picture
camera da	bedroom	**se**	if
letto *f*		**sedia** *f*	chair
Che carino!	How nice!	**sempre**	always
chiave *f*	key	**soggiorno** *m*	living room
Complimenti!	Congratulations!	**tappeto** *m*	carpet
complimento *m*	compliment	**tavolo** *m*	table
cucina *f*	kitchen	**tè** *m*	tea
davvero	really	**televisione** *f*	TV
freddo	cold	**treno** *m*	train
frigorifero *m*	refrigerator	**tuo**	your
giornale *m*	newspaper	**zia** *f*	aunt
grande	big, large	**zio** *m*	uncle

Hospitality Italian hospitality is well-known, and rightly so. Guests and friends enjoy lavish meals with multiple courses prepared for them, and everything is well arranged to make them feel welcome. Italians love to sit and talk so that their meals can last for hours. In return, visitors are expected to pay their hosts compliments and show their appreciation of the good food, the lovely home, the tasteful decorations etc. Italian praise usually is exuberant and very emotional.

Che tipo è Alessandra?

Alessandra è molto gentile e simpatica. Ora lei abita a
Milano, ma solo per tre mesi, per lavoro.
Alessandra è molto sportiva: gioca a tennis e a pallavolo e fa
joga. Suona anche il pianoforte, ma non molto bene.
Qualche volta guarda la televisione: lo sport e molti film. E
poi ama la natura: quando ha tempo fa lunghe passeggiate.
E naturalmente ama anche gli animali, soprattutto i gatti.
Parla inglese, francese, italiano e tedesco. Per questo viaggia
molto per lavoro: spesso è a Parigi, a Londra e a Milano.
Alessandra mangia volentieri la pizza e i dolci, ma quando
fa la dieta mangia solo insalata.

What type of person is Alexandra?

Alexandra is very kind and likeable. At the moment she lives
in Milan, but only for three months, because of her job.
Alexandra is very athletic: She plays tennis and volleyball and does
yoga. She also plays the piano, but not very well. Occasionally she

watches television: sport and lots of movies. And then she loves nature: When she finds the time she goes on long walks. Of course she also loves animals, above all cats. She speaks English, French, Italian and German. Therefore a lot of her travels are job related; she's often in Paris, London and Milan. Alexandra likes eating pizza and sweets, but when she goes on a diet, she eats only salad.

Conjugations

Italian has three different conjugations. Each of these conjugation groups has a different ending in the infinitive:

1. conjugation　　　　　*2. conjugation*　　　　　*3. conjugation*

-are　　　　　　　　　　**-ere**　　　　　　　　　　**-ire**

1. Conjugation – present indicative

	1. -are **parlare** (to speak)
io	parl**o**
tu	parl**i**
lui, lei, Lei	parl**a**
noi	parl**iamo**
voi	parl**ate**
loro	parl**ano**

Other verbs of this conjugation group include *lavorare, abitare, mangiare, viaggiare, guardare, amare* ...

fare	(to do)
io	faccio	noi	facciamo
tu	fai	voi	fate
lui, lei, Lei	fa	loro	fanno

▪ **Fare** is a verb with many uses. Becoming familiar with its different forms is important because they can be employed in many different situations.

fare la spesa (to go shopping)
   la maglia (to knit)
   una passeggiata (to go for a walk)
   le vacanze (to spend a holiday/ to go on vacation)
   freddo/caldo (to be cold/warm; it's cold = fa freddo)

Fill in the blanks.

Exercise 1

	guardare		
io	guardo	mangio	
Carla			abita
Valentina e Franco	guardano		

Insert the appropriate verb forms.

Exercise 2

1. Paolo .... a tennis. (giocare)

2. Marina non .... gli animali. (amare)

3. Gli amici di Valentina non .... tedesco. (parlare)

4. Io .... inglese. (parlare)

5. (Tu) ....il pianoforte. (suonare)

6. Guido .... in un ristorante. (lavorare) ▶

7. Valentina .... a Milano.
(abitare)

8. (Noi) .... spesso la televisione. (guardare)

9. (Voi) .... la natura. (amare)

10. (Io) .... a Milano. (lavorare)

Exercise 3

Fill in the appropriate forms of *fare*.

1. Simona .... le vacanze a Sanremo.

2. Valentina e Stefano .... la spesa.

3. Che cosa .... (tu) stasera?

4. Oggi .... freddo.

5. (Voi) .... ancora joga?

6. (Noi) .... una passeggiata.

Exercise 4

Complete the following text.

Che tipo è Valentina?

Valentina .... una ragazza ....
Lei .... a Milano. .... 23 anni e
non .... molto sportiv... ....
italiano e inglese e .... molto bene la
chitarra. Lei .... sempre la dieta e
.... insalata. .... spesso la
televisione e .... joga. Non ....
volentieri passeggiate. La mamma e il
papà di Valentina .... a Milano e
.... molto gentil... .

Write something about Paolo using the following words.

amico – Valentina – abitare Milano – 25 anni – sportivo – parlare italiano – non suonare chitarra – mangiare molti dolci – guardare – televisione.

Paolo è ....
....

Exercise 5

Cardinal numbers (21 – 100)

21	ventuno	27	ventisette	50	cinquanta
22	ventidue	28	ventotto	60	sessanta
23	ventitré	29	ventinove	70	settanta
24	ventiquattro	30	trenta	80	ottanta
25	venticinque	31	trentuno	90	novanta
26	ventisei	40	quaranta	100	cento

Write out the following numbers in full words.

13 ....   77 ....   66 ....

38 ....   92 ....   57 ....

54 ....   40 ....   99 ....

19 ....   23 ....   61 ....

27 ....   81 ....

46 ....   72 ....

Exercise 6

abitare	to live	**dieta** *f*	diet
amare	to love	**dolce** *m*	sweets *Br* /
anche	also		candy *Am*
animale *m*	animal	**ed**	and
caldo	warm	**fa freddo/**	it is cold/
che	which/who	**caldo**	warm
chitarra *f*	guitar	**fare**	to do

Vocabulary

fare la maglia	to knit	**per questo**	therefore
fare la spesa	to go shopping	**pianoforte** *m*	piano
		pizza *f*	pizza
fare le vacanze	to spend a holiday *Br* / to go on vacation *Am*	**qualche volta**	sometimes
		quando	when, if
		ristorante *m*	restaurant
film *m*	film, movie	**simpatico**	likeable
gatto *m*	cat	**solo**	only
giocare	to play	**soprattutto**	above all
giocare a pallavolo	to play volleyball	**spesa** *f*	shopping
		spesso	often
giocare a tennis	to play tennis	**sport** *m*	sport
		sportivo	sporty, athletic
guardare	to look	**suonare**	to play (an instrument), to ring
insalata *f*	salad, lettuce		
lavorare	to work		
maglia *f*	knitting	**tempo** *m*	time, weather
mangiare	to eat	**tipo** *m*	type
mese *m*	month	**vacanza** *f*	holiday *Br* / vacation *Am*
natura *f*	nature		
naturalmente	naturally	**viaggiare**	to travel, journey
papà *m*	father		
parlare	to speak	**volentieri**	gladly, like to
passeggiata *f*	walk		

The Italian family

The family continues to play a very prominent role in Italian life. Even today, many young Italians continue to live with their parents until they get married. Thereafter, the family network is relied upon for the upbringing of the children as well as the care of the elderly and sick. Most Italians, therefore, have a strong affinity to their hometown and are unlikely to move far away from it.

A tavola!

Valentina:	Mamma, ho fame. La cena è pronta?
Piera:	Sì, subito. Dov'è Stefano?
Valentina:	È in soggiorno con Alessandra. Sentono un po' di musica. Che cosa mangiamo stasera?
Piera:	Minestrone di verdura e saltimbocca alla romana. Stefano, Alessandra, la cena è pronta!!
Stefano:	Arriviamo, mamma. Il papà non torna a casa per cena?
Piera:	No, torna tardi. Ha molto lavoro.
Alexandra:	Buon appetito!
Tutti:	Grazie, altrettanto.
Alexandra:	Mmm, che buono questo minestrone!

Piera:	Grazie Alessandra. Preferisci l'acqua o il vino?
Alexandra:	Il vino, grazie, ma solo un bicchiere!
Piera:	Allora cin-cin, Alessandra.
Alexandra:	Alla vostra salute!
Piera:	Stefano, non spegni la televisione?
Stefano:	Non adesso, mamma, c'è lo sport.

Dinner is ready!

Valentina:	Mum, I am hungry. Is dinner ready?
Piera:	In a minute. Where is Stefano?
Valentina:	He is in the living room with Alexandra. They are listening to music. What's for dinner tonight?
Piera:	Vegetable soup and (Roman-style) veal cutlets. Stefano, Alexandra, dinner is served!
Stefano:	We're coming, mum. Is dad not coming home for dinner?
Piera:	No, he'll be back later. He's got a lot of work.
Alexandra:	Enjoy your dinner!
Alle:	Thanks, same to you.
Alexandra:	Hmmm, this vegetable soup is delicious!
Piera:	Thanks, Alexandra. Do you prefer water or wine?
Alexandra:	Wine, thank you, but just one glass.
Piera:	Cheers, Alexandra.
Alexandra:	To your health!
Piera:	Stefano, can't you turn off the TV?
Stefano:	Not now, mum, I'm watching sport.

2nd and 3rd conjugation – Present indicative

	2. **-ere**	3. **-ire**	
	prendere	**sentire**	**preferire**
io	prend**o**	sent**o**	prefer**isco**
tu	prend**i**	sent**i**	prefer**isci**
lui, lei, Lei	prend**e**	sent**e**	prefer**isce**
noi	prend**iamo**	sent**iamo**	prefer**iamo**
voi	prend**ete**	sent**ite**	prefer**ite**
loro	prend**ono**	sent**ono**	prefer**iscono**

A number of verbs from the 3rd conjugation have the syllable **– isc –** between the stem and the ending. Among them are verbs such as **capire** (to understand), **finire** (to end) and **pulire** (to clean).

Fill in the infinitive form.	**1.** capiscono	**6.** prendete ....
	2. torna	**7.** vedete ....
	3. finisce	**8.** guarda ....
	4. vendono	**9.** lavorate ....
	5. sente	**10.** credete ....

Exercise 1

Match the corresponding parts.

1. Stasera Marco   **a** guardo la televisione.

2. Voi   **b** sta la nonna?

3. Come   **c** capiscono il francese?

4. Qualche volta (io)   **d** parlate tedesco.

5. Silvia e Stefano   **e** non torna a casa.

6. Noi   **f** facciamo molto sport.

Exercise 2

Fill in the correct endings.

1. Stefano e Alexandra sent..... un po' di musica.

2. Il papà non torn..... a casa stasera.

3. Donatella prefer..... la birra.

4. Sandra e Guido guard..... la televisione.

5. (Tu) Cap..... l'italiano?

6. Tiziana pul..... la casa.

7. (Voi) Prend..... un caffè?

8. Alexandra arriv..... stasera.

Exercise 3

Exercise 4

Fill in the correct verb forms of *guardare – abitare – sentire – dormire – capire – preferire*.

1. La nonna è sorda, non .... molto bene.

2. (Voi) .... molto bene l'inglese.

3. (Io) .... volentieri la tele-visione.

4. I ragazzi .... la birra.

5. Stefano non .... molto la notte.

6. Sergio e Pietro .... a Napoli.

Exercise 5

Write up a short text from the pieces of information provided in the table below. The marked boxes indicate what the respective person is doing.
For example: Marco capisce il francese, non dorme molto e non guarda la TV.

	Marco	tu	Stefano e Valentina	la nonna
capire il francese	X	X		X
dormire molto		X	X	
guardare la tv		X		X

Write the
appropriate answers
to the questions.

1. Il papà torna a casa stasera per cena?
(No – tornare – tardi)

....

2. Stefano guarda la televisione?
(No – sentire – musica)

....

3. Alexandra beve la birra?
(No – preferire – acqua)

....

4. Simona parla tedesco?
(Sì   todesco – molto bene)

....

5. Hai fame? (Sì – fame)

....

Exercise 6

More cardinal numbers

101	centouno	100.000	centomila
126	centoventisei	300.000	trecentomila
200	duecento	1.000.000	un milione
300	trecento	5.000.000	cinque milioni
1000	mille	1.000.000.000	un miliardo
2000	duemila		

Note that Italian uses a comma instead of a decimal point,
and a period or space to indicate thousands.

Exercise 7

Write out the numerical values.

1. Ottocentonovantaquattro ....

2. Seicentotrentacinque ....

3. Duecentoventisette ....

4. Tremilanovecentosettantasei

   ....

5. Un milione seicentonovantamila-quattrocento

   ....

6. Millesettecentocinquanta

   ....

7. Tre milioni centotrentamila

   ....

8. Seicentosessantasettemilasette-centosessantasei

   ....

Vocabulary

acqua *f*	water	credere	to believe
adesso	now	dormire	to sleep
alla salute	to your health	espresso *m*	espresso
		finire	to end
altrettanto	to you too	minestrone *m*	minestrone, vegetable soup
appetito *m*	appetite		
arrivare	to arrive		
birra *f*	beer	musica *f*	music
buono	good	notte *f*	night
caffè *m*	coffee	per cena	for dinner
capire	to understand	preferire	to prefer
cappuccino *m*	coffee (with frothy milk)	primo *m*	(here:) first course
cena *f*	dinner	pronto	ready
che cosa	what	pulire	to clean
cin-cin	cheers		

saltimbocca alla romana *f*	Roman style veal cutlet	**tardi**	late
salute *f*	to your health	**tavola** *f*	dinner table
		tornare	to return
secondo *m*	(here:) second course	**tv** *f*	TV, to watch TV
		un po' di (+noun)	a little
sentire	to hear, feel	**vedere**	to watch, see
spegnere	to arrange, agree	**vendere**	to sell
		verdura *f*	vegetable
stasera	tonight	**vino** *m*	wine
subito	immediately	**vostro**	your

Buon appetito!

Most Italians start their day with a cup of coffee *(cappuccino, espresso)*, which they take in a bar on their way to work.

Lunch usually extends over two courses *il primo* – starters or appetizers, usually a plate of pasta – and *il secondo* – the second course of meat or fish with vegetables.

Before dinner, friends often meet up in a bar for a drink or an aperitif. Dinner also usually extends over a *primo* and a *secondo* course. The *primo* course will often be a warm dish, such as *minestrone* or noodle soup while the *secondo* course might just be something small, such as cheese or cold ham, but is also often another full dish. Meals are finished off with coffee *(espresso)*.

Mealtimes vary greatly between northern and southern Italy. Lunch *(pranzo)* is between 12:30 and 1:30 p.m., while dinner *(cena)* is between 7:30 and 8:30 p.m. In southern Italy, however, mealtimes can be even later.

Test 1

1 Choose the correct answer on square 2, then go on to the square with the number of your answer.

2 John è un ragazzo ... .

inglese ➪ 8
ingleso ➪ 15

6 Wrong!

Go back to number 8.

7 Wrong!

Go back to number 4.

11 Wrong!

Go back to number 29.

12 Very good! Continue:
... zio di Paolo è americano.
Lo ➪ 16
Il ➪ 24

16 Good! Continue:

Ciao, come ... ?
stai ➪ 19
hai ➪ 18

17 Wrong!

Go back to number 19.

21 Wrong!

Go back to number 13.

22 Correct!

End of exercise!

26 Wrong!

Go back to number 30.

27 Good! Contin
Stefano e Mar
sono ... .

italiane ➪ 23
italiani ➪ 12

Wrong! back to nber 5.	**4** Good! Continue: ... amico di Valentina è a Londra. L' ⇨ 20 Il ⇨ 7	**5** Correct! Continue: Alexandra è ... . biondo ⇨ 3 bionda ⇨ 13
Correct! Continue: arco ... la birra. efere ⇨ 6 eferisce ⇨ 25	**9** Wrong! Go back to number 25.	**10** Wrong! Go back to number 14.
Correct! Continue: arco ... un caffè. ndo ⇨ 21 nde ⇨ 29	**14** Very good! Continue: Noi ... la televisione. guardate ⇨ 10 guardiamo ⇨ 30	**15** Wrong! Go back to number 2.
Wrong! back to mber 16.	**19** Good! Continue: ... due camere da letto. C'è ⇨ 17 Ci sono ⇨ 22	**20** Great! Continue: In bagno c'è ... specchio. uno ⇨ 5 un ⇨ 28
Wrong! o back to umber 27.	**24** Wrong! Go back to number 12.	**25** Very good! Continue: Marco ... 15 anni. ha ⇨ 14 è ⇨ 9
Wrong! o back to umber 20.	**29** Great! Continue: Loro ... l'italiano. capano ⇨ 11 capiscono ⇨ 27	**30** Correct! Continue: ... tappeto è verde. Lo ⇨ 26 Il ⇨ 4

Una telefonata

Piera: Pronto?

Paolo: Buonasera signora, sono Paolo.
C'è Valentina per favore?

Piera: Ciao Paolo, un momento eh ... Valentina,
telefonooo! Tutto bene? I genitori come stanno?

Paolo: Bene grazie, sono in vacanza.

Piera: Oh, che bello! Ecco Valentina, a presto Paolo.

Valentina: Ciao, come stai?

Paolo: Benissimo e voi?

Valentina: Qui tutto tranquillo! La mamma cucina,
Stefano studia, io ascolto un po' di musica e
Alessandra guarda un film. Papà non è ancora
a casa.

Paolo: Come sta Alessandra? È contenta?

Valentina: Sì, molto. Domani andiamo in centro, così
vede un po' Milano. E lunedì comincia a
lavorare. E tu cosa fai?

Paolo: In questi giorni lavoro molto, ma perché sabato non facciamo una passeggiata o prendiamo
un caffè insieme al bar?

Valentina:	Un secondo, chiedo a Alessandra ...
	Dice che è d'accordo.
Paolo:	Benissimo, allora scegliete voi se preferite la
	passeggiata o il caffè.
Valentina:	Va bene, un bacione!
Paolo:	Ciao!

A telephone call

Piera:	Hello?
Paolo:	Good evening. This is Paolo.
	Is Valentina there?
Piera.	Hello Paolo, just a moment ... Valentina,
	telephone! Everything OK? How are your parents?
Paolo:	Fine thanks, they're on holiday (vacation).
Piera:	Oh, how nice! Here's Valentina, see you soon Paolo.
Valentina:	Hi, how are you?
Paolo:	Great, and what about you?
Valentina:	Everything's quiet around here! Mum's cooking, Stefano is studying, I am listening to some music and Alexandra is watching a movie. Dad is not home yet.
Paolo:	How is Alexandra? Is she happy?
Valentina:	Yes, very much so. Tomorrow we're going to the city centre so that she can see a little of Milan. She's starting work on Monday. And how are you doing?
Paolo:	I've got a lot of work these days, why don't we go for a walk on Saturday or have coffee together at a bar?
Valentina:	Just a second, I'll ask Alexandra ...
	She says that's fine with her.
Paolo:	Great, then you decide whether you'd rather go for a walk or have coffee.
Valentina:	OK, big kiss to you!
Paolo:	Bye!

Some irregular verbs

	dare (to give)	**dire** (to say)	**scegliere** (to choose)
io	do	dico	scelgo
tu	dai	dici	scegli
lui, lei, Lei	dà	dice	sceglie
noi	diamo	diciamo	scegliamo
voi	date	dite	scegliete
loro	danno	dicono	scelgono

	tenere (to hold, keep)	**salire** (to go/come up)
io	tengo	salgo
tu	tieni	sali
lui, lei, Lei	tiene	sale
noi	teniamo	saliamo
voi	tenete	salite
loro	tengono	salgono

Verbs ending in -care and -gare

Verbs ending in **-care** and **-gare** have an **-h** inserted before the ending **-i** or **-e**.

	giocare (to play)	**pagare** (to pay)
io	gioco	pago
tu	giochi	paghi
lui, lei, Lei	gioca	paga
noi	giochiamo	paghiamo
voi	giocate	pagate
loro	giocano	pagano

Special nouns

Nouns ending in **-a** that are masculine: *il cinema*
                                               il problema
Nouns ending in **-o** that are feminine: *la radio*

Some nouns share the same masculine and feminine form.
Among these are nouns ending in
-ista or **-ante**:   *il dentista   la dentista*
                                il cantante   la cantante

■ Special plural forms

masculine

-io	**-i**	*il negozio*	*i negozi*	**but:**	*lo zio*	*gli zii*
-co	**-chi**	*il tedesco*	*i tedeschi*	**but:**	*l'amico*	*gli amici*
-go	**-ghi**	*il lago*	*i laghi*			
-co	**-ci**	*l'austriaco*	*gli austriaci*	(if the stress is on		
-go	**-gi**	*l'asparago*	*gli asparagi*	the third last syllable)		

feminine

-ca	**-che**	*l'amica*	*le amiche*	
-ga	**-ghe**	*la strega*	*le streghe*	
-cia	**-ce**	*l'arancia*	*le arance*	(if preceded by
-gia	**-ge**	*la spiaggia*	*le spiagge*	a consonant)
-cia	**-cie**	*la camicia*	*le camicie*	(if preceded by
-gia	**-gie**	*la valigia*	*le valigie*	a vowel)

no change

il caffè	*i caffè*	(if the last vowel is
la città	*le città*	stressed or the if
il bar	*i bar*	the noun ends in
		a consonant)

But also: *il cinema/i cinema*
                la foto/le foto

irregular plural
l'uomo   gli uomini
l'uovo   le uova

Exercise 1

Complete the sentences by filling in the correct verb forms.

1. Maria .... (dare) la chitarra a Giovanni.

2. Che cosa (voi) .... (scegliere)?

3. (Io) .... (tenere) le bibite in frigorifero.

4. Oggi .... (pagare) noi la cena.

5. I genitori di Fabio .... (giocare) volentieri a tennis.

6. Laura .... (salire) le scale a piedi.

7. Scusa, che cosa (tu) .... (dire)?

8. (pagare) .... tu o (pagare) .... io?

Exercise 2

Match the corresponding parts to form sentences.

1. Alexandra dice   **a** prendete?

2. Dove tengono   **b** che è d'accordo.

3. Perché non sali   **c** a tennis?

4. Giochi volentieri   **d** le sigarette?

5. Che cosa   **e** in macchina?

6. Preferisci   **f** i genitori?

7. Come stanno   **g** acqua o vino?

Complete the crossword puzzle.

CRUCIVERBA

Exercise 3

Orizzontali

4. dire (io)

5. dire (loro)

8. pagare (noi)

9. tenere (io)

11. salire (io)

12. scegliere (lui)

13. salire (voi)

14. giocare (tu)

Verticali

1. dare (tu)

2. tenere (voi)

3. scegliere (loro)

4. dare (lei)

5. dare (noi)

6. pagare (voi)

7. giocare (noi)

10. dare (voi)

Exercise 4

Put these senten-
ces into the plu-
ral.

1. La valigia è leggera.

....

2. Il film è interessante.

....

3. La foto è molto bella.

....

4. L'arancia è buona.

....

5. Il medico è bravo.

....

6. L'amico di Marco è simpatico.

....

7. L'armadio è grande.

....

8. Il lago è vicino.

....

Exercise 5

Three short dialo-
gues have been
mixed up. Can you
separate them
again?

– Preferisci acqua o vino?
– No, grazie, non ancora.
– Ecco. Allora cin-cin!
– I genitori stanno bene?
– Dov'è la cucina?
– Che bello!
– La cucina è qui a destra. Hai fame?
– Vino, grazie.
– Sì grazie, sono in vacanza.

1. ....

....

....

2. ....

....

....

3. ....

....

....

a piedi	on foot	dare	to give
a presto	see you soon	dentista *m/f*	dentist
allora	so, then	dire	to say
arancia *f*	orange	domani	tomorrow
ascoltare	to listen, hear	foto *f*	photo
asparago *m*	asparagus	genitori *m/pl*	parents
austriaco *m*	Austrian	giorno *m*	day
bacione *m*	big kiss	in questi giorni	these days
bar *m*	(coffee) bar	insieme	together
bibita *f*	drink	interessante	interesting
bravo	good	lago *m*	lake
camicia *f*	shirt	lunedì *m*	Monday
cantante *m/f*	singer	momento *m*	moment
centro *m*	centre	negozio *m*	shop, store
che	that	o	or
Che bello!	How nice!	pagare	to pay
chiedere	to ask	per favore	please
cinema *m*	cinema	perché	why, because
città *f*	city, town	prendere	to take
cominciare	to start	problema *m*	problem
contento	happy, satisfied	pronto	hello (on the phone)
cucinare	to cook	radio *f*	radio
d'accordo	agreed	sabato *m*	Saturday ▶

salire	to go/come up	**telefonata** *f*	telephone call
scala *f*	stair	**telefono** *m*	telephone
scegliere	to choose, select	**tenere**	to hold
		tranquillo	calm, quiet
scusa	excuse me	**tutto**	all, whole
secondo *m*	second	**uomo** *m*	human being, man
sigaretta *f*	cigarette		
spiaggia *f*	beach	**uovo** *m*	egg
strega *f*	witch	**va bene**	OK
studiare	to study, learn	**vicino**	near (by)

"Pronto"!

When answering the phone in Italy, the standard response is "Pronto", which means "I am ready/I am prepared". As the person initiating the call your reply would be simply to greet the person and state who you are: *Ciao, sono ...* or in a more formal context *Buongiorno/Buonasera, sono ...*

La famiglia Simoni

La famiglia Simoni comprende cinque persone: la nonna Carlotta, la mamma Piera, il papà Luigi e i figli Valentina e Stefano.

La signora Carlotta è la mamma di Luigi; da tre anni vive con la famiglia del figlio perché ha alcuni problemi di salute e non è più giovane. Ma anche a ottantatré anni ha ancora molti interessi: guarda i film romantici alla televisione e cucina molto volentieri.

Piera è casalinga e quando ha un po' di tempo libero dipinge o incontra le amiche per prendere un tè insieme.

Luigi è dentista, lavora molto ma guadagna anche bene. È tifoso di calcio e qualche volta, come molti altri italiani, la domenica guarda la partita alla televisione; lui e la moglie amano molto l'opera.

Valentina ha 23 anni e studia economia. È fidanzata con Paolo. Ascolta volentieri musica rock con gli amici; ama sciare d'inverno e nuotare al mare d'estate.

Stefano ha 18 anni e frequenta l'ultimo anno di liceo. Legge molto, soprattutto libri di storia e ama viaggiare.

La famiglia Simoni vive a Milano in un grande appartamento, non proprio in centro ma in un quartiere molto tranquillo. I Simoni hanno anche una piccola casa per le vacanze in montagna.

The Simoni family

There are five people in the Simoni family: grandmother Carlotta; Piera, the mother; Luigi, the father; and Valentina and Stefano, the children.

Mrs. Carlotta is Luigi's mother. She has been living with her son's family for three years now because she has some health problems and because she is not so young any more. Yet even at the age of 83 she still has many interests. She watches romantic movies on TV and she enjoys cooking very much.

Piera is a housewife. In her spare time she enjoys painting or meeting with friends to have a cup of tea together.

Luigi is a dentist. He works a lot but also has a good income. He is a soccer fan, who, like many other Italians, sometimes watches games on TV on Sunday. He and his wife also love the opera.

Valentina is 23 years old and is studying economics. She is engaged to Paolo. She enjoys listening to rock music with her friends, she loves to go skiing in the winter and swimming in the sea in the summer.

Stefano is 18 years old and is in his last year of secondary school. He reads a lot, above all history books, and he loves to travel.

The Simoni family lives in a large flat (apartment) in Milan not close to the centre of town but in a very quiet neighbourhood.

The Simoni family also has a small holiday (vacation) home in the mountains.

Questions (II)

Chi?	Who?	*Chi è?* *È Stefano, il fratello di Valentina.*
Che cosa? **Che?** **Cosa?**	What?	*Che cosa/Che/Cosa mangi?* *Mangio una banana.*
Dove?	Where?	*Dov'è la cucina?* *La cucina è qui a destra.*
Come?	How?	*Come sta Piera?* *Sta bene, grazie.*
Perché?	Why?	*Perché non mangi la pizza?* *Perché sono a dieta.* ▶

| **Quando?** | When? | *Quando guardi la televisione?* |
| | | *Qualche volta, la sera.* |

Quale?	Which?	*Quale/Che vino prendi,*
Che?		*rosso o bianco?*
		Rosso, grazie.

Quanto/a/i/e	How much?	*Quanto costa? Dieci euro.*
	How many?	*Quanti figli ha? Tre.*
		Quanti anni ha? Trentacinque.

■ The regular order of words in questions with interrogative pronouns is:

Interrogative pronoun + verb + subject:

Che cosa fa Marla?

■ Questions without an interrogative pronoun generally have the same word order as the statement. (See Lesson 2.)

Franco è italiano? **question**
Franco è italiano. **statement**

How often?

non....mai	never	*Non mangio mai la pasta.*
raramente	seldom	*Leggo raramente.*
qualche volta	occasionally	*Qualche volta prendo l'autobus.*
spesso	often	*Lavoro spesso la domenica.*
sempre	always	*Parlo sempre italiano.*

Times of the day

il mattino/la mattina	early morning/morning
il pomeriggio	afternoon
la sera	evening
la notte	night

Exercise 1

Fill in the correct interrogative pronouns.

1. .... suoni il pianoforte? La domenica.

2. ....fate d'estate? Facciamo un viaggio.

3. .... fate le vacanze? In Francia.

4. .... anni ha la nonna? Ottantatré.

5. .... studi l'italiano? Perché è una bella lingua.

6. .... è la signora con la valigia? È la signora Bruni.

7. .... camera hai? La camera numero dodici.

8. .... stai? Non c'è male.

Exercise 2

Answer the following questions as in the example given.

Quando guardi la televisione?   (mai)
Non guardo mai la televisione.

1. Quando fate una passeggiata?
                    (spesso)

    ....

2. Quando mangi gli spaghetti?   (mai)

    ....

3. Quando legge il giornale Marco?
                          (sempre)

....

4. Lavori il sabato?   (qualche volta)

....

5. Viaggiate spesso? (raramente)

....

Repeat the three different forms of conjugations using these three new verbs.	*fumare* (to smoke), *chiudere* (to close), *aprire* (to open)		
	FUMARE	CHIUDERE	APRIRE
io	....	....	....
tu	....	....	....
lui, lei, Lei	....	....	....
noi	....	....	....
voi	....	....	....
loro	....	....	....

Exercise 3

Calculate the simple arithmetics and write out the result in words.

1. 35 + 42 =

....

2. 69 + 110 =

....

3. 1.350 + 800 =

....

4. 7.500 + 5.400 =

....

▶

Exercise 4

5. $41 + 86 =$

....

6. $10.900 + 4.700 =$

....

Exercise 5

The list includes a number of familiar words. Fill in the definite article and then give the plural form.

1. ..... mamma ....

2. ..... spagnolo ....

3. ..... animale ....

4. ..... bagno ....

5. ..... aranciata ....

6. ..... vacanza ....

7. ..... televisione ....

8. ..... appartamento ....

9. ..... bar ....

10. ..... valigia ....

Exercise 6

Rephrase the sentences by putting the nouns into the plural.

1. La signora ha una macchina.

....

2. L' appartamento è piccolo.

....

3. Il gatto sta bene.

....

4. Il libro è interessante.

....

5. La ragazza gioca a tennis.

.... ▶

6. Mangio sempre la pizza.

. . . .

7. L'amica di Mara è gentile.

. . . .

alcuni	a few	**in montagna**	in the mountains
altro	others		
aprire	to open	**incontrare**	to meet
autobus *m*	bus	**interesse** *m*	interest
banana *f*	banana	**leggere**	to read
bianco	white	**libro** *m*	book
calcio *m*	football (soccer)	**liceo** *m*	secondary school (high school)
casalinga *f*	housewife		
chi	who	**lingua** *f*	language
chiudere	to close	**macchina** *f*	car
comprendere	to consist of, understand	**mai**	never
		mare *m*	sea
costare	to cost	**mattina** *f*	morning
d'estate	in the summer	**mattino** *m*	early morning
		moglie *f*	wife
d'inverno	in the winter	**montagna** *f*	mountain
da tre anni	since three years	**numero** *m*	number
		nuotare	to swim
dipingere	to paint	**opera** *f*	opera
domenica *f*	Sunday	**partita** *f*	match *Br* / game *Am*
economia *f*	economics		
famiglia *f*	family	**pasta** *f*	pasta
fidanzato	engaged	**persona** *f*	person
figlio *m*	son	**piccolo**	small
fratello *m*	brother	**più**	more
frequentare	to visit	**pomeriggio** *m*	afternoon
fumare	to smoke	**proprio**	straight, exact
giovane	young	**quale**	which
guadagnare	to earn	**quanto**	how much

quartiere *m*	neighbourhood	**tempo**	free time,
raramente	seldom	**libero** *m*	leisure time
romantico	romantic	**tifoso** *m*	football *Br* /
rosso	red		soccer *Am* fan
sciare	to ski	**ultimo**	last
sera *f*	evening	**vivere**	to live
storia *f*	history		

One child ... "e basta"

Contrary to popular belief, the Italian extended family has also become a thing of the past. For years now Italy has ranked as one of the countries with the lowest birth rate. The nuclear family with its single child has become the standard family size. One major factor in this development is the improved education and professional status of women. To the Italian sentiment, though, **la famiglia** still stands as a cherished institution.

A Milano in giro per negozi

Alexandra:	Valentina! Sono qui!
Valentina:	Ciao Alessandra, come stai?
Alexandra:	Bene, grazie. Allora, vieni in centro a fare un giro per negozi?
Valentina:	Sì, vengo volentieri, così faccio anche qualche commissione. Prendiamo il tram?
Alexandra:	Forse la metropolitana è più veloce. D'accordo?
Valentina:	D'accordo, andiamo.

Alexandra:	Quanti negozi di abbigliamento! E tutti molto eleganti!
Valentina:	Eh sì e ... costosi! Guarda che bel vestito azzurro; è di Giorgio Armani.
Alexandra:	Sì, ma anche la ditta dove lavoro io fa vestiti molto belli e più a buon mercato!
Valentina:	Hai proprio ragione. Senti, io vado in banca e poi in farmacia a comprare una medicina.

	Fai un giro da sola?
Alexandra:	Certo, a più tardi.
Valentina:	Ciao.
Alexandra:	Scusi, c'è una libreria qui vicino?
1°Passante:	Mi dispiace signorina, non lo so, non sono di Milano.
Alexandra:	Non importa, grazie ... Scusi, c'è una libreria da queste parti?
2°Passante:	Sì, sempre dritto e poi la seconda strada a destra, no ... a sinistra. La libreria è sull'angolo.
Alexandra:	Grazie mille. Arrivederci.
2°Passante:	Prego, arrivederci.

A stroll through downtown Milan

Alexandra:	Valentina! Over here!
Valentina:	Hello Alexandra, how are you?
Alexandra:	Fine, thanks. Do you want to come with me for a stroll through the city?
Valentina:	Sure, I'd love to and I can run a few errands. Shall we take the tram?
Alexandra:	The subway might be quicker, don't you think?
Valentina:	OK, let's go.
Alexandra:	So many clothing stores! And they're all so elegant!
Valentina:	Oh yes, and ... expensive! Look here, what a marvellous blue dress; it's from Giorgio Armani.
Alexandra:	Yes, but the company where I work also makes nice clothes and what's more, they are cheaper!
Valentina:	You're absolutely right. Listen, I have to go to the bank and then to the chemist's (pharmacy) to buy some medicine. Can you walk around on your own?
Alexandra:	Sure, see you later.
Valentina:	Bye.
Alexandra:	Excuse me, is there a bookshop around here?
1ˢᵗ passer-by:	I am sorry, m'am, I don't know, I am not from Milan.
Alexandra:	That's OK, thanks ... Excuse me, is there a bookshop in the area?

▶

2nd passer-by:	Yes, straight ahead and then the second street on the right, no ... left. The bookshop is at the corner.
Alexandra:	Thank you very much. Goodbye.
2nd passer-by:	You're welcome, goodbye.

andare	**(to go, drive)**		
io	*vado*	*noi*	*andiamo*
tu	*vai*	*voi*	*andate*
lui, lei, Lei	*va*	*loro*	*vanno*

venire	**(to come)**		
io	*vengo*	*noi*	*veniamo*
tu	*vieni*	*voi*	*venite*
lui, lei, Lei	*viene*	*loro*	*vengono*

Prepositions

Sono/vado	**in**	*Italia.*	(in/to Italy)
I am/go	**in**	*centro*	(in/into the centre)
I am/go	**in**	*ufficio*	(in/into the office)
I am/go	**in**	*treno, macchina*	(in the train/by car)

Sono/vado	**a**	*Napoli.*	(in/to Naples)
I am/go	**a**	*casa*	(at home/home)
I am/go	**a**	*teatro*	(in/to the theatre)
I am/go	**a**	*letto*	(in/to bed)
I am/go	**a**	*piedi*	(on foot)

▪ **In** is used with country names, **a** with city names.

Sono	**di**	*Palermo.*	(I'm from Palermo.)
Vado	**da**	*Barbara.*	(I'm going to Barbara.)

Ordinal numbers

1. primo	**5.** quinto	**9.** nono
2. secondo	**6.** sesto	**10.** decimo
3. terzo	**7.** settimo	**11.** undicesimo
4. quarto	**8.** ottavo	**100.** centesimo

■ From eleven on, ordinal numbers are formed by dropping the last letter of the cardinal number and adding the ending **-esimo**:

　　　　dodici ☐ *dodicesimo*

Ordinal numbers agree in gender and number with the noun that they refer to:

　　　　　　　la prima strada　　　the first street
　　　　　　　il primo giorno　　　the first day

Exercise 1

Fill in the correct form of andare.

1. Marina e Laura .... a lavorare.

2. (Io) .... a letto molto tardi.

3. Domenica Paolo .... in centro.

4. (Tu) .... sempre a Palermo in vacanza.

5. Anche noi .... a scuola.

6. Sabato sera Anna .... da Alberto.

7. (Voi) .... spesso a teatro in taxi.

Various verb forms of *venire* are concealed here. Find them. They can be written from left to right, top to bottom or in any direction diagonally.

a	v	e	n	g	o	m	i	v
t	v	e	h	i	l	v	g	e
t	p	g	n	l	i	e	z	n
v	v	e	v	i	e	n	e	i
h	i	n	f	g	t	a	v	t
v	e	n	i	a	m	o	n	e
o	i	v	e	n	g	o	n	o

Complete the following sentences by inserting *a, di, in* or *da*.

1. Matteo e Luca vanno ...... Firenze ...... treno.

2. Jane è ...... Boston ma abita ...... Verona.

3. Vengo ...... casa subito.

4. Roberto va ...... Paola a cena.

5. Quando vai ...... ufficio?

6. Luisa va ...... letto presto.

Complete the sentences with the verbs provided.

andate – facciamo – guardo – hanno – sei – vengono – ama – prende – stanno.

1. Laura e Giorgio .... molto bene.

2. Questa sera (io) .... un film alla televisione.

3. (Loro) .... a casa in macchina.

4. E tu Manuela, ... di Venezia?

5. Dove (voi) .... in vacanza?

6. Franco .... lo sport. ▶

7. Il papà e la mamma di Elena

.... una casa a Roma.

8. Anna .... spesso la metropoli-tana.

9. Oggi (noi) .... una passeggiata con gli amici.

Exercise 5

Match the answer to the corresponding question.

1. Scusi, c'è un ristorante qui vicino?

2. Andiamo a piedi?

3. Mi scusi, dov'è la chiesa di San Paolo?

4. Come stai?

5. Questo è Sandro?

a Non c'è male.

b Mi dispiace, non lo so.

c No, in tram.

d No, è Giovanni, un amico di Valentina.

e Sì, sempre dritto, la prima strada a destra, è un ristorante cinese.

Exercise 6

Which word is out of line?

1. cucina – camera da letto – tavolo – bagno

2. mamma – figlia – nonna – ragazza

3. inglese – Germania – francese – italiano

4. pizza – lasagne – aranciata – insalata

5. ciao – grazie – buonasera – arrivederci

a buon mercato	cheap	lasagne *f pl*	lasagne
a più tardi	see you later	libreria *f*	bookshop
abbiglia- mento *m*	clothing	medicina *f*	medicine, drugs
andare	to go, drive	metropolitana *f*	subway
angolo *m*	corner	non importa	it doesn't matter, it's not important, that's OK
arrivederci	goodbye		
azzurro	blue		
banca *f*	bank		
certo	certainly, sure	non lo so	I don't know
		più veloce	quicker, faster
cinese	Chinese		
commissione *f*	errand	prego	you're welcome, my pleasure, please
comprare	to buy		
costoso	expensive		
da queste parti	in this area		
da solo	alone	qualche	some
ditta *f*	company	qui vicino	nearby
dritto	straight ahead	sapere	to know
elegante	elegant	strada *f*	street
fare un giro per negozi	to go for a stroll through the city	sull'angolo	at the corner
		taxi *m*	taxi
		teatro *m*	theatre
farmacia *f*	chemist's *Br* / pharmacy *Am*	tram *m*	tram
		ufficio *m*	office
giro *m*	stroll, tour	veloce	fast, quick
grazie mille	many thanks	venire	to come
		vestito *m*	dress
hai proprio ragione	you are absolutely right		

Shopping in Italy

When shopping in Italy be aware of the local opening hours. Virtually all stores close between 1 and 3:30 p.m. for an extended lunch break. Post offices are open to the public only until 2 p.m. If you need to change money bear in mind that banks, likewise, are open only in the morning and for one hour in the afternoon.

Shops and stores are generally open on Saturday afternoons; some are open on Sundays.

Although large supermarket chains and department stores are increasing in Italy, the majority of Italians still prefer to do their shopping in small family-owned stores.

Primo giorno in ufficio

Oggi è lunedì: il primo giorno di lavoro di Alessandra. Alle sette (7.00) si alza, fa la doccia e fa colazione con la famiglia Simoni. A colazione tutti prendono solo un tè o un caffè con alcuni biscotti; anche Alessandra non ha molta fame perché è un po' nervosa a causa del nuovo lavoro. Ma è già così tardi! Alessandra prende di corsa la metropolitana per andare in ufficio dove arriva puntuale, alle otto e mezza (8.30).

E che sorpresa! L'ufficio è nuovo, i colleghi e le colleghe sono molto simpatici, il lavoro davvero interessante e ... il tempo vola! Sono già le dodici e trenta (12.30); Alessandra e Laura, la segretaria del direttore, vanno insieme a pranzo in mensa. Poi per un espresso al bar »Roma«, dove fanno amicizia con Marco, un ragazzo molto simpatico. Marco è medico e lavora lì vicino in un ospedale; invita Alessandra a uscire con lui mercoledì prossimo.

Anche il pomeriggio passa velocemente e alle cinque (17.00) Alessandra torna a casa.

La signora Simoni prepara una buona cena per festeggiare il primo giorno di lavoro di Alessandra; dopo cena, alle nove e mezzo (21.30), i ragazzi guardano un vecchio film con Sofia Loren alla tv. Un vecchio film, ma che brava attrice!

Alle undici (23.00) Alessandra va a letto: è molto stanca ma contenta.

The first day at the office

Today is Monday: Alexandra's first day at work. She gets up at seven in the morning, takes a shower and has breakfast with the Simoni family. Everyone has just a cup of tea or coffee and a few biscuits (biscotti) for breakfast; Alexandra is not very hungry because she feels a little nervous about her new job. Oh dear, it's already late!

Alexandra rushes to catch the subway which takes her to the office where she arrives right on time, at half past eight.

What a nice surprise! The office is new, the colleagues are all very nice, the job is really interesting and ... time just flies by! It's already half past twelve. Alexandra and Laura, the director's secretary, go to have lunch together at the cafeteria. Afterwards they have coffee at the bar "Roma" where they make friends with Marco, a really nice young man. Marco is a doctor and works in a nearby hospital. He invites Alexandra to go out with him next Wednesday.

The afternoon also whizzes by and at five o'clock Alexandra goes home.

Mrs. Simoni prepares a fine meal to celebrate Alexandra's first day at work. After dinner at nine thirty, the young people watch an old movie with Sophia Loren on TV. It may be an old movie, but what an actress! At eleven o'clock Alexandra goes off to bed. She is very tired but happy.

Reflexive verbs

		lavarsi		to wash onself	
io	**mi**	lavo	I	wash	myself
tu	**ti**	lavi	you	wash	yourself
lui, lei, Lei	**si**	lava	he, she,	washes	him/herself
			you (formal)	wash	yourself
noi	**ci**	laviamo	we	wash	ourselves
voi	**vi**	lavate	you *(plural)*	wash	yourselves
loro	**si**	lavano	they	wash	themselves

▶

Reflexive verbs carry the object pronouns *mi, ti, si, ci, vi, si*.
They are positioned in front of the conjugated verb.
Mi *lavo alle sette.*   I wash myself at seven.

In the infinitive, the pronouns are attached to the verb:
*lavar**si**.*   to wash oneself
*vestir**si**.*   to dress (oneself)

▧ Some verbs are reflexive in Italian but not in English:

chiamarsi	to call
alzarsi	to get up
svegliarsi	to wake up
addormentarsi	to fall asleep

The days of the week

lunedì	Monday
martedì	Tuesday
mercoledì	Wednesday
giovedì	Thursday
venerdì	Friday
sabato	Saturday
domenica	Sunday

The days of the week are usually listed without an article,
except for days with a regularly recurring action.

Oggi è sabato.   It is Saturday today.
La domenica vado al cinema.   I go to the cinema on
                                              Sundays.

Telling the time

Che ora è?	*È l'una. (1:00/13:00)*
Che ore sono?	*Sono le nove. (9:00/21:00)*
What time is it?	*Sono le nove e cinque. (9:05)*
	Sono le nove e un quarto. (9:15)
	Sono le nove e mezza/o. (9:30)
	Sono le dieci meno venti. (9:40)
	Sono le dieci meno un quarto. (9:45)
	È mezzogiorno. (12:00)
	È mezzanotte. (24:00)
A che ora?	*A mezzogiorno. (12:00)*
At what time?	*Alle sette. (7:00)*

Exercise 1

Complete the text by filling in the correct verb forms in the 1st person singular.

La mattina (alzarsi) .... alle sette, (andare) .... in bagno, (vestirmi) .... e poi (fare) .... colazione. Alle otto e mezzo (portare) .... mio figlio Luca a scuola e (andare) .... a lavorare. (Essere) .... impiegata in un ufficio dove (lavorare) .... fino alle due. Il pomeriggio (fare) .... la spesa, (prendere) .... un caffè con le amiche, (riposarsi) .... e spesso (leggere) .... un buon libro. ▶

Alle sette e mezza (mangiare) ....

con Luca e poi (giocare) .... con

lui. Più tardi (guardare) .... un film

alla televisione o (andare) ....

a teatro con amici. A mezzanotte (andare)

.... a letto e (addormentarsi)

....

Using the follo-
wing example,
write short senten-
ces.

Alexandra – impiegata – 9.00
Alexandra è impiegata e va a lavorare alle
nove.

1. Mario – medico – 8.15

....

2. Franca – cameriera – 16.00

....

3. Silvia – insegnante – 8.30

....

4. Andrea – architetto – 9.15

....

5. Francesco – cantante – 10.00

....

6. Teresa – infermiera – 6.45

....

7. Sara – dentista – 9.30

....

Exercise 2

Exercise 3

Fill in the correct forms of the reflexive verbs.

1. La signora Rossi .... (addormentarsi) sempre alle dieci.

2. Laura e Mario .... (svegliarsi) molto presto.

3. (Noi) .... (alzarsi) alle sette e mezza, ... (vestirsi) e poi andiamo a lavorare.

4. (Io) .... (chiamarsi) Renzo.

5. (Voi) non .... (riposarsi)?

Exercise 4

Che ora è?
Write out the following times.

1. 6.35 ....

2. 21.03 ....

3. 9.15 ....

4. 24.00 ....

5. 11.40 ....

6. 13.30 ....

7. 15.10 ....

8. 12.00 ....

9. 8.00 ....

Exercise 5

Arrange the words to form complete sentences.

1. la metropolitana – non – ma va – a piedi – Alexandra – prende – in ufficio.

....

2. si – poi – lava – fa colazione – Valentina – si alza – e – alle sette.

....

3. alla televisione – Masi – un film – Dopo cena – guarda – la famiglia.

....▶

4. chiama – La nuova – si – di Alexandra – amica – Laura.

....

5. a letto – A mezzanotte – va – perché – Alexandra – è stanca.

....

a causa di	because of	**impiegata** *f*	employee
addormentarsi	to fall asleep	**infermiera** *f*	nurse
alzarsi	to get up	**insegnante** *m/f*	teacher
amicizia *f*	friendship	**invitare**	to invite
architetto *m*	architect	**lavarsi**	to wash oneself
attore *m*	actor		
attrice *f*	actress	**lì**	there
biscotto *m*	biscuit *Br* / cookie *Am*	**martedì** *m*	Tuesday
		medico *m*	doctor
cameriera *f*	waitress	**mensa** *f*	cafeteria
Che ora è?	What time is it?	**mercoledì** *m*	Wednesday
		mezzanotte *f*	midnight
Che sorpresa!	What a surprise!	**mezzogiorno** *m*	midday
		nervoso	nervous
chiamarsi	to call	**nuovo**	new
colazione *f*	breakfast	**ora di punta** *f*	rush hour
collega *m/f*	colleague	**ora** *f*	hour
di corsa	in a hurry	**ospedale** *m*	hospital
direttore *m*	director	**passare**	to go by (time)
doccia *f*	shower		
dopo	after(wards)	**pendolare** *m*	commuter
fare amicizia	to make friends	**portare**	to bring
		pranzo *m*	lunch
fare la doccia	to take a shower	**preparare**	to prepare
		prossimo	next
festeggiare	to celebrate	**puntuale**	on time
fino a	until	**ragazzo** *m*	boy, young man
giovedì *m*	Thursday		
il tempo vola	time flies	**riposarsi**	to rest

▶

segretaria *f*	secretary	**venerdì** *m*	Friday
svegliarsi	to wake up	**vestirsi**	to get dressed
uscire	to go out	**volare**	to fly
velocemente	quick, fast		

Commuting in Italy

The public transport systems in Italian cities are often not as extensive as in other European cities. Commuters *(pendolari)*, therefore, have to spend considerable time on their way to work. Many employees consequently opt to take their own car to drive to work, which often causes traffic jams and gridlock on major roads during rush hour *(ora di punta)*.

Business hours, especially for offices, start relatively late, generally at 9 o'clock in the morning and employees leave correspondingly later in the evening.

La sera, in un locale

Marco: Ci sediamo a questo tavolo, va bene?
Alexandra: Certo. Che bel locale, vieni spesso qui?
Marco: Sì, è il mio locale preferito; l'ambiente è simpatico, il mercoledì e il sabato suona un gruppo jazz molto bravo e poi è vicino a casa mia.
Cameriere: Buonasera, che cosa desiderate?
Marco: Io ho fame, vorrei ... un piatto di tagliatelle verdi e da bere una birra scura media. E tu Alessandra, prendi qualcosa?
Alexandra: Sì, volentieri. Vorrei un succo di frutta e un gelato misto.
Cameriere: Va bene.

Alexandra: Marco, che cosa fai di solito nel tuo tempo libero?
Marco: Lavoro molto in ospedale in questo periodo, ma quando ho un po' di tempo leggo volentieri un buon libro, ascolto musica jazz e gioco a tennis con mio fratello e con due colleghi di lavoro.

▶

Alexandra:	Anch'io gioco a tennis, ma qui a Milano non conosco nessuno.
Marco:	Vieni a giocare con noi, giochiamo sempre il sabato mattina alle dieci.
Alexandra:	È un'ottima idea. Vengo senz'altro.
Marco:	Oh, ecco il tuo gelato e il succo di frutta. E questa è la mia pasta e la birra. Grazie. Ah, scusi vorrei ancora un'acqua minerale naturale.
Cameriere:	Arriva subito.
Alexandra:	Sei d'accordo se andiamo a casa? È già piuttosto tardi.
Marco:	Certo, anch'io sono un po' stanco. Cameriere, il conto per favore.
Cameriere:	Fanno diciannove euro.
Marco:	Ecco a Lei. Arrivederci.
Cameriere:	Arrivederci e grazie.
Alexandra:	Grazie per l'invito e la bella serata Marco. Allora, ci vediamo sabato per il tennis?
Marco:	Sì, ti telefono venerdì sera.
Alexandra:	Ok. A venerdì.
Marco:	Ciao e buonanotte.

An evening at a restaurant

Marco:	Let's sit down at this table, OK?
Alexandra:	Sure. What a lovely restaurant. Do you come here often?
Marco:	Yes, it's my favourite restaurant; the atmosphere is nice. On Wednesdays and Saturdays they have a very good jazz band playing, and it's very close to my place.
Waiter:	Good evening, what would you like?
Marco:	I'm hungry; I'd like ..."tagliatelle verdi" and a half a litre of dark beer. And what about you Alexandra, are you going to have something?

Alexandra:	Yes, I'd like fruit juice and mixed ice cream.
Waiter:	OK.
Alexandra:	Marco, what do you normally do in your spare time?
Marco:	At the moment I work long hours at the hospital but when I have a little spare time, I enjoy reading a good book, listening to jazz and playing tennis with my brother and two colleagues from work.
Alexandra:	I also play tennis but I don't know anyone here in Milan.
Marco:	Come and play with us, we always play Saturday mornings at 10.
Alexandra:	That's a great idea. I'll definitely come.
Marco:	Oh, here's your ice cream and fruit juice. And that's my pasta and the beer. Thank you.
	Excuse me, I would also like a non-carbonated mineral water.
Waiter:	Coming right up.
Alexandra:	Is it OK with you if we go home? It's already pretty late.
Marco:	Of course, I am a little tired, too.
	Waiter, the bill please.
Waiter :	That'll be 19 euros.
Marco:	Here you are. Goodbye.
Waiter:	Goodbye and thank you.
Alexandra:	Thanks for the invitation and the nice evening, Marco. Well, we'll see each other for tennis on Saturday then?
Marco:	Yes, I'll call you Friday evening.
Alexandra:	OK, until Friday.
Marco:	Ciao and good night.

bere	**(to drink)**		
io	bevo	*noi*	beviamo
tu	bevi	*voi*	bevete
lui, lei, Lei	beve	*loro*	bevono

Possessive pronouns

singular
masculine   *feminine*

il **mio**	my (mine)	la **mia**	my (mine)
il **tuo**	your(s)	la **tua**	your(s)
il **suo**	his/her(s)/your(s)	la **sua**	his/her(s)/your(s)
il **nostro**	our(s)	la **nostra**	our(s)
il **vostro**	your(s)	la **vostra**	your(s)
il **loro**	their(s)	la **loro**	their(s)

plural
masculine   *feminine*

i **miei**	my (mine)	le **mie**	my (mine)
i **tuoi**	your(s)	le **tue**	your(s)
i **suoi**	his/her(s)/your(s)	le **sue**	his/her(s)/your(s)
i **nostri**	our(s)	le **nostre**	our(s)
i **vostri**	your(s)	le **vostre**	your(s)
i **loro**	their(s)	le **loro**	their(s)

In Italian the possessive pronouns take their gender and number from the object they refer to.

il suo letto   his/her bed
la sua casa   his/her house

Loro remains unchanged.

Possessive pronouns are normally used with the definite article in Italian.

la mia macchina   my car

Exception: the article is omitted with relatives.

mio padre   my father

Always use the article:
– with **loro**   **la loro figlia**   their daughter
– with names of relatives in the plural
                i vostri figli   your sons
– with exactly defined names of relatives or with
  affectionate forms

il mio fratello maggiore   my oldest brother
la mia mammina   my mum

▶

The article can be omitted when referring to a possession that has been previously mentioned, in which case **essere** + **possessive pronoun** are used.

Di chi è questa bicicletta? Whose bicycle is this?
È (la) mia. It belongs to me./It is mine.

The possessive pronoun can also be used without an article in various idiomatic expressions:

Mamma mia! Oh my God./Oh dear!
A casa mia. At my place.

Complete the sentences by filling in the correct form of the possessive pronoun – with or without the article.

Exercise 1

mio

1. Oggi vado a giocare a golf con .... amica Silvia.

2. .... collega è davvero antipatico.

3. Carla viene a cena a casa ....

4. Faccio un giro in centro con .... fratelli.

tuo

1. Di chi è questo vestito? È .... ?

2. Vado due settimane a San Remo con

.... sorella.

3. Sono belle .... fotografie?

4. .... padre ti telefona domani.

nostro

1. Vado a fare una passeggiata con

.... bambine.

2. Ecco .... amici italiani!

3. .... televisione è rotta.

4. .... fratelli si chiamano Marco e
Luigi.

vostro

1. .... casa è molto bella.

2. Come stanno .... sorelle?

3. .... lavoro è davvero interessante.

4. Dove sono .... valigie?

Exercise 2

Fill in the correct
form of *suo* and
loro.

1. Antonella e Ivano vanno a trovare

.... genitori.

2. Sono i libri di Gabriele? Sì sono

....

3. Maria ascolta .... dischi di musica
classica.

4. I signori Rossi vengono a Monaco con

.... macchina.

5. Lei abita a casa di .... sorella.

6. Laura e Marta amano .... nonni.

Which parts belong together?	**1.** Vorrei	**a** gioco a tennis con mia sorella.	Exercise 3
	2. Scusi,	**b** grazie.	
	3. Buonasera, che cosa	**c** il mio bar preferito.	
	4. Mille	**d** una coca-cola, per favore.	
	5. La domenica	**e** c'è un ristorante qui vicino?	
	6. Questo è	**f** prendete?	

Use the correct form of *bere* to create complete sentences.	Il tuo amico Marco		un caffè	Exercise 4
	Tu		un'aranciata	
	Paola		un martini	
	Voi	**bere**	un tè	
	Andrea e Luca		una cioccolata	
	Noi		un cognac	
	Io		un'acqua minerale	
	I miei genitori		un cappuccino	

Do you recall how these numbers were written out?	**1.**	89	Exercise 5
	2.	146	
	3.	1.580	
	4.	120.000	
	5.	376	
	6.	5.300.000	
	7.	2.610	
	8.	21.000	

Exercise 6

Form four groups, each consisting of four related words.

letto	metropolitana	zucchini	fratello
zio	autobus	sedia	arancia
broccoli	macchina	treno	tavolo
insalata	lampada	figlia	nonno

....

....

....

....

Vocabulary

acqua minerale naturale *f*	non-carbonated mineral water	golf *m*	golf
ambiente *m*	atmosphere	gruppo *m*	group
anch'io	me too	invito *m*	invitation
antipatico	unpleasant	lampada *f*	lamp
bambino *m*	child	locale *m*	restaurant, bar
bere	to drink		
bicicletta *f*	bicycle	mancia *f*	tip
broccolo *m*	broccoli	media	(here:) half a litre of beer
buonanotte	good night		
cameriere *m*	waiter	mio	my, mine
ci vediamo	we'll see each other	non nessuno	no one
		nonni *m pl*	grandparents
cioccolata *f*	hot chocolate	ottimo	excellent
conoscere	to know, get to know	periodo *m*	time, period
		piatto *m*	plate, dish
conto *m*	bill *Br* / check *Am* (in restaurant)	piuttosto	rather
		preferito	favourite
		qualcosa	something
desiderare	to wish, desire	rotto	broken
di solito	normally	scuro	dark
fotografia *f*	photo	senz'altro	definitely
gelato misto *m*	mixed ice cream	serata *f*	evening
		sorella *f*	sister
		succo di frutta *m*	fruit juice

tagliatelle *f pl*	tagliatelle pasta	**vorrei**	I would like to
telefonare	to phone *Br* / to call *Am*	**zucchino** *m*	courgette *Br* / zucchini *Am*
ti telefono	I'll call you		
verde	green		

Who pays?

Never ask for separate bills for the different members of a party in an Italian restaurant; either one person pays for it all – albeit in the expectation that it is his turn to be invited the next time – or the bill is divided up internally among those sitting at the table *(pagare alla romana)*.

The traditional male-female role model still prevails in that the general expectation is for the man to invite the woman. A tip for the waiter, *la mancia*, is certainly expected by the serving staff, even though there is no set rule about the size of the tip. Never add the tip to the bill, though; simply put it on the table after you've paid.

Test 2

1 Choose one of the two answers, then go to the square with the number of your answer.

2 ... in treno.

Ando ⇨ 9
Vado ⇨ 13

6 Good! Continue: Vado a lavorare alle ... (8.30).

otto e mezza ⇨ 8
nove e mezza ⇨ 28

7 Wrong!

Go back to number 27.

11 Wrong!

Go back to number 22.

12 Wrong!

Go back to number 17.

16 Wrong!

Go back to number 13.

17 Good! Con▪

Prendo le tue ... .

valigie ⇨ 25
valige ⇨ 12

21 Wrong!

Go back to number 29.

22 Very good! Continue:

Sono ... Napoli.

da ⇨ 11
di ⇨ 20

26 Wrong!

Go back to number 4.

27 Correct! Continue:
Sara e Luca ... a ca
domani.
vengono ⇨ 4
veniamo ⇨ 7

Wrong! back to nber 24.	**4** Great! Continue: A che ora vai ... letto? in ⊳ 26 a ⊳ 17	**5** Wrong! Go back to number 20.
Great! Continue: do a pranzo ... mia figlia ⊳ 27 la mia figlia ⊳ 19	**9** Wrong! Go back to number 2.	**10** Correct! Continue: Sandro ... alle sette. ti alzi ⊳ 14 si alza ⊳ 22
Good! Continue: anni hai? ali ⊳ 16 anti ⊳ 24	**14** Wrong! Go back to number 10.	**15** Correct! Continue: Rita va ... ufficio a piedi. in ⊳ 10 a ⊳ 23
Great! Continue: ai stasera? i ⊳ 30 e cosa ⊳ 6	**19** Wrong! Go back to number 8.	**20** Very good! Continue: Noi ... a tennis. giociamo ⊳ 5 giochiamo ⊳ 29
Wrong! back to nber 15.	**24** Good! Continue: Kurt e Andreas sono ... . tedeschi ⊳ 15 tedesci ⊳ 3	**25** Correct! End of exercise!
Wrong! back to mber 6.	**29** Great! Continue: I signori Donati prendono ... macchina. la sua ⊳ 21 la loro ⊳ 18	**30** Wrong! Go back to number 18.

11 Un fine settimana al mare

Alexandra: Che cosa fai questo fine settimana?

Valentina: Niente di speciale, e tu? Devi lavorare?

Alexandra: No, voglio fare una gita, forse visitare una città. Vuoi venire con me?

Valentina: Perché no? Però fa un po' troppo caldo per passare il fine settimana in città!

Alexandra: Ho un'idea! Perché non andiamo due giorni al mare? Possiamo prendere il treno venerdì pomeriggio e tornare domenica sera.

Valentina: È un'ottima idea. Possiamo andare a Lerici; conosco una piccola pensione vicino alla spiaggia, è tranquilla e costa poco. Devo prenotare due camere?

Alexandra: Sì, e io compro i biglietti e prenoto i posti in treno.

Valentina: Che bello! Possiamo andare in spiaggia, prendere il sole, nuotare, andare al ristorante e poi voglio anche andare dalla mia amica Elisabetta. Non vedo l'ora!

Portiere:	Pensione Rosina, buongiorno.
Valentina:	Buongiorno, vorrei prenotare due camere singole per venerdì e sabato.
Portiere:	Mi dispiace abbiamo solo camere doppie o matrimoniali.
Valentina:	Allora prendo una doppia, per favore. Ha il bagno?
Portiere:	Sì, e anche un balcone con vista sul mare.
Valentina:	Quanto costa?
Portiere:	Cinquantacinque euro a notte, compresa la prima colazione.
Valentina:	Va bene, allora grazie e ... a venerdì.
Portiere:	Grazie a Lei. Buona giornata.

A weekend by the sea

Alexandra:	What are you doing over the weekend?
Valentina:	Nothing special, and you? Do you have to work?
Alexandra:	No, I want to take a trip, maybe visit a city. Do you want to come along?
Valentina:	Why not? But it's a little too hot to spend the weekend in the city.
Alexandra:	I have an idea! Why don't we go to the seaside for two days? We could take the train on Friday afternoon and come back Sunday evening.
Valentina:	That's a great idea. We could go to Lerici. I know a little guesthouse right by the beach. It is quiet and not expensive. Shall I reserve two rooms?
Alexandra:	Yes, and I'll buy the tickets and book the seats on the train.
Valentina:	How lovely! We can go to the beach, lie in the sun, swim and go to the restaurant. And then I also want to visit my friend Elisabetta. I can hardly wait!
Receptionist:	Guesthouse Rosina, good morning.
Valentina:	Good morning, I would like to book two single rooms for Friday and Saturday.
Receptionist:	I am sorry, but we only have double rooms and rooms with double beds.

▶

Valentina:	Well I'll take a double room, please. Does it have a bathroom?
Receptionist:	Yes, and also a balcony with an ocean view.
Valentina:	How much is it?
Receptionist :	55 euros per night, including breakfast.
Valentina:	OK, thank you ... see you Friday.
Receptionist:	Thank you too. Have a nice day.

---

sapere

io	*so*	*noi*	*sappiamo*
tu	*sai*	*voi*	*sapete*
lui, lei, Lei	*sa*	*loro*	*sanno*

The verb *sapere* means both, **to know** as well as **to be able to** in which case it is used with an infinitive construction:

> *Non lo so.*   I don't know.
> *Non so nuotare.* I cannot swim.

Modal verbs

	potere	volere	dovere
io	*posso*	*voglio*	*devo*
tu	*puoi*	*vuoi*	*devi*
lui,lei,Lei	*può*	*vuole*	*deve*
noi	*possiamo*	*vogliamo*	*dobbiamo*
voi	*potete*	*volete*	*dovete*
loro	*possono*	*vogliono*	*devono*

The verbs **volere, dovere, potere,** are used with the infinitive:

Devo andare a casa.   I have to go home.   ▶

Potere means **to be able to** and **to be allowed to**.

Dovere means **must/to have to**.

Vorrei is often used instead of **voglio** as a more polite form:
Vorrei un caffè.   I would like a coffee.

Prepositions + definite article

	il	*lo*	*l'*	*la*	*i*	*gli*	*le*
di	**del**	**dello**	**dell'**	**della**	**dei**	**degli**	**delle**
a	**al**	**allo**	**all'**	**alla**	**ai**	**agli**	**alle**
da	**dal**	**dallo**	**dall'**	**dalla**	**dai**	**dagli**	**dalle**
in	**nel**	**nello**	**nell'**	**nella**	**nei**	**negli**	**nelle**
su	**sul**	**sullo**	**sull'**	**sulla**	**sui**	**sugli**	**sulle**

When the prepositions **di, a, da, in, su** are used with the definite article they combine into one word: **a + il = al mare**

The preposition **con** can also be combined with the articles **il** and **i**:

*Faccio una passeggiata **col** cane/**coi** cani.*
I go for a walk with the dog/dogs.

Fill in the correct form of the modal verb.

(Io) .... (volere) comprare un biglietto per Venezia. (Io)
.... (potere) partire sabato mattina ma .... (dovere)
già tornare lunedì sera. (Io) .... (dovere) comprare un
dizionario perché non .... (sapere) parlare bene l'italiano.

Exercise 1

Exercise 2

Repeat exercise 1 again, this time fill in the 3ʳᵈ person singular and plural.

(Lui) ....

....

(Loro) ....

....

Exercise 3

Complete the sentences with the verb forms provided.

volete – so – puoi – devo – dovete – sappiamo – posso – vogliono.

1. Se (voi) .... andare in macchina

.... pagare la benzina.

2. (Loro) .... comprare una casa nuova.

3. Mi dispiace, non .... venire al

cinema, ... lavorare.

4. (Noi) non .... giocare a tennis.

5. (Tu) .... aprire la porta?

6. (Io) .... parlare bene l'inglese.

Exercise 4

Fill in the correct form of the preposition + the definite article.

A

Andiamo ..... mare. Vengo ..... stazione. Vanno ..... mercato. Vado ..... zoo.

DI

Tom è il cane ..... mia amica. Questo è il bar .... albergo. Prendi i libri .... studenti.

DA

Va ..... dentista. Veniamo ..... stazione. Vado ..... miei amici.

IN

La sedia è ..... nostra camera. La birra è ..... frigorifero. Vado ..... musei. ▶

SU

Il giornale è ..... tavolo. La camera ha
un balcone .... mare. I fiori sono .... scrivania.

**Which prepositions –
with or without an
article – are missing?**

1. Vado ..... Genova ..... treno.

2. Pietro e Susanna vanno ..... cinema
..... loro amici francesi.

3. Sei ..... Milano? Sì ma vivo .....
Napoli.

4. Per favore, vai ..... supermercato e
compra una bottiglia ..... vino.

Exercise 5

Che cosa fa Giovanni questa settimana?
Write short sentences.

Lunedì mattina alle otto e mezza Giovanni va all'università.

	mattina	pomeriggio	sera
lunedì	8.30 Università	16.30 medico	
martedì			teatro
mercoledì		19.30 tennis!	
giovedì			opera
venerdì	11.15 parco		
sabato		13.00 pranzo da Carla	
domenica		16.00 partita di calcio	

Exercise 6

---

a notte	per night	**camera**	double room
balcone *m*	balcony	**doppia** *f*	
benzina *f*	petrol *Br* /	**camera**	room with a
	gasoline *Am*	**matrimoniale** *f*	double bed
biglietto *m*	ticket	**camera**	single room
bottiglia *f*	bottle	**singola** *f*	

Vocabulary

cane *m*	dog	**poco**	a little
compreso	inclusive	**ponte** *m*	bridge
con me	with me	**posto** *m*	position, place
dizionario *m*	dictionary		
dovere	to have to, must	**potere**	to be able/ allowed to
ferie *f pl*	holidays	**prendere il sole**	to lie in the sun
fiore *m*	flower		
giornata *f*	day	**prenotare**	to book, reserve
gita *f*	trip		
mercato *m*	market	**prima colazione** *f*	breakfast
museo *m*	museum		
niente	nothing	**scrivania** *f*	desk
niente di speciale	nothing special	**sul mare**	by the sea
		supermercato *m*	supermarket
non vedo l'ora	I can hardly wait	**troppo**	too much
		università *f*	university
parco *m*	park	**visitare**	to visit
passaporto *m*	passport	**vista** *f*	view
pensione *f*	guesthouse	**volere**	to want
però	but	**zoo** *m*	zoo

Holidays "all'italiana"

In Italy, August is *the* holiday month: not only do most offices and factories close down, but virtually all shops are **chiuso per ferie**. The 15th of August, called **Ferragosto**, is the peak of the holiday season when the Italian cities are more or less abandoned! Italians actually enjoy travelling throughout the year. Going on short vacations between two weekends, **fare il ponte,** is very popular especially when there is a public holiday mid-week and one can take two days additional vacation.

Il lunedì in ufficio

Laura:	Ciao Alessandra.
Alexandra:	Ciao.
Laura:	Sei in ritardo oggi!
Laura:	Sono in ritardo perché non ho sentito la sveglia. Ieri sera sono andata a letto molto tardi.
Laura:	Ah ah, e che cosa hai fatto?
Alexandra:	Ho passato il fine settimana con Valentina al mare e siamo arrivate a casa solo a mezzanotte.
Laura:	Dove siete state?
Alexandra:	A Lerici, in Liguria.
Laura:	E che cosa avete fatto di bello? Sicuramente avete preso il sole, sei abbronzata.
Alexandra:	Eh sì, il tempo è stato davvero bello, ma non siamo state solo al sole. Sabato siamo andate

	a visitare il paese e poi abbiamo fatto una gita in barca; la sera abbiamo mangiato dell'ottimo pesce in un ristorante all'aperto e dopo siamo andate a ballare con degli amici di Valentina. Domenica abbiamo dormito fino a tardi e poi siamo andate ancora un po' in spiaggia; abbiamo preso il sole e giocato a pallavolo! Mi sono proprio divertita!
Laura:	Che fortuna! Se penso che io sabato ho lavorato tutto il giorno ...
Alexandra:	Oh, mi dispiace. E ieri che cosa hai fatto?
Laura:	Sono andata da mia sorella, sul lago di Como e alla sera al cinema con il mio ragazzo.
Alexandra:	Allora hai passato anche tu una bella domenica.
Laura:	Eh sì, ma purtroppo oggi è lunedì e dobbiamo proprio cominciare a lavorare!

Monday in the office

Laura:	Hello Alexandra.
Alexandra:	Hello.
Laura:	You're late today!
Alexandra:	I'm late because I didn't hear the alarm. I went to bed very late last night.
Laura:	I see, and what did you do?
Alexandra:	I spent the weekend at the seaside with Valentina and we got back only at midnight.
Laura:	Where did you stay?
Alexandra:	In Lerici, in Liguria.
Laura:	And what nice things did you do? You must have been sunbathing; you have a tan.
Alexandra:	Sure, the weather was really nice, but we didn't only lie around in the sun. On Saturday we went to the country and then we took a boat trip.

▶

	In the evening we had excellent fish in an outdoor restaurant and then went dancing with some friends of Valentina's. On Sunday we slept late and then went to the beach where we lay in the sun and played volleyball. I really enjoyed myself!
Laura:	Lucky you! I was just thinking that I had to work all day Saturday ...
Alexandra:	Oh, I am sorry. What did you do yesterday?
Laura:	I went to see my sister at Lake Como, and in the evening I went to the movies with my boyfriend.
Alexandra:	Well then, you had a nice Sunday as well.
Laura:	Yes I did, but unfortunately it's Monday today and we really have to start working!

Perfect tense (I)

		mangiare		**andare**
io	**ho**	mangiato	**sono**	andato/a
tu	**hai**	mangiato	**sei**	andato/a
lui, lei, Lei	**ha**	mangiato	**è**	andato/a
noi	**abbiamo**	mangiato	**siamo**	andati/e
voi	**avete**	mangiato	**siete**	andati/e
loro	**hanno**	mangiato	**sono**	andati/e

In Italian the perfect tense is formed with the present of the auxiliary verbs **avere** or **essere** and the **past particple** of the respective verb.
Past participles are formed from the stem of the infinitive.

1. conj.	**-ato**	mangiare	mang**iato**
2. conj.	**-uto**	avere	av**uto**
3. conj.	**-ito**	dormire	dorm**ito**

▶

■ Many verbs have irregular past participles.

essere	**stato**	stare	**stato**	fare	**fatto**
leggere	**letto**	venire	**venuto**	vedere	**visto**
aprire	**aperto**	scrivere	**scritto**	perdere	**perso**
prendere	**preso**	mettere	**messo**	chiedere	**chiesto**
chiudere	**chiuso**	rispondere	**risposto**		

Past participles formed with **avere** remain unchanged:
> Laura ha lavorato molto.
> Marco e Pietro hanno lavorato molto.

Past participles formed with **essere**, however, agree with the gender and number of the subject:
> Carlo è andato a scuola.
> Silvia è andata a scuola.
> Aldo e Gino sono andati a scuola.
> Anna e Assunta sono andate a scuola.

Exercise 1

Fill in the missing infinitives and past participles.

1. guardare ....

2. .... letto

3. scrivere ....

4. .... chiuso

5. dormire ....

6. .... aperto

7. essere ....

8. .... suonato

9. prendere ....

10. .... visitato

Complete the following sentences by inserting the participle.
Pay close attention to the endings!

1. fare — Maria ha .... una gita in montagna.

2. sentire — (Io) ho .... musica classica tutta la domenica.

3. andare — Matteo e Paolo sono .... a Torino.

4. prendere — (Voi) avete .... il sole in spiaggia.

5. lavorare — Non (loro) hanno .... ieri?

6. essere — La nonna non è mai .... In America.

7. arrivare — (Noi) siamo .... alle nove e mezza.

8. chiudere — (Tu) hai .... la finestra?

Exercise 2

Rewrite the sentences in the perfect tense.

avere	*essere*
1. Tua madre guarda la tv.	**2.** (Io) vado al mare.
....	....
3. Tu senti la radio.	**4.** (Voi) tornate a casa.
....	....
5. (Loro) prendono il tram.	**6.** Massimo viene con noi.
....	....
7. (Noi) apriamo la porta.	**8.** Loro arrivano alle sette.
....	....

Exercise 3

Exercise 4

Rewrite the following sentences in the perfect tense.

Lisa mette i vestiti nell'armadio.
❑ Lisa ha messo i vestiti nell'armadio.

1. Rispondo alla lettera di mio papà.

....

2. (Tu) chiedi al cameriere una birra.

....

3. Nora perde l'autobus.

....

4. Massimo scrive un libro di storia.

....

5. (Noi) mettiamo la televisione in soggiorno.

....

Exercise 5

Form the past tense of the verbs and rearrange the sentences in their proper sequence.

1. Al pomeriggio Francesco legge un libro e Alberta scrive alcune lettere.

2. Arrivano a casa alle undici e mezzo e vanno subito a letto.

3. Alberta e Francesco fanno colazione a letto.

4. All'una vanno insieme a pranzo dalla zia di Alberta.

5. Alle otto vanno a teatro e poi a cena in un ristorante messicano.

6. Dopo colazione Alberta va in chiesa e Francesco fa una passeggiata in centro.

Che cosa hanno fatto domenica
Alberta e Francesco?

1. Alberta e Francesco hanno fatto
colazione a letto.

2. ....

....

Choose the appropriate prepositions.

Exercise 6

alla	**a**	**in**	**nell'**	**dallo**
dai	**di**	**del**	**sul**	**con**

1. La lampada è .... tavolo.

2. I signori Battaglia sono andati ....
banca.

3. I bicchieri sono .... armadio.

4. Siamo andati .... piedi.

5. Questa è la bicicletta .... mia
sorella.

6. Antonio e Vincenzo vanno .... loro
genitori.

7. Mia sorella è andata al mare ....
Nicola.

8. Venite anche voi .... stazione.

9. Stasera vado .... zio a cena.

10. Questo è Paolo, il figlio .... nostro
dottore.

abbronzato	tanned	**messicano**	Mexican
all'aperto	outdoors	**mettere**	to put
America *f*	America	**paese** *m*	village,
ballare	to dance		country(side)
barca *f*	boat, ship	**pensare**	to think
Che fortuna!	(here:)	**perdere**	to lose, miss
	"Lucky you!"	**pesce** *m*	fish
chiesa *f*	church	**purtroppo**	unfortunately
classico	classic(al)	**rispondere**	to answer
divertirsi	to have fun,	**ritardo** *m*	delay
	enjoy	**scrivere**	to write
dottore *m*	GP *Br* /	**sicuramente**	certain
	doctor *Am*	**sul lago**	at the lake
essere in ritardo	to be late	**sveglia** *f*	alarm clock
finestra *f*	window	**tifoso** *m*	(sports)fan
ieri	yesterday	**tutto il giorno**	the whole day
lettera *f*	letter		

"Tifosi" – everywhere!

Monday morning there is but one topic of conversation in most of Italy: *calcio* – football (soccer). Be prepared!
On Sunday afternoon you'll notice how many Italians walk around with their portable radios turned on just to be up with the action. As the week progresses everything revolves around tips and forecasts for the *schedina del Totocalcio* (football lottery ticket). The latter in itself has become something of a national pastime sport!

Lo zio d'America

Alexandra:	Stefano, ieri sera ho guardato le vecchie fotografie della vostra famiglia e in una c'è un signore coi baffi davanti alla statua della libertà a New York. Ma chi è?
Stefano:	Ah, è il famoso zio Gianni.
Alexandra:	Uno zio? E perché è famoso?
Stefano:	A dire la verità non è mio zio, è lo zio della mamma ed è famoso perché ha avuto una vita piuttosto movimentata.
Alexandra:	Davvero? Racconta!
Stefano:	È nato in piccolo paese vicino a Milano, il 3 febbraio 1910 (millenovecentodieci) – lo so perché il 3 febbraio è anche il mio compleanno – e a diciotto anni è andato via di casa, o meglio è emigrato in America.
Alexandra:	Beh, questo non è strano, molti italiani sono emigrati in America tra la fine del 1800 e l'inizio del 1900.
Stefano:	È vero ma lo zio Gianni ha fatto fortuna ed è diventato molto ricco! Ha aperto una pasticceria e poi due, tre, e così via. Un giorno ha conosciuto una ragazza argentina, ha venduto tutto e si è trasferito in Sud America.
Alexandra:	E poi?

▶

Stefano:	Ha comprato una fattoria e della terra ed è diventato ... un contadino! Ha viaggiato molto ma non è mai tornato in Italia. È morto solo cinque anni fa.
Alexandra:	Ha avuto dei figli?
Stefano:	Sì, figli e nipoti.
Alexandra:	Allora hai dei cugini in Argentina?
Stefano:	Sì, non ci siamo mai visti, ma ci scriviamo sempre gli auguri di Natale.
Alexandra:	Perché non fai un viaggio in Argentina?
Stefano:	Hai ragione, è una bella idea; forse dopo gli esami di maturità, se papà paga il viaggio!!

The uncle from America

Alexandra:	Stefano, last night I was looking through some old pictures of your family and in one of them there was this man with a moustache in front of the Statue of Liberty in New York. Who is he?
Stefano:	Oh, that's our famous Uncle Gianni.
Alexandra:	An uncle? Why is he famous?
Stefano:	To tell you the truth, he is not my uncle, he is my mother's uncle, and he is famous because he had a rather exciting life.
Alexandra:	Really? Tell me more!
Stefano:	He was born in a small village near Milan on February 3rd 1910 – I know that because the 3rd of February is also my birthday – and at the age of 18 he left home, or shall we say, he emigrated to America.
Alexandra:	Well, that's not unusual, many Italians immigrated to America at the end of the 19th and the early 20th century.
Stefano:	That's right but my uncle Gianni made a fortune there and became very rich! He opened one pastry shop, then two, three and so on. One day he met a girl from Argentina, sold everything and moved to South America.
Alexandra:	And then?
Stefano:	He bought a farm and land and ... became a farmer.

	He travelled a lot but never returned to Italy. He died just five years ago.
Alexandra:	Did he have any children?
Stefano:	Yes, children and grandchildren.
Alexandra:	So you have cousins in Argentina?
Stefano:	Yes, though we've never seen each other we always write each other Christmas cards.
Alexandra:	Why don't you take a trip to Argentina?
Stefano:	You're right, that's a good idea. Maybe after my final exams, if dad pays for the trip!!

Perfect tense (II)

The Italian present perfect tense is a compound tense that uses ***essere*** and ***avere*** as auxiliary verbs and the past participle of the verb (see also Lesson 11). As a guideline, many English verbs share the same auxiliary verbs (to be or to have) when forming the perfect tense.

The following verbs are conjugated with ***essere***:

reflexive verbs	*Noi non siamo visti.*
	(We haven't seen each other.)
costare	*L'albergo è costato poco.*
	(The hotel was cheap.)
mancare	*Luisa è mancata a scuola.*
	(Luisa was absent from school.)

The following verbs are conjugated with ***avere***:

viaggiare	*Ha viaggiato molto.*
	(He travelled a lot.)
camminare	*Ho camminato lungo il fiume.*
	(I walked along the river.)
nuotare	*Abbiamo nuotato in piscina.*
	(We swam in the swimming pool.)

Irregular participles are:

nascere	**nato**
morire	**morto**

Some expressions of time relating to the past

ieri mattina
(yesterday morning)
ieri pomeriggio
ieri sera

l'altro ieri
(the day before yesterday)
l'altro giorno

l'anno scorso
(last year)
il mese scorso
la settimana scorsa
martedì scorso

un'ora fa
(an hour ago)
una settimana fa
tre giorni fa

Months and seasons

gennaio	**luglio**	**primavera**
febbraio	**agosto**	**estate**
marzo	**settembre**	**autunno**
aprile	**ottobre**	**inverno**
maggio	**novembre**	
giugno	**dicembre**	

Dates

Dates are given with cardinal numbers except for the first day of the month.

What date is it today?
Qual è la data di oggi?

Today is the first　　12th　　30th of January 2006.
Oggi è il　　primo　　dodici　　trenta gennaio 2006.

The preposition da

The preposition **da** is used:

with locations	meaning **from**	*Vengo **dalla** America.*
	meaning **to**	*Vado **da** Mauro.*
with times	meaning **for/since**	*Abito a Roma **da** tre anni.*
as indication of a purpose		*Gli occhiali **da** sole.*
as indication of a feature		*Il signore **dai** capelli biondi.*
in some idioms		*Vado in vacanza **da** solo.*
meaning **as**		***da** bambino*

Which of the following verbs is conjugated with *essere*?

Exercise 1

dormire, arrivare, scrivere, essere, fare, andare, nuotare, mangiare, lavarsi, leggere, tornare, prendere, visitare, riposarsi, sapere, comprare, viaggiare, costare, fumare, aprire, vedere, sentire.

....

Put the verbs into the perfect tense.

Exercise 2

Anna Ferrero racconta: Io .... (nascere) il 27 luglio 1932 in un piccolo paese in Piemonte, vicino a Torino. I miei genitori .... (trasferirsi) a Genova nel 1938. (Io)................. (frequentare) la scuola, il liceo e l'università a Genova; .... (studiare) medicina e .... (diventare) pediatra. Nel 1958 .... (sposarsi) e io e mio marito .... (andare) a vivere a Bologna. (Noi) .... (comprare) una casa in campagna e il 7 ottobre 1962 .... (nascere) le nostre figlie Marina e Stefania, due gemelle. (Io) .... (lavorare) in un ospedale di Bologna per 35 anni.

Exercise 3

Describe what Mrs. Bianchi did yesterday.

ore 7.00	svegliarsi	ore 7.15	fare la doccia
ore 7.30	prendere un caffè	ore 8.00	andare in ufficio in macchina
ore 12.30	in mensa	ore 13.30	fare una passeggiata
ore 17.00	andare in centro	ore 19.00	tornare a casa
ore 20.30	cenare	ore 23.00	andare a letto
ore 23.15	addormentarsi		

Start like this: Alle sette la signora Bianchi si è svegliata.

Alle sette e un quarto ....

Exercise 4

What happened when? Write down the corresponding questions as shown in the example.

(Venire a casa / loro)
☐ Quando sono venuti a casa? Tre ore fa.

1. (nascere / lo zio Gianni)

....

Il 3 febbraio 1910.

2. (andare in America / lei)

....

L'anno scorso.

3. (pranzare / loro)

....

Un'ora fa.

4. (leggere il giornale / voi)

....

Fill in the correct preposition, with or without the article.

1. Vive a Roma .... febbraio.

2. Anna è .... Bari.

3. Ieri sono andata .... medico.

4. Silvio si è trasferito .... Sud America.

5. Sono arrivato a casa .... sette.

Exercise 5

Which parts belong together?

1. occhiali	**a** da bagno
2. costume	**b** da letto
3. macchina	**c** da sole
4. camicia	**d** da notte
5. camera	**e** da scrivere

Exercise 6

Vocabulary

a dire la verità	to be honest, tell the truth	**davanti a**	before
		dicembre *m*	December
agosto *m*	August	**diventare**	to become
andare via	to leave	**e così via**	and so on
aprile *m*	April	**emigrare**	to emigrate
argentino *m*	Argentinian	**esame** *m*	exam, test
augurio *m*	wish	**estate** *f*	summer
autunno *m*	autumn *Br* / fall *Am*	**famoso** *f*	famous
		fattoria *f*	farm
baffi *m pl*	moustache	**febbraio** *m*	February
camminare	to walk, go on foot	**fine** *f*	end
		fortuna *f*	fortune
capello *m*	hair	**gemello** *m*	twin
cenare	to eat dinner	**gennaio** *m*	January
compleanno *m*	birthday	**giugno** *m*	June
contadino *m*	farmer	**inizio** *m*	start, beginning
costume da bagno *m*	bathing suit	**inverno** *m*	winter
cugino *m*	cousin	**l'altro ieri**	day before yesterday ▶
data *f*	date		

libertà *f*	freedom	**ottobre** *m*	October
luglio *m*	July	**pasticceria** *f*	pastry shop
macchina da scrivere *f*	typewriter	**pediatra** *m/f*	pediatrician
		pranzare	to eat lunch
maggio *m*	May	**primavera** *f*	spring (time)
mancare	to lack, miss	**raccontare**	to tell,
marito *m*	husband		narrate
marzo *m*	March	**ricco**	rich
maturità *f*	secondary school exam	**scorso**	past
		scriversi	to write
meglio	better	**settembre** *m*	September
morire	to die	**sposarsi**	to marry
movimentato	(here:) exciting	**statua** *f*	statue
		strano	strange,
nascere	to be born		unusual
Natale *m*	Christmas	**terra** *f*	earth
nipote *m/f*	grandchild, niece, nephew	**tra**	between
		trasferirsi	to move
		vedersi	to see (each
novembre *m*	November		other)
occhiali da sole *m pl*	sunglasses	**verità** *f*	truth
		vita *f*	life

Immigration in Italy

Virtually everyone in Italy has some ancestor who emigrated to the USA or Argentina in the last 100 years.
Yet now Italy itself has become a country full of immigrants, legal and illegal. As its long extended coast lines are hard to patrol, Italy is experiencing a wave of illegal immigrants from non-EU countries, the so-called ***extracomunitari***. Support for these immigrants comes mainly from private initiatives and associations rather than the government.

Al mercato rionale

Fruttivendolo: Buongiorno signora, che cosa Le posso dare?
Piera: Vorrei un chilo di pomodori, due chili di patate e dell'insalata.
Fruttivendolo: Non vuole delle melanzane? Sono belle fresche!

Piera: Quanto costano? Non c'è il prezzo.
Fruttivendolo: 3 euro al chilo.
Piera: Un po' care, ma ne prendo due. Alessandra, guarda che bella frutta. Che cosa mangi volentieri?
Alexandra: Mi piacciono molto le albicocche.
Piera: Sono buone le albicocche? Sembrano un po' troppo mature.
Fruttivendolo: No, sono ottime signora, vengono dalla Riviera e sono dolcissime. Ne vuole assaggiare una?

Piera:	No, no, Le credo. Ne prendo un chilo e vorrei anche delle fragole, due cestini.
Fruttivendolo:	Desidera altro?
Piera:	No, grazie. Quant'è?
Fruttivendolo:	9 euro e 70 centesimi.
Piera:	Mi dà una borsa per favore?
Fruttivendolo:	Certo, ecco. Grazie e arrivederci.
Piera:	Arrivederci. Bene, abbiamo frutta e verdura ma devo ancora andare dal macellaio a comprare della carne: hai voglia di andare in panetteria a prendere un po' di pane, Alessandra?
Alexandra:	Volentieri. Prendo anche dei grissini?
Piera:	Sì, e la focaccia per Stefano, gli piace così tanto!
Alexandra:	Va bene, a più tardi.
Piera:	Grazie dell'aiuto, ciao.

At the local market

Fruit vendor:	Good morning, what can I offer you?
Piera:	I'd like a kilo of tomatoes, two kilos of potatoes and (a head of) lettuce.
Fruit vendor:	You don't want any aubergines (eggplants)? They are very fresh!
Piera:	How much are they? There's no price tag.
Fruit vendor:	Three euros a kilo.
Piera:	A little expensive but I'll take two. Alexandra, look at the lovely fruit. What kind do you like eating?
Alexandra:	I love apricots.
Piera:	Are the apricots any good? They seem to be somewhat overripe.
Fruit vendor:	No, they are excellent; they're from the Riviera and are very sweet. Would you like to try one?
Piera:	No, no I believe you. I'll take one kilo and I'd like strawberries as well, two punnets (baskets).
Fruit vendor:	Anything else?

Piera:	No thanks. How much is it?
Fruit vendor:	9 euros and 70 cents.
Piera:	Could you give me a bag, please?
Fruit vendor:	Of course, here you are. Thanks and goodbye.
Piera:	Goodbye. Well, we have fruit and vegetables but I still have to go to the butcher's to buy some meat. Alexandra, would you like to go to the bakery and buy some bread?
Alexandra:	Yes, I'll do that. Shall I also get some breadsticks?
Piera:	Yes and flat bread for Stefano, he likes it so much!
Alexandra:	OK, see you later.
Piera:	Thanks for your help, ciao.

The partitive article

The partitive article is used to designate an unspecified or unknown quantity. The English equivalent would be "some" or "any".

The partitive article is formed with the preposition **di** and the definite article.

	singular	*plural*
masculine	**del**	**dei**
	dello	**degli**
	dell'	**degli**
feminine	**della**	**delle**
	dell'	**delle**

Vorrei dello zucchero.	I'd like [some] sugar.
Vorrei delle melanzane.	I'd like [some] aubergines (eggplants).

ne

The pronoun **ne** refers to a previously mentioned object, group of objects or persons. It can cover a wide range of meanings such as **some, any, of (something)**:

Le albicocche sono dolci.
***Ne** prendo un chilo.* (I'll take one kilo of them.)

Sul tavolo ci sono quattro foto.
***Ne** vedo solo due.* (I can only see two of them.)

It can also mean **about (something)**.

Voglio comprare una macchina.
*Che cosa **ne** dici?* (What do you say about that?)

Indirect object pronouns

Indirect object pronouns generally **precede the verb**.

mi	me	*Mi piace la frutta.* (The fruit tastes good to me./I like fruit.)
ti	you	*Non ti credo.* (I don't believe you.)
gli	him	*Gli scrivo una lettera.* (I am writing him a letter.)
le	her	*Le porto dei fiori.* (I bring her flowers.)
Le	you	*Che cosa Le do, signora Bia?* (What can I give you, Mrs. Bia?)
ci	us	*Ci porti due caffè.* (Bring us two coffees.)
vi	you	*Vi presento Aldo Rei.* (I introduce you to Aldo Rei.)
gli	them	*Gli credo.* (I believe them.)

piacere

In Italian the verb **piacere** (to like/enjoy) is always formed with an indirect pronoun.

– **Indirect pronoun** + **piace** + **singular**
Mi piace la pasta. (I like pasta.)

– **Indirect pronoun** + **piacciono** + **plural**
Ti piacciono le tagliatelle? (Do you like tagliatelle?)

– **Indirect pronoun** + **piace** + **infinitive**
Gli piace ballare. (He likes dancing.)

The perfect tense of **piacere** is formed with **essere**:
Le è piaciuto il film? No, non mi è piaciuto.
(Did you enjoy the film? No I didn't like it.)

Quantities

> **un chilo** *di pomodori* (a kilo of tomatoes)
> **un etto** *di prosciutto* (100 grammes of ham)
> **mezzo chilo** *di fragole* (half a kilo of strawberries)
> **un pacco** *di pasta* (one packet of pasta)
> **un vasetto** *di marmellata* (one jar of jam)
> **un litro** *di vino bianco* (one litre of white wine)
> **mezzo litro** *di latte* (half a litre of milk)
> **una bottiglia** *di olio* (one bottle of oil)
> **una lattina** *di birra* (a can of beer)

Exercise 1

Write a shopping list by inserting the appropriate partitive article.

Devo comprare:

della	carne	......	carote
......	pane	......	aceto
......	prosciutto	......	zucchero
......	birra	......	fragole
......	vino	......	zucchini
......	biscotti		

Exercise 2

Fill in the correct indirect personal pronoun.

1. Quando scrivete ai signori Rossi?

   ...... scriviamo stasera.

2. Ti piace la musica classica?

   Sì, ... piace molto.

3. Signor Marchi, che cosa prende?

   ...... porti un tè.

4. Avete già scritto a Lisa?

   No, ... scriviamo domani.

5. Marco, ... piace il gelato?

6. Che cosa ci avete portato?

   ...... abbiamo portato dei fiori.

7. Vi piacciono le fragole?

   No, non ...... piacciono.

8. Hai dato i libri a Giorgio?

   Sì, ... ho dato i libri e anche i dischi.

Complete the sentences with *gli*, *le*, *Le* or *ne*.

Exercise 3

1. Hai scritto a Giovanni?
   No, ... scrivo domani.

2. Quante sigarette fumi? ...... fumo 10.

3. Maria, prendi un cioccolatino?
   Grazie ...... prendo due.

4. Signora, ... porto la macchina lunedì mattina.

5. A Maria piace la musica?
   Sì, ... piace.

6. Avete scritto a Carlo? Sì ...... abbiamo scritto.

Fill in *mi piace* or *mi piacciono*.

Exercise 4

1. .... molto i fiori.

2. Non .... il calcio.

3. .... nuotare in piscina.

4. .... la frutta fresca.

5. Non .... le macchine da corsa.

6. .... viaggiare.

Which parts match?

Exercise 5

Dove comprate queste cose?

1. Compro i grissini   **a** al mercato

2. Compro la frutta   **b** all'ufficio postale

3. Compro le medicine **c** in farmacia

4. Compro la carne   **d** in panetteria

5. Compro i francobolli **e** in macelleria

Vocabulary

aceto *m*	vinegar	**marmellata** *f*	jam
aiuto *m*	help	**maturo**	ripe
albicocca *f*	apricot	**melanzana** *f*	aubergine *Br* /
assaggiare	to taste, try		eggplant *Am*
borsa *f*	bag	**mezzo**	half
carne *f*	meat	**ne**	some, any, of
carota *f*	carrot		(something)
cestino *m*	punnet *Br* /	**olio** *m*	oil
	basket *Am*	**pacco** *m*	package
chilo *m*	kilo(gramme)	**pane** *m*	bread
dolcissimo	very sweet	**panetteria** *f*	bakery
etto *m*	100 grammes	**patata** *f*	potato
focaccia *f*	flat bread	**piacere**	to like, enjoy
fragola *f*	strawberry	**pomodoro** *m*	tomato
francobollo *m*	postage stamp	**presentare**	to present,
fresco	fresh		introduce
frutta *f*	fruit	**prezzo** *m*	price
fruttivendolo *m*	fruit vendor	**prosciutto** *m*	ham
grissino *m*	breadstick	**Quant'è?**	How much is
latte *m*	milk		it?
lattina *f*	can	**rionale**	local
litro *m*	litre	**sembrare**	to seem
macchina da	racing car	**ufficio postale** *m*	post office
corsa *f*		**vasetto** *m*	glass/jar
macellaio *m*	butcher	**zucchero** *m*	sugar
macelleria *f*	butcher's		

A buon mercato! Weekly markets are a common feature of all Italian towns. The bigger cities actually have itinerate markets throughout the week, serving a different neighbourhood every day.

These markets offer everything from food such as fruit and vegetables, meat and bread to shoes, table linen, clothing, cutlery and crockery. If you are looking for a bargain that's the place to search for it: **a buon mercato!**

Dove andiamo stasera?

Marco:	Allora ragazze, cosa facciamo stasera?
Alexandra:	Mah, non so, tu Laura hai un'idea?
Laura:	Perché non andiamo al cinema? All'Ariston danno l'ultimo film di Pupi Avati, deve essere molto bello.
Alexandra:	Non lo conosco, chi è?
Laura:	È un giovane regista italiano.
Marco:	Ma dobbiamo proprio andare al cinema? Io non ho molta voglia, preferisco il teatro. Al Nazionale c'è una commedia di Pirandello.
Alexandra:	Io sono d'accordo.
Laura:	Anch'io, ma chi compra i biglietti?
Marco:	Li prendo io oggi pomeriggio.
Alexandra:	A che ora comincia lo spettacolo?
Marco:	Ora guardo sul giornale ... alle 20.30. Prendi tu la macchina?

Laura:	Sì, la prendo io perché passo a prendere il mio ragazzo Giorgio e dopo vengo da Alessandra. Marco, puoi venire a casa di Alessandra alle otto meno un quarto?
Marco:	Certo. Allora compro quattro biglietti?
Laura:	Sì, grazie.
Alexandra:	E forse dopo possiamo andare a mangiare qualcosa in birreria.
Laura:	Senz'altro, e fare quattro salti in discoteca! Allora a stasera, io suono e vi aspetto sotto.
Alexandra:	Va bene, ciao.
Marco:	Ciao.

Where're we going tonight?

Marco:	OK guys, what are we doing tonight?
Alexandra:	I don't know. Do you have any ideas, Laura?
Laura:	Why don't we go to the cinema? At the Ariston they're showing the latest film by Pupi Avati. It's supposed to be very good.
Alexandra:	I don't know him. Who is he?
Laura:	He is a young Italian director.
Marco:	Do we really have to go to the cinema? I'm not in the mood for that, I'd rather go to the theatre. There's a comedy by Pirandello at the Nazionale Theatre.
Alexandra:	I'm with you.
Laura:	Me too, who is buying the tickets?
Marco:	I'll get them in this afternoon.
Alexandra:	What time does the show start?
Marco:	Just a minute, I'll check the paper ... at 8:30 p.m. Are you going by car?
Laura:	Yes, I am, because I'll be picking up my friend Giorgio on the way and then I'll go to Alexandra's place. Marco, can you be at Alexandra's at a quarter to eight?

Marco:	Sure. I'll get four tickets then?
Laura:	Yes, thanks.
Alexandra:	Maybe we can go and have something to eat in a pub afterwards?
Laura:	We certainly can, and then go dancing in a club! Well, until tonight then, I'll ring the bell and wait for you downstairs.
Alexandra:	OK, ciao.
Marco:	Ciao.

Direct object pronouns

Direct object pronouns generally **precede the verb**.

mi	me	*Mi senti?*	Can you hear me?
ti	you	*Ti accompagno.*	I accompany you.
lo	him/it	*Non lo conosco.*	I don't know him.
la	her/it	*Non la mangio.*	I don't eat it.
La	you	*La aspetto, dottore.*	I am expecting you, doctor.
ci	us	*Ci sentite?*	Can you hear us?
vi	you	*Non vi capisco.*	I don't understand you.
li	them *(m.)*	*Li conosco.*	I know them. (Marco and Alberto)
le	them *(f.)*	*Non le capisco.*	I don't understand them. (Maria and Laura)

Infinitive constructions

Some Italian infinitive constructions are formed with or without prepositions.

with **a**	**andare a**	*Vado a mangiare in mensa.* (I am going to eat in the cafeteria.)
	aiutare a	*Aiutiamo Maria a lavare la macchina.* (We help Maria to wash the car.)
with **di**	**avere voglia di**	*Ho voglia di giocare.* (I'm in the mood to play.)
	avere tempo di	*Hai tempo di fare la spesa?* (Do you have time to go shopping?)
without preposition	**preferire**	*Preferisco viaggiare in treno.* (I prefer to travel by train.)
	desiderare	*Desidera bere qualcosa?* (Would you like something to drink?)
	piacere	*Mi piace cantare.* (I like to sing.)

Exercise 1

Answer the following questions using the correct personal pronoun.

1. Chi compra il giornale?

   ...... compra il nonno.

2. Accompagnate a casa Marisa e Ada?

   ...... accompagniamo subito.

3. Pronto, ci senti?

   Sì, adesso ...... sento.

4. Mamma, mamma, mi aspetti?

   Certo, ... aspetto in macchina.

▶

5. Ti porto a scuola domani?

No, grazie ...... porta Alexandra.

6. Vi conoscete già?

Sì, ... conosciamo, abitiamo vicino.

Qual è la tua opinione? Fill in the correct pronoun and choose the adjective that you think fits best.

Exercise 2

Ti piace il cinema? ☐ **Lo** trovo divertente / noioso

1. Ti piace Roma? .... trovo interessante / caotica

2. Ti piacciono le lasagne? .... trovo saporite / troppo pesanti

3. Ti piace lo sport? .... trovo sano / faticoso

4. Ti piacciono i computer? .... trovo utili / inutili

5. Ti piace il deserto? .... trovo affascinante / pericoloso

6. Ti piace la moda italiana? .... trovo elegante / troppo cara.

Complete the following sentences using the correct direct pronoun (*lo, la, La, li,le*) or the correct indirect pronoun (*gli, le, Le*).

Exercise 3

1. Perché non aiuti papà a lavare la macchina?

Va bene, ... aiuto.

2. Quando telefonate alla vostra amica tedesca?

...... telefoniamo domenica pomeriggio.

3. Ascolti i dischi di musica lirica?

Sì, ... ascolto molto volentieri.

▶

4. Non avete ancora parlato a Massimo?

No, purtroppo non ...... abbiamo ancora parlato.

5. Signora, ... posso aiutare?

6. Quando ringraziate le vostre amiche per il regalo?

...... ringraziamo domani.

7. Tuo zio ti ha scritto una lunga lettera.

...... hai risposto?

8. Ho chiesto a Monica un favore.

Che cosa ...... hai chiesto?

Exercise 4

Write complete sentences as in the example. Pay attention to the correct use of the prepositions!

Massimo / avere voglia / andare in vacanza
Massimo ha voglia di andare in vacanza.

1. I nonni / andare / vedere un film al cinema

....

2. Nadia / non avere tempo / suonare il pianoforte

....

3. (Loro) / preferire / mangiare / in pizzeria

....

4. (Io) / aiutare i miei genitori / pulire l'appartamento

....

5. Nicola / non avere voglia / andare a scuola

....

Vocabulary

accompagnare	to accompany	**inutile**	useless
affascinante	fascinating	**lavare**	to wash
aiutare	to help	**musica lirica** *f*	opera music
avere voglia	to want to do	**noioso**	boring
birreria *f*	pub, bar	**passare a**	to pick up,
cantare	to sing	**prendere**	collect
caotico	chaotic	**pericoloso**	dangerous
commedia *f*	comedy	**pesante**	heavy
dare (al cinema)	to show (in	**regalo** *m*	gift, present
	the cinema)	**regista** *m/f*	(film) director
discoteca *f*	disco,	**ringraziare**	to thank
	(night)club	**sano**	healthy
divertente	funny,	**saporito**	tasty
	amusing	**spettacolo** *m*	show,
fare quattro	to go for a		presentation
salti	dance	**utile**	useful
faticoso	exhausting		
favore *m*	favour		

Going to the movies

Italy still has plenty of historical movie theatres recalling the heyday of moving pictures. During the summer months, many cinemas offer outdoor screenings, *cinema all'aperto.* When getting tickets bear in mind that these can be bought only at the ticket counter at the cinema on the night of the viewing itself. Most Italian cinemas don't take any reservations. Although there are no long-winded commercials before a movie, the screening itself is often interrupted at regular intervals for smokers to go out and have a cigarette.

Test 3

1 Choose one of the two answers, then go to the square with the number of your answer.

2 I bambini va... ... zoo.

allo ⮕ 24
al ⮕ 14

6 Correct! Continue:

Andiamo ... stazione.

a ⮕ 26
alla ⮕ 10

7 Wrong!

Back to number 30.

11 Wrong!

Go back to number 24.

12 Correct! Continue:

Non ho voglia ... .

di mangiare ⮕ 8
mangiare ⮕ 19

16 Wrong!

Go back to number 10.

17 Good! Conti... Elena e Paola sono ... in tram.

venuto ⮕ 23
venute ⮕ 4

21 Wrong!

Go back to number 13.

22 Very good! Continue: Compri i biglietti? Sì, ... compro.

gli ⮕ 9
li ⮕ 12

26 Wrong!

Go back to number 6.

27 Correct! Conti... Compro i griss... in ...

farmacia ⮕ 3
panetteria ⮕ 17

Wrong!

back to
mber 27.

---

4 Very good!
Continue:

Non ... il francese.

posso ⤳ 28
so ⤳ 20

---

5 Wrong!

Go back to
number 25.

Great!
Continue:
ai telefonato a Mario?
, ... ho telefonato.
i ⤳ 15
⤳ 29

---

9 Wrong!

Go back to
number 22.

---

10 Great!
Continue:

Quando ... arrivato?

sei ⤳ 30
hai ⤳ 16

Very good!
Continue:
rrei ... albicocche.

l' ⤳ 21
le ⤳ 6

---

14 Wrong!

Go back to
number 2.

---

15 Correct!

End of exercise!

Wrong!

back to
mber 20.

---

19 Wrong!

Go back to
number 12.

---

20 Good! Continue:

... la musica jazz?

Ti piacciono ⤳ 18
Ti piace ⤳ 13

Wrong!

back to
mber 17.

---

24 Correct!
Continue:
Avete ... questo libro?

letto ⤳ 27
leggiuto ⤳ 11

---

25 Great!
Continue.
La macchina ...
costata poco.
ha ⤳ 5
è ⤳ 22

Wrong!

o back to
mber 4.

---

29 Wrong!

Go back to
number 8.

---

30 Good!
Continue:
L'anno ... sono andata
in Sicilia.
fa ⤳ 7
scorso ⤳ 25

16 In macchina in città

Alexandra: Buongiorno, il pieno per favore.
Benzinaio: Subito signorina. Senza piombo, vero?
Alexandra: Sì, grazie. E controlli anche l'olio per favore.
Valentina, sei sicura di sapere che strada
dobbiamo prendere? Io non conosco ancora
abbastanza bene Milano e poi viaggio
sempre in metropolitana.
Valentina: Magari è meglio se chiediamo, così non
sbagliamo strada.
Alexandra: Senta, scusi, vorrei un'informazione.
Benzinaio: Se posso, volentieri.
Alexandra: Per andare in
piazza Santa
Chiara che
strada devo
prendere?

Benzinaio: Allora, ... prenda la prima strada a sinistra e
vada sempre dritto fino al parco; subito
dopo, davanti alla chiesa, giri a sinistra,
continui dritto fino al primo semaforo e alla
sua destra c'è piazza Santa Chiara.
Alexandra: Va bene, grazie molte.
Benzinaio: Però faccia attenzione: fino alle 12.00 c'è
divieto di sosta sulla piazza. Provi a

	parcheggiare dietro la chiesa, qualche volta c'è un posto libero.
Alexandra:	Grazie del consiglio … Quanto Le devo?
Benzinaio:	40 euro. Olio ne ha ancora abbastanza.
Alexandra:	Arrivederci.
Benzinaio:	Arrivederci e buona giornata.
…	
Alexandra:	C'è molto traffico oggi. Hai capito bene che strada dobbiamo prendere?
Valentina:	Beh, più o meno, ma forse chiediamo ancora a un vigile.
Alexandra:	Almeno sai dov'è l'ufficio dove dobbiamo andare?
Valentina:	Ma certo, proprio sulla piazza, di fronte al cinema. Ehi, guarda, là c'è un vigile; sii gentile, accosta un attimo così gli chiediamo. Senta, mi scusi …
Alexandra:	Che stress! Domani prendo di sicuro la metropolitana!

Driving in the city

Alexandra:	Good morning, fill it up please.
Attendant:	Right away. Unleaded, right?
Alexandra:	Yes, thank you. And check the oil as well, please. Valentina, are you sure you know which street we have to take? I don't know Milan well enough yet and besides, I always take the subway.
Valentina:	We'd better ask so we don't get lost.
Alexandra:	Excuse me, I need some information.
Attendant:	If I can help, certainly.
Alexandra:	Which street do I have to take to get to Santa Chiara square?
Attendant:	OK, … take the first street on the left and then go straight ahead up to the park. Immediately turn left in front of the church and continue until you come to the first set of traffic lights. Santa Chiara square is to your right.

Alexandra:	OK, thank you very much.
Attendant:	But watch out: you're not allowed to park on the square before 12 o'clock. Try to park behind the church; you might find a free parking space there.
Alexandra:	Thanks for the tip ... How much do I owe you?
Attendant:	40 euros. You still have enough oil.
Alexandra:	Goodbye.
Attendant:	Goodbye and have a nice day.
...	
Alexandra:	Lots of traffic today. Did you understand which street we have to take?
Valentina:	Well, more or less, but perhaps we should also ask a policeman.
Alexandra:	Do you at least know where the office is that we have to go to?
Valentina:	Sure, directly on the square opposite the cinema. Hey, there's a policeman. Be nice and pull over and we'll ask him. Excuse me, ...
Alexandra:	This is too stressful for me! Tomorrow I'll definitely take the subway!

Imperative

guardare	**prendere**	**sentire**	**finire**
(tu) guard**a**	prend**i**	sent**i**	finis**ci**
(Lei) guard**i**	prend**a**	sent**a**	finis**ca**
(noi) guard**iamo**	prend**iamo**	sent**iamo**	fin**iamo**
(voi) guard**ate**	prend**ete**	sent**ite**	fin**ite**
(loro) guard**ino**	prend**ano**	sent**ano**	finis**cano**

The 1st and 2nd person plural are formed like the present tense. The negative imperative is formed by simply inserting **non** before the verb. In the informal **tu** form, the negative imperative is formed with **non** +infinitive:

| *Signor Risi, **non fumi** così tanto!* | (Mr. Risi, don't smoke so much!) |
| *Marco, **non fumare** così tanto!* | (Marco, don't smoke so much!) |

The imperative of some irregular verbs:

	andare	venire	stare	fare
(tu)	vai/va'	vieni	stai/sta'	fai/fa'
(Lei)	vada	venga	stia	faccia
(noi)	andiamo	veniamo	stiamo	facciamo
(voi)	andate	venite	state	fate
(loro)	vadano	vengano	stiano	facciano

	dire	dare	avere	essere
(tu)	di'	dai/da'	abbi	sii
(Lei)	dica	dia	abbia	sia
(noi)	diciamo	diamo	abbiamo	siamo
(voi)	dite	date	abbiate	siate
(loro)	dicano	diano	abbiano	siano

Prepositions defining location

vicino a	vicino al ristorante	(near the restaurant)
accanto a	accanto al bar	(next to the bar)
di fronte a	di fronte alla banca	(opposite the bank)
davanti a	davanti a casa mia	(in front of my house)
dietro a	dietro alla chiesa	(behind the church)
tra/fra	tra/fra Milano e Torino	(between Milan and Turin)
in mezzo a	in mezzo alla piazza	(in the centre of the square)
fino a	fino al semaforo	(up to the traffic lights)
in fondo a	in fondo alla strada	(at the end of the street)

Exercise 1

Fill in the corresponding imperative forms.

1. chiudere: Marco, ... la porta!

2. scrivere: Ragazzi, ... una cartolina a Maria.

3. portare: Beppe, ... il caffè a papà.

4. raccontare: Mamma, ... una favola a Paolo.

5. dormire: .... bene, Marina.

6. telefonare: Signora Dossi, ... a mia moglie, per favore.

Watch out here!

7. venire: Laura .... subito a casa!

8. dare: Luigi, ... questi libri a tua sorella.

9. dire: Per favore, signor Bui .... a Luca che è ora di pranzo!

10. avere: Bambini, ... un po' di pazienza.

11. andare: Graziella, ... a fare la spesa.

12. fare: Elena, ... una passeggiata.

Exercise 2

Complete the sentences using the correct imperative forms.

Alcuni consigli per la signora Pozzi:

1. .... (fare) molte passeggiate.

2. Non .... (fumare) troppo.

3. .... (mangiare) poca carne.

4. .... (prendere) le medicine.

5. .... (dormire) molto.

6. Non .... (bere) vino.

7. .... (andare) in vacanza al mare.

8. Non .... (mangiare) dolci.

Which of these conversations are business-related and which are private?

1. Telefoni al Dottor Rosso, per favore.

2. Vieni subito alla stazione!

3. Venga in ufficio alle 8.30.

4. Scriva a macchina questa lettera.

5. Telefona a Silvia e Gino.

6. Finisca questo lavoro.

business: ....

private: ....

Study the map on page 144, then answer the following questions.

1. Dov'è la pizzeria?

È accanto ....

2. Dov'è il parcheggio?

....

3. Dov'è la chiesa?

....

4. Dov'è la banca?

....

5. Dov'è il supermercato?

....

6. Dov'è la farmacia?

....

**Write complete
sentences using
the following
example.**

macelleria / davanti a / bar
La macelleria è davanti al bar.

1. cinema / in fondo a / strada

....

2. ristorante / di fronte a / scuola

....

3. casa di Luca / dietro a / chiesa

....

4. panetteria / accanto a / negozio di
abbigliamento

....

5. farmacia / tra / supermercato e banca

....

Which sentences belong together?

1. Che strada devo prendere?
2. Sono molto stanca.
3. Desidera?
4. Fa molto caldo qui!
5. Posso fumare?
6. Non sto molto bene.

a Controlli l'olio per favore.
b Apri la finestra.
c Va' a dormire.
d Fuma pure.
e Vai dal medico.
f Vada sempre dritto e giri la terza strada a destra.

abbastanza	enough	**favola** *f*	story
accanto a	besides	**fra**	between
accostare	to pull over	**girare**	to turn
almeno	at least	**in mezzo a**	in the middle of
attenzione *f*	attention, care	**informazione** *f*	information
attimo *m*	moment	**là**	there
benzinaio *m*	attendant (at petrol *Br* / gas *Am* station)	**libero**	free
		magari	maybe
		parcheggiare	to park
cartolina *f*	postcard	**parcheggio** *m*	parking space
consiglio *m*	advice	**pazienza** *f*	patience
continuare	to drive on	**piazza** *f*	square
controllare	to control	**piombo** *m*	lead
di fronte a	opposite	**pure**	if you want
di sicuro	certainly	**quanto Le devo?**	how much do I owe you?
dietro a	behind	**sbagliare**	to err, be mistaken
divieto di sosta	no parking		
fare attenzione	to pay attention, watch out	**sbagliare strada**	to get lost
		scrivere a macchina	to write with a typewriter
fare il pieno	to fill up	**semaforo** *m*	traffic lights ▶

senza	without	**vicino a**	near
senza piombo	unleaded	**vigile** *m*	traffic
sicuro	certain(ly), sure		policeman
traffico *m*	traffic		

Driving in Italy

Driving a car in Italy is a costly undertaking given the motorway tolls and high petrol (gas) prices. More and more inner-city areas are being made into traffic-free zones, at least during certain hours. When driving a car in the city, finding a parking space can be a daunting task.

Petrol stations, on the other hand, still offer their customers a wide range of services. Self-service stations are rare in Italy. Car drivers are instead expected to remain seated in their cars and tell the attendant what they need done. The windscreen is habitually cleaned and the oil and cooling water levels are checked. When asking for petrol, unleaded, *senza piombo,* is also often referred to as *verde*.

Una gita a Firenze

Marco:	Due biglietti di andata e ritorno per Firenze, per favore.
Impiegato:	Di prima o seconda classe?
Marco:	Di seconda classe. Mi sa dire a che ora parte il prossimo treno?
Impiegato:	Un momento prego, glielo dico subito ... Il prossimo parte alle 8.38, ma deve cambiare a Bologna. Altrimenti deve aspettare quello delle 9.00. È un Intercity e arriva a Firenze alle 11.53. Ma deve pagare il supplemento.
Marco:	Allora due biglietti per quello delle 9.00, per favore.
A Firenze:	
Marco:	Eccoci in piazza della Signoria!
Alexandra:	E qual è la galleria degli Uffizi?
Marco:	Eccola, proprio davanti a te!
Alexandra:	Entriamo, voglio visitarla subito! Mi puoi fare il biglietto, per favore?
Marco:	Sì, certo, te lo faccio io ... Due biglietti, per favore. Scusi, a che ora chiude la galleria?

Impiegata:	Alle cinque.
Marco:	Allora abbiamo tempo!
Impiegata:	Lei scherza, vero? Per visitare gli Uffizi non bastano tre giorni!

Dopo alcune ore:

Alexandra:	Marco, tu non sei un po' stanco?
Marco:	Stanco? Sono stanco morto!! Non possiamo fare una pausa?
Alexandra:	Ma certo, usciamo e andiamo a mangiare qualcosa.
Marco:	Buona idea. Che cosa vuoi vedere dopo?
Alexandra:	Dunque... il Duomo, il giardino di Boboli, il Ponte Vecchio e il Mercato Nuovo! Voglio toccare il muso del porcellino: porta fortuna!
Marco:	Perché, sei superstiziosa?
Alexandra:	Non molto, ma un po' di fortuna fa sempre bene!

A trip to Florence

Marco:	Two return tickets to Florence, please.
Rail employee:	First or second class?
Marco:	Second class. Can you tell me when the next train leaves?
Rail employee:	One moment please, I'll tell you in a minute ... The next train leaves at 8:38 a.m. but you'll have to change in Bologna. Otherwise you have to wait until nine o'clock. That's an intercity which arrives in Florence at 11:53 a.m. but you will have to pay a surcharge.
Marco:	OK, I'll take two tickets for the nine o'clock train, please.

In Florence:

Marco:	Here we are at the Piazza della Signoria!
Alexandra:	And which one is the Uffizi Gallery?
Marco:	Here, facing you!
Alexandra:	Let's go inside, I want to see it right now! Can you get me the admission ticket, please?

▶

Marco:	Sure, I'll get it for you ... Two tickets, please. Excuse me, what time does the gallery close?
Employee:	At five o'clock.
Marco:	We have time then!
Employee:	You're kidding, right? Not even three days would be enough time to see the Uffizi!

After a few hours:

Alexandra:	Marco, aren't you a little tired?
Marco:	Tired? I'm dead tired!! Can't we take a break?
Alexandra:	Sure, let's go outside and eat something.
Marco:	Good idea. What do you want to see afterwards?
Alexandra:	Well... the Duomo (cathedral), Boboli gardens, Ponte Vecchio (bridge) and Mercato Nuovo (market). And I want to touch the piglet's snout; it's said to be lucky.
Marco:	Why? Are you superstitious?
Alexandra:	Not really, but it's always good to have some luck!

Double pronouns

When two object pronouns occur together, the indirect pronoun precedes the direct pronoun. The pronouns change accordingly:

mi + lo (la / li / le / ne)	**me lo (me la / me li / me le / me ne)**
ti + lo	**te lo**
gli + lo	**glielo**
ci + lo	**ce lo**
vi + lo	**ve lo**
gli + lo	**glielo**
si + lo	**se lo**

– *Mario **mi** presenta **suo padre**.* → *(Mario)* **me lo** *presenta.*
     Mario introduced him (to me).

– *Mario **mi** presenta **sua madre**.* → **Me la** *presenta.*
– *Mario **mi** presenta **i suoi fratelli**.* → **Me li** *presenta.*
– *Mario **mi** presenta **le sue sorelle**.* → **Me le** *presenta.*
– *Mario **ti** presenta **suo padre**.* → **Te lo** *presenta.*

Infinitive + pronoun

When using a pronoun together with an infinitive, the pronoun is added to the ending of the verb by omitting the final vowel of the infinitive form:

È meglio **parcheggiare la macchina** qui.
➔ È meglio **parcheggiarla** qui.

With the modal verbs *dovere, potere, volere*, there are two different ways to add the pronoun:

– either in front of the modal verb:
   La voglio parcheggiare qui.

– or attached to the infinitive (the final vowel of the infinitive is omitted):
   Voglio parcheggiar**la** qui.

Ecco!

Italians regularly use the expression **ecco** in their speech. It can be broadly translated as "here/there/that/this is (are); look, see". It is worthwhile to take a closer look at its usage.

Ecco is used above all to refer to or point at something or to emphasize something just said.

– **Ecco** il tuo quaderno! (Here is your exercise book!)

– **Ecco** Mario! (Here is Mario!)

– Tutto è andato bene, ma **ecco** che lui ha sempre da protestare! (Everything went well but nevertheless he always has to protest!)

Eccolo!

It is also possible to attach an object pronoun to *ecco*:

Ecco il duomo! → *Eccolo!* (Here is the cathedral!/
Here it is!)

Ecco la galleria! → *Eccola!* (Here is the gallery!/
Here it is!)

Ecco i giardini! → *Eccoli!* (Here are the gardens!/
Here they are!)

Ecco le ragazze! → *Eccole!* (Here are the girls!/
Here they are!)

Additional idiomatic expressions:

Eccomi!	Here I am!
Eccoti!	Here you are!
Eccoci!	Here we are!
Eccovi!	Here you (plural) are!
EccoLe il resto!	Here is the rest (for you)!

Fill in *ecco* and the corresponding pronoun.

1. Hai visto la mia borsa? Sì, ...

2. Dove sono i miei figli? ....

3. Hai una matita, per favore?

   Certo, ...

4. Scusi, sa dov'è il duomo?

   Certo: ....!

5. Marco, Marco, dove sei?

   .... mamma!

6. .... qui, ci avete cercato?

7. Dove sono le fragole? ....

Exercise 1

Exercise 2

Replace the underlined words with the appropriate pronouns. Rearrange the word order where necessary.

Compro <u>il giornale</u>. → **Lo** compro.

1. Mangio <u>l'insalata</u>. . . . .

2. Devo comprare <u>il caffè</u>. . . . .

3. Che cosa regali <u>a Silvia</u>? . . . .

4. Vuoi anche tu <u>una birra</u>? . . . .

5. <u>A Marco</u> piace molto la musica jazz.

. . . .

6. È meglio prendere <u>il tram</u>. . . . .

7. Anche Alexandra mangia <u>i biscotti</u>.

. . . .

8. <u>Ai miei figli</u> piace giocare a tennis.

. . . .

Exercise 3

Fill in both object pronouns in their correct order when answering the questions.

1. Marco mi regala un disco?

   Sì, ...

2. Andrea le porta i fiori?

   No, ...

3. Giovanni si lava sempre i denti?

   Sì, ...

4. Chi mi porta i giornali?

   . . . . Carlo.

5. Mi scrivi una lettera?

   Sì, ...

6. Mi dai le chiavi, per favore?

   Sì, ... subito.

Replace the underlined words with the appropriate pronouns.

Exercise 4

Dario non dice <u>la verità alla mamma</u>. ➔ Dario non **gliela** dice.

1. Piero racconta <u>una favola a suo figlio</u>. ....

2. Il signor Cattaneo scrive <u>una lettera al direttore</u>. ....

3. Andrea chiede <u>a Maria un piacere</u>. ....

4. La mamma insegna <u>a Fabio l'alfabeto</u>. ....

5. Presento <u>Stefano a mia madre</u>. ....

Translate the English sentences in the dialogue.

Exercise 5

A: Buongiorno.

B: Good afternoon. A ticket to Bologna, please.

....

A: Di prima o seconda classe?

B: Second class.

....

A: Ecco a Lei. Fanno 18,50 euro.

B: Excuse me, do you know what time the next train leaves?

....

A: Il prossimo parte alle 14.18, dal binario tredici.

B: Thank you very much. Goodbye.

....

alfabeto *m*	alphabet	**matita** *f*	pencil
altrimenti	otherwise	**militare** *m*	soldier
andata e ritorno	return *Br* / round-trip *Am* ticket	**muso** *m*	snout, mouth
		orario di apertura *m*	opening hours
antico	old, antique	**orario** *m*	schedule
aspettare	to wait	**pausa** *f*	break, pause
bastare	to suffice, be enough	**pensionato** *m*	senior citizen
biblioteca *f*	library	**porcellino** *m*	piglet
cambiare	to change, switch	**protestare**	to protest
		quaderno *m*	exercise book
chiuso	closed	**ridotto**	discounted admission ticket
classe *f*	class		
comunale	municipal		
dente *m*	tooth	**scherzare**	to joke
dunque	well then	**sconto** *m*	reduction
eccoci	here we are	**stanco morto**	dead tired
eccola	here she is	**superstizioso**	superstitious
entrare	to enter	**supplemento** *m*	surcharge
far bene	to do good	**toccare**	to touch
galleria *f*	gallery		
giardino *m*	garden		
invalido *m*	disabled person		

Tourist information   Though Italian museums don't have uniform opening hours, they are generally closed during lunch breaks and on Mondays. Most museums and cinemas offer discounts *(sconti/ ridotti)* for the disabled *(invalidi)*, senior citizens *(pensionati)*, soldiers *(militari)* and larger groups. Most churches are open during the day. Excessively casual dress, such as shorts, strapless tops and dresses, plastic flip-flop sandles etc. is discouraged.

Una telefonata di lavoro

Segretaria:	Pronto, P.T.R. Italia, buongiorno.
Alexandra:	Buongiorno, sono Alexandra Jansen, vorrei parlare con il signor Arturi. È in ufficio?
Segretaria:	Attenda un attimo, per favore, devo guardare ... No, mi dispiace, in questo momento è in riunione, può telefonare più tardi?
Alexandra:	Sì, certo. Tra mezz'ora va bene?
Segretaria:	Sì, benissimo.
Alexandra:	A più tardi, allora.
Segretaria:	A più tardi.

Segretaria:	Pronto, P.T.R. Italia, buongiorno.
Alexandra:	Buongiorno, sono ancora Jansen. Vorrei parlare con il signor Arturi. Me lo può passare?
Segretaria:	Mi dispiace, ma il signor Arturi è ancora in riunione.
Alexandra:	Posso lasciare un messaggio?
Segretaria:	Certamente!
Alexandra:	Dunque, gli dica che confermo l'appuntamento del 10 maggio alle 10.30.

▶

Segretaria:	Bene: ha detto il 10 maggio, vero?
Alexandra:	Sì.
Segretaria:	Mi può ripetere il Suo nome, per favore?
Alexandra:	Alexandra Jansen.
Segretaria:	Scusi, come si scrive il suo cognome?
Alexandra:	Jansen. I lunga, A come Ancona, N come Napoli, S come Savona, E come Empoli e N come Napoli.
Segretaria:	Jansen. Perfetto. Il signor Arturi La deve richiamare?
Alexandra:	No, grazie, non è necessario.
Segretaria:	Arrivederci, allora.
Alexandra:	Arrivederci.

A business call

Secretary:	P.T.R. Italy, good morning.
Alexandra:	Good morning, I am Alexandra Jansen. I'd like to speak to Mr. Arturi. Is he in his office?
Secretary:	Just a moment, please, I have to check ... No, I am sorry, he is in a meeting right now. Can you call back later?
Alexandra:	Yes, of course. Let's say in half an hour?
Secretary:	Yes, very well.
Alexandra:	Until later then.
Secretary:	Yes, until later.
Secretary:	P.T.R. Italy, good morning.
Alexandra:	Good morning, it's me again, Jansen. I would like to speak to Mr. Arturi. Can you put me through to him?
Secretary:	I am sorry, but Mr. Arturi is still in a meeting.
Alexandra:	Can I leave a message?
Secretary:	Yes, of course!
Alexandra:	Well then, could you please let him know that I'm confirming the appointment on the 10th of May at 10:30 a.m.
Secretary:	OK, you said the 10th of May, right?
Alexandra:	Yes.

▶

Secretary:	Could you repeat your name for me, please?
Alexandra:	Alexandra Jansen.
Secretary:	I'm sorry, how do you spell your last name?
Alexandra:	Jansen. J, A as in Ancona, N as in Naples, S as in Savona, E as in Empoli and N as in Naples.
Secretary:	Jansen. Perfect. Do you want Mr. Arturi to call you back?
Alexandra:	No, thank you, that's not necessary.
Secretary:	Goodbye then.
Alexandra:	Goodbye.

Postion of pronouns in the imperative

When using the imperative be careful where to position the object pronoun (*mi, ti, gli, le, Le, ci, vi, si, la, lo, li, le, ci, ne*):

(tu) guarda**lo**	prendi**lo**	senti**lo**
(Look at it/him!)	(Take it/him!)	(Listen to him!)
(Lei) **lo** guardi	**lo** prenda	**lo** senta
(noi) guardiamo**lo**	prendiamo**lo**	sentiamo**lo**
(voi) guardate**lo**	prendete**lo**	sentite**lo**
(loro) **lo** guardino	**lo** prendano	**lo** sentano

In the second person singular *(tu)* and the first and second person plural *(noi, voi)* the object pronouns are attached directly to the verb. In the third person singular and plural *(Lei* and *loro)* they remain in their normal position in front of the verb.

The negative of the second person singular is formed with the infinitive (see also Lesson 16). The last letter of the infinitive is dropped and the pronoun is attached directly to the verb: *non guardar**lo**, non prender**lo**, non sentir**lo**!*
With the abbreviated imperative in the second person singular of the verbs *andare, dare, dire, fare, stare (va', da', di', fa', sta')* the first letters of the pronoun are **doubled** (except with *gli*):

di'+ mi → dimmi (tell me), **fa'+ lo → fallo** (do it),
da'+ le → dalle (give her)

Spelling words in Italian

A (a)	come Ancona	**N** (enne)	come Napoli
B (bi)	come Bologna	**O** (o)	come Otranto
C (ci)	come Cagliari	**P** (pi)	come Palermo
D (di)	come Domodossola	**Q** (qu)	come Quarto
E (e)	come Empoli	**R** (erre)	come Roma
F (effe)	come Firenze	**S** (esse)	come Savona
G (gi)	come Genova	**T** (ti)	come Torino
H (acca)		**U** (u)	come Udine
I (i)	come Imola	**V** (vu/vi)	come Venezia
J (i lunga)		**W** (vu doppia)	
K (cappa)		**X** (ics)	
L (elle)	come Livorno	**Y** (ipsilon)	
M (emme)	come Milano	**Z** (zeta)	come Zara

Exercise 1

The following exercise includes a number of tips for the preparation of salads. Replace *insalata* with the pronoun *la* and make sure to place it in the right position.

Compra l'insalata. → Comprala!

1. Lava l'insalata.

. . . .

2. Non lavare l'insalata con l'acqua calda.

. . . .

3. Taglia l'insalata.

. . . .

4. Metti l'insalata in un'insalatiera.

. . . .

5. Condisci l'insalata con olio, aceto, pepe e sale.

. . . .

6. Assaggia l'insalata.

. . . .

7. Porta l'insalata in tavola.

. . . .

8. Mangia l'insalata.

. . . .

Repeat exercise 1
using the third
person singular
(Lei).

Compra l'insalata. → La compri!

1. . . . .
2. . . . .
3. . . . .
4. . . . .
5. . . . .
6. . . . .
7. . . . .
8. . . . .

Exercise 2

Form the imperative in the second and third person singular
(**tu** and **Lei**). Match the following verbs to fit the items listed
below: *bere, mangiare, provare, assaggiare, comprare, pagare,
prendere, guardare, leggere.* Use the appropriate pronouns
(e. g. *Caffè: Bevilo!/Lo beva!; Compralo!/Lo compri!* etc.).

Exercise 3

1. caffè   **2.** scarpe   **3.** spaghetti   **4.** libro

. . . .	. . . .	. . . .	. . . .
. . . .	. . . .	. . . .	. . . .
. . . .	. . . .	. . . .	. . . .
. . . .	. . . .	. . . .	. . . .
. . . .	. . . .	. . . .	. . . .

Exercise 4

Answer the questions using the imperative.
Be careful when to apply "tu" or "Lei".

1. Scusi, posso aprire la finestra?
   Certo, ... pure.

2. Mamma, posso mangiare una caramella? Sì, ...

3. Scusa, posso fumare una sigaretta?
   Ma certo, ...

4. Cristina, cosa mi consigli, compro questa gonna o no? No, ...

5. Le dispiace se chiudo la porta?
   No, no, prego .... pure.

6. Roberto ti ha scritto una lettera, posso leggerla? Sì, certo, ...

Exercise 5

Your friend Piero has a lot of problems and is asking you for advice. Use the expressions suggested in the imperative.

1. La mia macchina è rotta. (portare in officina)

   ....

2. Ho litigato con la mia ragazza. (scrivere una lettera)

   ....

3. Ho finito il dentifricio. (comprare)

   ....

4. Il mio appartamento è in disordine. (pulire)

   ....

5. Il 10 aprile è il compleanno di mia mamma. (regalare un mazzo di fiori)

   ....

Complete the following sentences using the imperative forms *dammi*, *fammi* and *dimmi*.

1. Ti prego .... un piacere!

2. Non so cosa fare, ... un consiglio!

3. Marco, ... subito il mio diario!

4. .... la verità questa volta!

5. .... un po' di tempo!

6. È troppo pesante, ... una mano, per favore.

Which parts go together to form complete sentences?

1. Buongiorno, vorrei   **a** ho chiamato?

2. Mi dispiace,   **b** il suo nome?

3. Mi sa dire quando   **c** tardi, allora.

4. Provi   **d** lo posso trovare?

5. Può dirgli che   **e** tra un'ora.

6. Sì, certo, qual è   **f** non c'è.

7. A più   **g** arrivederci.

8. Grazie,   **h** parlare con il direttore.

appuntamento *m*	appointment	**diario** *m*	diary
attendere	to wait	**disordine** *m*	disorder
caramella *f*	sweet *Br* / hard candy *Am*	**edicola** *f*	newsstand
		gettone	telephone
cellulare *m*	mobile *Br* / wireless *Am* phone	**telefonico** *m*	token
		gonna *f*	skirt
		lasciare	to leave (behind)
certamente	certain(ly)		
cognome *m*	surname	**litigare**	to quarrel
condire	to prepare (salad)	**mano** *f*	hand
		mazzo *m*	bouquet (flowers)
confermare	to confirm		
dentifricio *m*	toothpaste	**messaggio** *m*	message

▶

mezz'ora	half hour	**ripetere**	to repeat
necessario	necessary	**riunione** *f*	meeting
nome *m*	name	**sale** *m*	salt
officina *f*	repair shop	**tagliare**	to cut
passare	to connect with	**telefonino** *m*	mobile *Br* / wireless *Am* phone
pepe *m*	pepper		
perfetto	perfect	**tra**	in
provare	to try (out)	**trovare**	to find
regalare	to give (as a present)	**volta** *f*	time
richiamare	to call back		

On the phone

In the past, public phone boxes (booths) were a common feature in most Italian bars, tobacco stores and newsstands *(edicole)*. These phones often had to be operated with special coins/tokens *(gettoni telefonici)* or chip cards, both of which have been virtually phased out. If you want to make a phone call from the phone in a bar or pub you will be charged according to the units you use, indicated by the unit counter *(telefono a scatti)*.

Today, mobile (wireless) phones *(telefonino/cellulare)* have become a fashionable accessory. They can be heard virtually everywhere but their use is considered impolite in certain environments such as restaurants.

Davanti al televisore

Alexandra:	Ah, sei qui, Valentina! Che cosa stai facendo?
Valentina:	Sto guardando la televisione.
Alexandra:	Non esci stasera?
Valentina:	No, preferisco restare in casa.
Alexandra:	Che cosa stai guardando?
Valentina:	Un film americano degli anni trenta, in bianco e nero. Hai voglia di guardarlo anche tu?
Alexandra:	Mah, non so. Sai che non guardo mai questo genere di film alla televisione. Non capisco niente e mi annoio.
Valentina:	Ma qui la storia è molto semplice! Dunque, Rosemarie, la ragazza, è innamorata di Peter e lo vuole sposare, ma il padre non è d'accordo. Ecco, adesso lei sta andando dal suo fidanzato per dirgli che vuole scappare con lui. Ma il padre ha capito tutto e ha deciso di seguirla.
Alexandra:	Su che canale è?
Valentina:	Sul primo.

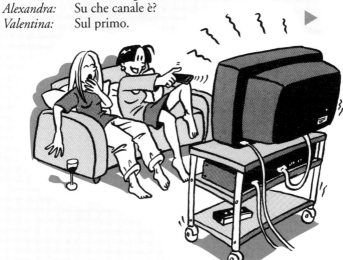

Alexandra:	Non vuoi guardare che cosa c'è sul secondo?
Valentina:	Aspetta, questa scena è molto divertente: la figlia è andata in una chiesa dove l'aspetta il suo fidanzato. Ma anche suo padre è lì, vestito da prete, e lei non l'ha riconosciuto e gli sta chiedendo un consiglio.
Alexandra:	E dov'è il suo fidanzato?
Valentina:	Lui ha già riconosciuto il padre della ragazza e sta cercando di nascondersi.
Alexandra:	Dov'è il telecomando?
Valentina:	Non lo so. Ah, guarda, adesso anche lei ha riconosciuto suo padre ed è svenuta!
Alexandra:	È svenuta davvero?
Valentina:	Uffa, Alessandra! Se non smetti di parlare, non capisco niente neanch'io!!!

Watching TV

Alexandra:	Ah, there you are, Valentina! What are you doing at the moment?
Valentina:	I'm watching TV.
Alexandra:	You're not going out tonight?
Valentina:	No, I'd rather stay in.
Alexandra:	What are you watching?
Valentina:	An American movie from the thirties in black and white. Do you want to watch it, too?
Alexandra:	Oh, I don't know. You know that I never watch those kinds of movies on television. I don't understand anything and get bored.
Valentina:	But the story is very simple! Well, Rosemarie the girl is in love with Peter and wants to marry him but her father is against it. So she goes to her fiancé to tell him that she wants to run away with him. But her father figures that out and decides to follow her.
Alexandra:	What channel is this on?
Valentina:	Channel one.
Alexandra:	Don't you want to see what's on channel two?

Valentina:	Wait, this scene is very funny: the daughter goes to the church where her fiancé is waiting for her. But her father is there too, dressed up as priest, and she doesn't recognize him and now she's asking him for advice.
Alexandra:	And where is her fiancé?
Valentina:	He has already recognized the girl's father and is trying to hide.
Alexandra:	Where is the remote control?
Valentina:	I don't know. Look, she has just recognized her father and has fainted.
Alexandra:	Did she really faint?
Valentina:	Phew, Alexandra! If you don't stop talking I won't understand anything either!

The present progressive

In Italian, like in English, the present progressive tense expresses an action that is ongoing at the moment of speaking. It is formed with the conjugated verb **stare** (see Lesson 2) and the **gerund**:

guard-are	*prend-ere*	*sent-ire*
*guard-**ando***	*prend-**endo***	*sent-**endo***

Irregular gerund forms:

*bere – **bevendo***	*fare – **facendo***
*dire – **dicendo***	*tradurre – **traducendo***

stare + gerund

io	**sto**	***guardando*** *la televisione.*
		(I'm watching TV.)
tu	**stai**	***leggendo*** *il giornale.*
lui, lei, Lei	**sta**	***mangiando.***
noi	**stiamo**	***andando*** *a casa.*
voi	**state**	***parlando.***
loro	**stanno**	***dormendo.***

The corresponding pronouns can be positioned either in front of the verb *stare* or after the gerund:

*– **Lo** sto mangiando.*	*Sto mangiando**lo**.*

uscire	(to go out)		
io	**esco**	noi	**usciamo**
tu	**esci**	voi	**uscite**
lui, lei, Lei	**esce**	loro	**escono**

Double negatives

There are a number of situations in Italian when a double negative has to be used:

Non bevo **mai** il caffè. (I never drink coffee.)
Non compro **niente/nulla.** (I don't buy anything.)
Non conosco **nessuno.** (I don't know anyone.)
Non viene **nemmeno/neanche/neppure** Maria.
(Maria is also not coming.)

But:
In sentences starting with **mai, niente, nulla, nessuno, nemmeno, neanche, neppure** the **non** is omitted:

Nessuno ha telefonato. (No one called.)
Nemmeno Maria è venuta. (Maria did not come either.)
Neanche lei lo conosce. (She doesn't know him either.)

The preposition di

The preposition **di** is used:

– to express possession (genitive)
  la casa **di** Maria (Maria's house)
– for specification of material
  un maglione **di** lana (a wool pullover)
– to express time
  di mattina, **d'**estate (in the morning, in the summer) ▶

- to define where a person is from
  Sono di Palermo. (I'm from Palermo.)
- as a partitive article
  due chili di mele (two kilos of apples)
- after idiomatic expressions such as:

essere innamorato di (to be in love with)	*cercare di* + infinitive (to try to)
avere voglia di (to want to)	*finire di* + infinitive (to end)
avere paura di (to be afraid of)	*smettere di* + infinitive (to stop)
decidere di + infinitive (to decide to)	*sperare di* + infinitive (to hope to)
credere di + infinitive (to believe)	

Fill in the correct gerund form.

1. parlare ....
2. dare ....
3. dire ....
4. vedere ....
5. pulire ....
6. incontrare ....
7. venire ....

Exercise 1

Write the sentences in the present progressive using the following example.

Marco va in ufficio in macchina. →
Marco sta andando in ufficio in macchina.

1. Piera si veste in camera sua.

....

2. Zia Carla parte per le vacanze.

....

Exercise 2

3. Andiamo a fare la spesa al supermercato all'angolo.

....

4. Fa i compiti.

....

5. Telefonano a Carla per dirle di venire
più tardi.

....

6. Ascolti le notizie alla radio.

....

Exercise 3

**Answer the
questions using the
following example.**

Hai già letto questo libro?
No, lo sto leggendo adesso.

1. Hai già telefonato a Patrizia?

No, ...

2. Si è già alzata Marina?

No, ...

3. Hai già scritto a Silvia?

No, ...

4. Avete già bevuto il caffè?

No, ...

5. Maria è già uscita?

No, ...

6. Hai già preparato il pranzo?

No, ...

Insert *non* where necessary.

1. Piero ...... va mai al cinema.

2. Nessuno ...... è venuto a trovarmi.

3. Mi dispiace, ... voglio comprare niente.

4. Forse ...... ha invitato neanche Alexandra.

5. Neanche Marina ...... è stata invitata.

6. ...... sono mai stato in Cina.

7. Nessuno ...... l'ha visto.

8. ...... vuole mai niente.

Exercise 4

Fill in the correct prepositions.

1. Marco non ha paura ...... niente.

2. Vado ...... Firenze ...... treno.

3. Quando finisci ...... lavorare?

4. La macchina ...... Patrizia è parcheggiata qui ...... angolo.

5. Hai voglia ...... venire ...... cinema?

6. Mi dia mezzo chilo ...... ciliegie.

7. Vorrei tre cestini ...... fragole.

8. Torno ...... casa ...... otto.

Exercise 5

Which parts go together to form complete sentences?

1. Di solito Luca smette di   **a** andare in Venezuela.

2. Ho voglia di un   **b** Valentina.

3. Paolo è innamorato di   **c** dentista?

4. Stefania ha deciso di   **d** gelato.

5. Non hai paura del   **e** lavorare alle cinque.

Exercise 6

Vocabulary

americano	American	**notizia** *f*	news
anni trenta	thirties	**nulla**	nothing
annoiarsi	to be bored	**paura** *f*	fear
canale *m*	channel	**prete** *m*	priest
cercare di	to try	**restare**	to stay
ciliegia *f*	cherry	**riconoscere**	to recognize
compito *m*	homework	**scappare**	to flee, run away
decidere (di)	to decide		
fidanzato *m*	fiancé	**scena** *f*	scene
genere *m*	kind, genre	**seguire**	to follow
innamorato (di)	to be in love (with)	**smettere**	to stop
		sperare	to hope
maglione *m*	pullover *Br* / sweater *Am*	**sposare**	to marry
		svenire	to faint
nascondersi	to hide (oneself)	**telecomando** *m*	remote control
neanche	not even	**televisore** *m*	TV set
nemmeno	not even	**tradurre**	to translate
neppure	not even	**uffa**	phew
nero	black	**vestito da**	dressed up as
nessuno	no one		

Television in Italy

Television plays an important role in daily life in Italy. The national broadcasting corporation **Rai** (Radiotelevisione italiana) maintains three channels: **Raiuno, Raidue, Raitre** (the third one with regional programmes).

The number of private stations has risen considerably over the last few years resulting in a proliferation of quiz and talk shows and movie channels. In most Italian households the TV sets are kept turned on throughout the day and even during mealtimes without much attention being paid to what's on.

Un giorno di festa

Il 25 aprile è stata proprio una giornata speciale. Tutta la
famiglia Simoni si è alzata di buon'umore. Il papà ha
promesso di lavare la macchina (che miracolo!) e di fare
una partita a carte con la nonna. Valentina e Stefano
hanno deciso di preparare il pranzo per fare una sorpresa
alla mamma e l'hanno mandata con Alessandra a fare una
passeggiata. Poi sono andati in cucina e Valentina ha
iniziato a preparare le lasagne. Ma ha telefonato Paolo e
Valentina le ha dimenticate nel forno, così si sono bruciate.
Stefano invece ha preparato un arrosto di vitello con
patate. Purtroppo le patate le ha salate un po' troppo, ma
almeno non le ha dimenticate nel forno. Quando Piera e
Alessandra sono tornate tutta la famiglia si è seduta a
tavola. Che sorpresa per la mamma! Stefano e Valentina
hanno servito le lasagne bruciate e tutti le hanno mangiate
di gusto (soprattutto la mamma). Alla fine del pranzo
hanno portato in tavola una bellissima torta con la scritta
„Alessandra". L'hanno comprata in pasticceria e poi
l'hanno decorata con la panna. Alla sera è arrivato Marco.
È venuto per vedere Alessandra e l'ha portata
fuori a cena. Chissà a che ora sono tornati?!

A holiday

The 25th of April was really a special day. The entire Simoni family
got up in a good mood. Their father promised to wash the car
(a miracle!) and to play cards with grandma. Valentina and Stefano
decided to prepare lunch to surprise their mother whom they'd sent for
a walk with Alexandra. Then they went into the kitchen and Valentina
started to make lasagna but Paolo phoned and Valentina forgot to take
the lasagna out of the oven with the result that it got burnt. Stefano, on
the other hand, prepared roast veal with potatoes. Though he added
a little too much salt to the potatoes, he nevertheless did not forget to
take them out of the oven. When Piera and Alexandra returned home,
the whole family sat down at the table for a meal. And what a surprise it
was for their mother! Stefano and Valentina served the burnt lasagna
and everyone enjoyed eating it (especially mother). At the end of lunch
they presented a wonderful cake with "Alessandra" written on it which
they had bought in the pastry shop and then decorated with whipped
cream. Marco came in the evening. He came to see Alexandra and he
took her out for dinner. Who knows what time they came back?!

Perfect tense + pronouns

The endings of past participles that are formed with the
auxiliary verb *avere* can change if the conjugated verb in
the perfect tense is preceded by a direct object pronoun (*la,
le, lo, li, ne*):

Hai mangiato il pane? Sì, I'ho mangiato. (I' = lo)
Hai mangiato la pizza? Sì, I'ho mangiata tutta. (I' = la)
Hai comprato i biglietti? Sì, li ho comprati.
Quando hai visto Piera e Simona? Le ho viste ieri.

If the object **precedes** the verb, the appropriate pronoun is
also inserted:

Marco ha comprato le patate, Silvia ha comprato i piselli.
Le patate le ha comprate Marco, i piselli li ha comprati Silvia.

In the second example the words *patate* and *piselli* are
positioned at the beginning for emphasis.

The preposition a

The preposition **a** is used:

– to define the indirect object
Lo porto **a** Maria.   (I bring it to Maria.)

– to specify locations and directions
a Roma	(to/in Rome)
	(with cities and small islands)
al mercato	(to the market)
al mare	(to the sea)
al bar	(to/into the bar)
a scuola	(to/into the school)

– to define times
alle due e mezza	(at half past two)
a Natale	(at Christmas)
a maggio	(in May)

– as a specification of way and manner
saltimbocca **alla** romana
un vestito **a** righe (a striped dress)

– as an indication of means
andare **a** piedi   (to go on foot)

– with quantities
due euro **al** chilo	(two euros per kilo)
100 chilometri **all'**ora	(100 km/h)
una volta **al** mese	(once a month)

– after specific verbs, such as
cominciare **a** + **infinitive** (to start to)
continuare **a** + **infinitive** (to continue to)
riuscire **a** + **infinitive** (to succeed in)

The preposition *in*

The preposition **in** is used:
– to specify locations and directions

in *Italia*	(in/to Italy)	
	(with countries and larger islands)	
in *centro*	(in/into the centre)	
in *città*	(in/into the city)	
in *ufficio*	(at/into the office)	

– to define times

in *primavera*	(in springtime)
in *maggio*	(in May)
in *tre giorni*	(within three days)

– to specify mode of transportation

in *bicicletta*	(by bicycle)
in *treno*	(by train)

Exercise 1

Answer the questions.

Dove hai visto mia madre? (in giardino)
→ L'ho vista in giardino.

1. Hai già letto il giornale? (sì)

   ....

2. Quando hai sentito la radio? (stamattina)

   ....

3. Hai già fatto la spesa oggi? (no, non ancora)

   ....

4. Dove hai comprato queste melanzane? (al mercato)

   ....

5. Hai già visto l'Aida? (sì)

   ....

6. Hai già provato questi spaghetti? (sì)

....

7. Dove hai conosciuto i miei genitori?
(a Firenze)

....

Fill in the correct endings.

Exercise 2

Oggi Marco ha preparat.... (1) l'anatra all'arancia. Ha trovat....

(2) la ricetta in un vecchio libro di cucina, l'ha lett.... (3)

molto bene e poi ha iniziat.... (4) a cucinare. Ha preparat.... (5)

la carne poi l'ha mess.... (6) in forno. Dopo mezz'ora l'ha

pres.... (7) e l'ha mess.... (8) sul balcone. Ma un gatto l'ha

vist.... (9) e l'ha mangiat.... (10). Ecco perché oggi tutta la fami-

glia è andat.... (11) al ristorante.

**A page from
Alexandra's
diary (calendar).**
What did she do
yesterday?

Exercise 3

```
18   9ºº SVEGLIA
     10ºº PASSEGGIATA
          CON PIERA
     12³º PRANZO IN CASA
     14ºº TV
     19ºº MARCO!
          RISTORANTE
          "LE TRE NOCI"
     24ºº BUONA NOTTE !

19
```

Ieri Alessandra ....

....

....

Exercise 4

Put the following pronouns where they belong:
li – gli – gli – la – la – lo – l' – ti – le – te la.

1. Conosci Marina? Sì, ... conosco.

2. Quando hai telefonato a Marco?

   ..... ho telefonato alle tre.

3. Mi scrivi una lettera? Sì, ... scrivo.

4. Hai invitato Sandra e Paolo alla festa?

   No, non ..... ho invitati.

5. Dove hai comprato questa torta? .....

   ho comprata alla pasticceria Centrale.

6. Mi vedi bene, adesso?

   Sì, adesso ..... vedo benissimo.

7. Bevi il caffè? No, non ..... bevo mai.

8. Guardi spesso la televisione?

   Sì, ... guardo molto spesso.

9. Che cosa hai scritto a Gino?

   ..... ho scritto una cartolina.

10. Che cosa regali a Silvia per il suo

    compleanno? ..... regalo un libro.

Exercise 5

Rewrite the story in the past tense.

Oggi Roberto si alza presto. Fa colazione in un bar e poi va in ufficio. Alle 11.00 gli telefona Cristina e gli chiede di andare a pranzo insieme. Così si incontrano alle 12.30 al ristorante „Al Mulino" e mangiano una bella insalata. Poi Roberto torna in ufficio. Alle 18.00 esce e va a casa di Mariella. Loro chiacchierano un po' e poi vanno al cinema. Dopo il cinema vanno in un bar e a mezzanotte tornano a casa.

Ieri Roberto ....

Fill in the imperative of the verbs provided.

Oggi Piera è molto arrabbiata con Stefano e gli dice:(studiare)

.... un po', (pulire) .... la tua stanza, (non ascoltare)

.... sempre la musica, (fare) .... il tuo letto, (porta)

.... la nonna dal dottore, (leggere) .... un libro, (andare)

.... a letto presto, (non fumare) .... tante sigarette e

(ascoltare) .... un po' quando ti parlo!!!

Exercise 6

Fill in the missing parts of this interview.

A: Scusi, signora, ... ?

B: Abito a Milano.

A: .... ?

B: Sono nata a Pavia.

A: .... ?

B: Ho tre figli.

A: .... ?

B: Sì, lavoro in banca.

A: .... ?

B: Mi alzo alle sette.

A: .... ?

B: Comincio a lavorare alle nove.

A: .... ?

B: A mezzogiorno mangio in mensa.

A: .... ?

B: Finisco di lavorare alle 17.30.

Exercise 7

Exercise 8

Write Mrs. Rinaldi's personal history.

Use some of these expressions:

data di nascita = date of birth   frequentare = to visit
luogo di nascita = place of birth   sposarsi con = to marry
dal... al... = from... to...   lavorare come = to work as

NOME E COGNOME: FRANCESCA RINALDI
DATA DI NASCITA : 7 OTTOBRE 1958
LUOGO DI NASCITA: FOGGIA
DAL 1964 AL 1972: SCUOLA ELEMENTARE
                  E MEDIA A FOGGIA

DAL 1973 AL 1978: LICEO A BARI
1979:   MATRIMONIO CON
                  FABRIZIO DE SANTI
DAL 1980 AL 1986: IMPIEGATA ALLE
                  POSTE DI BARI
1986:   NASCITA DELLA
                  FIGLIA CRISTINA
DAL 1990 AL 1995: IMPIEGATA ALLE
                  POSTE DI BARI
1995:   NASCITA DEL
                  FIGLIO LUCA

Francesca Rinaldi è ....

Vocabulary

arrabbiato	angry, upset	**di buon'umore**	in a good mood
arrosto *m*	roast		
bruciare	to burn	**dimenticare**	to forget
carte *f pl*	cards	**festa** *f*	holiday, feast
chiacchierare	to chat	**forno** *m*	oven
chissà	who knows	**gusto** *m*	taste
dal... al...	from...to...	**lavorare come**	to work as
data di nascita *f*	date of birth	**luogo** *m*	place
decorare	to decorate		▶

luogo di nascita *m*	place of birth	**promettere**	to promise
mandare	to send	**ricetta** *f*	recipe
mangiare di gusto	to enjoy eating	**salare**	to salt
		scritta *f*	inscription / message
matrimonio *m*	wedding	**scuola elementare** *f*	elementary school
miracolo *m*	miracle		
mulino *m*	mill	**scuola media** *f*	middle school
nascita *f*	birth	**servire**	to serve
noce *f*	nut	**sorpresa** *f*	surprise
panna *f*	cream	**speciale**	special
pisello *m*	pea	**stanza** *f*	room
portare fuori	to take out	**torta** *f*	layered cake
posta *f*	post *Br* / mail *Am*	**umore** *m*	mood
		vitello *m*	veal

Italian holidays

January 1	*Capodanno*	New Year's Day
January 6	*Epifania*	Epiphany
	Pasqua	Easter
	Lunedì dell'Angelo (Pasquetta)	Easter Monday
April 25	*Anniversario della Liberazione*	(Anniversary of) Liberation Day
May 1	*Festa dei Lavoratori*	Labour Day
August 15	*Assunzione di Maria (Ferragosto)*	Assumption
November 1	*Ognissanti*	All Saints Day
December 8	*Immacolata Concezione*	Immaculate Conception
December 25	*Natale*	Christmas Day
December 26	*Santo Stefano*	St. Stephen's Day

Test 4

1 Choose one of the two answers, then go to the square with the number of your answer.

2 Dov'è Marco?

Lo ecco! ⇨ 14
Eccolo! ⇨ 23

6 Very Good! Continue:

... nessuno.
Non viene ⇨ 16
Viene ⇨ 19

7 Wrong!

Go back to number 4.

11 Good! Continue: Mi porti un caffè?
Sì, ... porto.

lo ti ⇨ 30
te lo ⇨ 4

12 Correct! Contin Signora, ... qui favore!

viene ⇨ 22
venga ⇨ 20

16 Great! Continue:
Sandra, ..., sono le otto.
svegliati ⇨ 29
ti sveglia ⇨ 21

17 Wrong!

Go back to number 24.

21 Wrong!

Go back to number 16.

22 Wrong!

Go back to number 12.

26 Very good! Continue:
Giulia, ... tardi!

non tornare ⇨ 9
non torna ⇨ 5

27 Wrong!

Go back to number 9.

Wrong!

back to
mber 13.

---

4 Good! Continue:

Che cosa stai ... ?

fando ▷ 7
facendo ▷ 13

---

5 Wrong!

Go back to
number 26.

Wrong!

o back to
umber 28.

---

9 Good! Continue:
La banca è ...
supermercato.

vicino al ▷ 12
vicino il ▷ 27

---

10 Wrong!

Go back to
number 20.

---

3 Good! Continue:
Finisco ... alle
.00.

vorare ▷ 3
lavorare ▷ 28

---

14 Wrong!

Go back to
number 2.

---

15 Correct! Continue:
Hai fame? ...
qualcosa.

Mangi ▷ 18
Mangia ▷ 26

Wrong!

o back to
umber 15.

---

19 Wrong!

Go back to
number 6.

---

20 Correct! Continue:

Marco, ... tutto.

mi di' ▷ 10
dimmi ▷ 24

---

3 Very good!
Continue:

conosco nessuno.

▷ 25
on ▷ 11

---

24 Good! Continue:

Ecco il caffè: ...!

bevilo ▷ 6
lo bevi ▷ 17

---

25 Wrong!

Go back to
number 23.

---

8 Very good!
Continue:
lai visto Simona?
, ...
ho vista ▷ 15
ho visto ▷ 8

---

29 Correct!

End of exercise!

---

30 Wrong!

Go back to
number 11.

21   La nonna racconta

Alla nonna piace molto stare insieme a tutta la famiglia a chiacchierare e giocare. In particolar modo le piace molto raccontare della sua giovinezza.

Carlotta: La mia famiglia viveva in un piccolo paese di pescatori. Amavamo molto il mare. Non avevamo tante cose ma ci divertivamo lo stesso. D'estate, la sera, noi ragazze ci sedevamo davanti alla porta di casa, ricamavamo o lavoravamo a maglia e guardavamo i ragazzi che passavano. La domenica andavamo a ballare sulla piazza del paese, mio papà non voleva, ma io andavo di nascosto. Un giorno mi ha visto. Non mi ha detto niente, ma quando sono tornata a casa mi ha proibito di uscire per quattro settimane. Non era cattivo, ma severo. Poi è scoppiata la guerra e la vita è cambiata per tutti.

Grandmother remembers

Grandmother likes to be together with the whole family, chatting and playing games. She especially likes to tell stories about her youth.

Carlotta: My family lived in a small fishing village. We loved the sea. We didn't have much but we still enjoyed ourselves. On summer evenings, we girls sat in front of the house, doing some embroidery or knitting and watching the boys passing by. On Sundays we went to the dance in the village square. My father didn't want me to go there but I went secretly. One day he saw me. He didn't say a word but when I returned home he didn't allow me to go out for four weeks. He wasn't mean but he was strict. Then the war broke out and life changed for everybody.

Imperfect tense

	guardare	leggere	dormire	essere
io	guardavo	leggevo	dormivo	ero
tu	guardavi	leggevi	dormivi	eri
lui, lei, Lei	guardava	leggeva	dormiva	era
noi	guardavamo	leggevamo	dormivamo	eravamo
voi	guardavate	leggevate	dormivate	eravate
loro	guardavano	leggevano	dormivano	erano

■ Irregular verbs
bere: bevevo, bevevi, beveva, bevevamo, bevevate,
bevevano
dire: dicevo, dicevi, etc.
fare: facevo, facevi, etc.
tradurre: traducevo, traducevi, etc.

The imperfect tense is used:

– to express a habit in the past
Da bambina giocavo sempre con le bambole.

– to describe a state in the past
La casa non era grande ma aveva un bel giardino.

– to indicate an action in the past that was not completed
when another action occurred
Mentre leggevo il giornale, è arrivato Paolo.

– to indicate an action in the past that was not completed at
a given moment in time
A mezzogiorno Fabio dormiva ancora.

while/during

The term **while** can be translated into Italian by using
mentre + verb:
*Ieri, **mentre** Marco **passeggiava** nel parco,
ha incontrato Fulvio.*

During is translated by
durante + noun:
*Ieri, **durante una passeggiata** nel parco,
Marco ha incontrato Fulvio.*

Prepositions relating to time

a = at		*Paolo torna alle cinque.*
da = since		*Lo conosco da tre anni.*
da...a = from...to		*Dal 1992 al 1995 ho lavorato a Pisa.*
fa = ago		*L'ho conosciuto due mesi fa.*
fra/tra = in		*Fra tre giorni vado al mare.*
in = in		*In primavera faccio molto sport.*
in = within		*Le fotografie sono pronte in tre giorni.*
per = for		*Alexandra resta a Milano per tre mesi.*

Exercise 1

Fill in the correct form of the imperfect tense.

Da bambina in estate .... (andare) sempre al mare con la
mamma. Il papà ci .... (accompagnare) in macchina, ma
lui .... (restare) solo due giorni e poi .... (tornare) in
città, perché .... (dovere) lavorare. (Noi) .... (andare)
sempre nello stesso posto. L'albergo .... (essere) piccolo
ma direttamente sul mare. La mattina (noi) .... (fare) colazione in terrazza, poi .... (andare) in spiaggia. La spiaggia non
.... (essere) molto grande, ma noi bambini .... (giocare)

felici tutto il giorno. La sera (noi) .... (telefonare) al papà e

gli .... (raccontare) le nostre avventure.

Imperfect or perfect tense? Fill in the correct form.

1. Al mare Valeria .... sempre al ristorante. (mangiare)

2. Mentre .... a casa, Simona

.... Gino. (tornare – incontrare)

3. Tutti i giorni, alle otto, Marco

.... di casa per andare a scuola. (uscire)

4. Da bambina Marta .... i capelli biondi. (avere)

5. Mentre Piera .... l'autobus,

.... (aspettare – svenire)

6. Ieri, mentre (io) .... la tele-

visione, ... Mario. (guardare – arrivare)

7. Da giovane mi .... andare a ballare. (piacere)

Exercise 2

Describe what is happening in scenes 1 to 4 on page 186.

Ieri, mentre ....

....

....

....

....▶

Exercise 3

Exercise 4

Fill in the correct prepositions of time.

1. Non vedevo mio zio ...... 1989.

2. Ieri, ... la lezione, il professore ha spiegato l'uso dell'imperfetto.

3. Ho fame, non mangio ...... tre giorni.

4. Ti ho aspettato ...... un'ora e poi sono andato a casa.

5. ...... venivo qui, ho visto tua madre.

6. ...... che ora inizia il film? ......10.00.

7. ...... una settimana parto per le vacanze.

Who's who? Choose the correct answers.

1. Il papà di mio marito?

   a mio padre   **b** mio suocero   **c** mio cognato

2. Il figlio della sorella di mia mamma?

   a mio fratello   **b** io   **c** mio cugino

3. La suocera di mia madre?

   a mia nonna   **b** mia zia   **c** mia cognata

4. La mamma del fratello di mio marito?

   a mia zia   **b** mia cognata   **c** mia suocera

Exercise 5

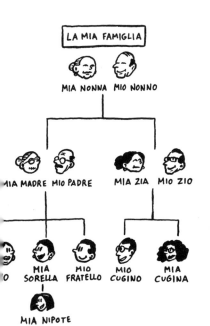

Vocabulary

avventura *f*	adventure	nonno *m*	grandfather
bambola *f*	doll	offrire	to offer
cattivo	nasty, mean, bad	onomastico *m*	name day
		pescatore *m*	fisherman
cognata *f*	sister-in-law	professore *m*	professor
cognato *m*	brother-in-law	proibire	to forbid, prohibit
cosa *f*	cause, matter	ricamare	to stitch, embroider
di nascosto	secretly		
direttamente	directly	scoppiare	to burst, break out
durante	during		
felice	happy, content	scoppia la guerra	the war breaks out
giovinezza *f*	youth	severo	strict
guerra *f*	war	solo	alone
iniziare	to start	spiegare	to explain
lezione *f*	lesson	suocera *f*	mother-in-law
lo stesso	anyway, nevertheless		
		suocero *m*	father-in-law
mentre	while	terrazza *f*	terrace
		uso *m*	use

Birthdays and name days

Birthdays are celebrated in Italy like everywhere else, even though the birthday party doesn't necessarily have to take place on the actual day itself but either before or after. Well-wishers congratulate with *auguri* and *buon compleanno*. One custom is to pinch the birthday child's ears by the number of years he has reached that day. In many Italian regions your name day *(onomastico)* constitutes another occasion for congratulations. Though presents are not normally given, one still congratulates with *Auguri!* or *Buon onomastico!* and makes a toast to the person in question who in turn invites his friends for a drink *(offrire da bere)*.

Sfilata di moda

Alexandra:	Buongiorno signor Arturi, sono Alexandra Jansen.
Signor Arturi:	Piacere signorina Jansen, finalmente ci conosciamo di persona. Si trova bene qui in Italia?
Alexandra:	Sì, grazie. Milano mi piace molto e il lavoro è veramente interessante. A proposito: ha già visto la nostra collezione autunno – inverno?
Signor Arturi:	No, aspettavo Lei.
Alexandra:	Allora possiamo cominciare ... Prego, signorina! ... Il primo modello è un cappotto di lana grigio scuro, giacca a righe verticali con gonna in tinta unita nera; una bella camicetta di seta bianca e accessori in pelle nera.
Signor Arturi:	Bel cappotto, molto elegante. In quali colori è disponibile?
Alexandra:	Oltre al grigio scuro, in marrone, beige e blu notte. Ecco il campionario; che colore Le piace di più?

Signor Arturi: Il blu e il marrone sono i più
belli, secondo me.

Alexandra: Veniamo al secondo modello: un maglione
di angora rosso, pantaloni scozzesi,
cappotto corto nero, borsa e scarpe col
tacco alto di camoscio.

Signor Arturi: Questo modello è più sportivo del
precedente, ma lo preferisco. Il cappotto
corto non è così elegante ma sicuramente
più pratico e si vende senz'altro bene.

Alexandra: Ha ragione anche se lo stesso modello in
verde scuro e in bianco è più elegante che
in nero. Ma passiamo al terzo modello ...

The fashion show

Alexandra: Good morning, Mr. Arturi, I am Alexandra Jansen.

Mr. Arturi: My pleasure Ms. Jansen, we are finally getting to know
one another personally. Do you like it here in Italy?

Alexandra: Yes, thank you. I like Milan a lot and my work is really
interesting. By the way, have you already seen our
autumn-winter collection?

Mr. Arturi: No, I was waiting for you.

Alexandra: Then we can begin ... Please ... The first style is a dark
grey wool coat, a jacket with vertical stripes and a plain
black skirt; a nice white silk blouse and accessories in
black leather.

Mr. Arturi: Nice coat, very elegant. In which colours is it available?

Alexandra: Besides dark grey, in brown, beige and deep blue.
Here's the catalogue with samples. Which colour do
you like best?

Mr. Arturi: The blue and brown ones are the prettiest, to my
mind.

Alexandra: Let's see the second model: A red angora wool pullover,
plaid trousers, a short black coat, suede handbag and
shoes with high heels.

Mr. Arturi: This style is sportier than the previous one but I prefer
it. The short coat isn't as elegant but certainly more
practical and will definitely sell well.

▶

Alexandra: You're right, even if the same model in dark green and
white is more elegant than the black. But let's go on to
the third model ...

Comparative and superlative

1. The comparative is formed by adding **più** (more) or **meno**
(less) before the adjective: **più** *bello*   nicer
                                   meno *bello*   less nice

2. The superlative is expressed by using the **comparative
with the definite article:**
                          *È **la più** bella casa della città.*
                          (It is the nicest house in the city.)

3. Italian also has an absolute superlative that is formed
with the ending **-issimo.** This form omits the
comparative and is used to express an extreme quality of
an object:
                          *È una casa bell**issima**.*
                          (It is a most beautiful house.)

Irregular comparatives

buono	**migliore**	**il migliore**	**ottimo**
(good)	(better)	(the best)	(very good)
cattivo	**peggiore**	**il peggiore**	**pessimo**
(bad)	(worse)	(the worst)	(very bad)

The regular comparative of **buono** (*più buono, buonissimo*)
and **cattivo** (*più cattivo, cattivissimo*) is only used in
reference to persons and food:
                    La pizza è buonissima.
                    Marco è più cattivo di suo fratello.   ▶

Other irregular comparatives

grande	più grande (greater, larger)	grandissimo
	maggiore (older, more significant)	massimo
piccolo	più piccolo (smaller)	piccolissimo
	minore (younger, lesser)	minimo
alto	più alto (higher, taller)	altissimo
	superiore (upper, better)	supremo, sommo
basso	più basso (lesser, lower)	bassissimo
	inferiore (lower, worse)	infimo

Comparative clauses

When comparing people or objects with **as ... as** use

(tanto) ... quanto oder **(così) ... come**
> *Gianni è (così) alto come suo padre.*
> *Margherita è (tanto) simpatica quanto Rosa.*

The English **than** is expressed in Italian with **di** when followed by a name, noun or pronoun. Before a preposition, adjective, adverb or verb use **che**:

*Roma è più grande **di** Venezia.* (Rome is larger than Venice.)
*Meglio tardi **che** mai.* (Better late than never.)

Colour adjectives

The following adjectives can **change their endings**:
bianco, rosso, nero, verde, giallo, grigio, azzurro, marrone.

These **always stay the same**: **blu, rosa, viola, beige** and combinations such as **verde chiaro** or **verde scuro**.

Irregular adjective forms

Generally the adjective follows the noun in Italian.
However, **bello, brutto, grande, buono** and **bravo** can also be
positioned in front of the noun in which case some of them
change their form.

	bello	*buono*
before masc. sing.	**bel** ragazzo	**buon** caffè
before masc. sing. with vowel	**bell'** uomo	**buon** amico
before masc. sing. with z, s+consonants, ps, gn	**bello** spettacolo	**buono** sconto
before masc. plur.	**bei** ragazzi	**buoni** caffè
before masc. plur. with vowel	**begli** uomini	**buoni** amici
before masc. plur. with z, s+consonants, ps, gn	**begli** spettacoli	**buoni** sconti
before fem. sing.	**bella** ragazza	**buona** pizza
before fem. sing. with vowel	**bell'** attrice	**buon'** amica
before fem. plur.	**belle** ragazze	**buone** pizze
before fem. plur. with vowel	**belle** attrici	**buone** amiche

The adjective **grande** can be abbreviated to **gran** before
nouns starting with a consonant (but not with **z** or
s + consonant):   **gran** signore
Adjectives can be apostrophized when positioned in front of
vowels: **grand'** uomo

Exercise 1

Form comparative sentences with the following adjectives.

vecchio   Paolo / Roberto
Paolo è più vecchio di Roberto

1. elegante   il cappotto / la giacca

....

2. comodo   aereo / treno

....

3. moderno   la lambada / il valzer

....

4. pratico   i pantaloni / la gonna

....

5. facile   l'inglese / l'italiano

....

Exercise 2

Che cosa ti piace di più?
Say what you like better. When do you use **di** and when **che**?

Le sigarette / i sigari ⬜ Mi piacciono di più le sigarette dei sigari.

1. andare a piedi / andare in macchina

....

2. la mia bicicletta / la tua

....

3. Venezia / Bologna

....

4. suonare il pianoforte / andare a un concerto

....

5. il cappuccino / il tè

....

Write questions with the words provided using the superlative as shown in the example.

città / grande / Francia

Qual è la città più grande della Francia?

1. vino / buono / Germania

....

2. montagna / alto / mondo

....

3. film / bello / anno

....

4. ristorante / cattivo / città

....

5. vestito / bello / negozio

....

Match the nouns with the different forms of *bello*.

Quanti complimenti!

Signora Simoni,

che bello ....   **a** casa

bei ....   **b** quadri

begli ....   **c** poltrone

bella ....   **d** ufficio

bell' ....   **e** armadi

belle ....   **f** specchio

---

a proposito	by the way	**angora** *f*	angora wool
a righe	striped	**basso**	low
accessorio *m*	accessory	**beige**	beige
aereo *m*	aeroplane *Br* / airplane *Am*	**blu**	blue
		brutto	ugly
alto	high	**camicetta** *f*	blouse

▶

camoscio *m*	suede	**modello** *m*	model
campionario *m*	sample catalogue	**moderno**	modern
		mondo *m*	world
cappotto *m*	coat	**oltre a**	except
chiaro	bright	**pantaloni** *m pl*	trousers
collezione *f*	collection	**pelle** *f*	leather
colore *m*	colour	**pratico**	practical
comodo	comfortable	**precedente**	previous
concerto *m*	concert	**rosa**	pink
conoscersi	to get to know one another	**scarpa** *f*	shoe
		scozzese	Scottish
corto	short	**secondo me**	to my mind
di persona	personally	**seta** *f*	silk
disponibile	available	**sfilata**	fashion show
erba *f*	grass	**di moda** *f*	
giacca *f*	jacket	**si**	one
giallo	yellow	**specchio** *m*	mirror
grigio	grey	**stesso**	the same
in tinta unita	uni-coloured	**stoffa** *f*	fabric
lana *f*	wool	**tacco** *m*	heel
marrone	brown	**trovarsi**	to be, feel
moda *f*	fashion	**viola**	violet

Italian fashion

Not only is Milan one of the world's fashion capitals but the whole of Italy is known for its good style. Many expensive brands originate in Italy and have a solid customer base in the country itself.
It comes as no surprise that Italy ranks as the European country with the highest budget for clothes and shoes per capita.

Una lettera

Cara Silvia,

ormai sono a Milano da due mesi e non sono ancora riuscita a scriverti, ma ho veramente pochissimo tempo a disposizione. Mi perdoni? Voglio raccontarti un sacco di cose, ma non so da dove cominciare! Vivo con i signori Simoni che sono davvero gentilissimi con me; la signora cucina dei piatti squisiti e... avevi ragione, in Italia si mangia veramente molto: devo assolutamente mettermi a dieta! Io e Valentina, la figlia dei Simoni, siamo diventate amiche e trascorriamo parecchio tempo insieme. Ho già visitato Milano e i dintorni, sono stata al mare, ho fatto una gita a Firenze e

sono stata sempre fortunata perché il tempo era splendido: sole e qualche nuvola, ma mai pioggia.

Anche il lavoro mi dà grosse soddisfazioni, i colleghi sono simpatici e c'è molto da imparare.

Quando ero a Firenze ho telefonato a tua sorella e mi ha detto che hai intenzione di venire una settimana in vacanza a giugno. È sicuro? Aspetto una tua risposta, così possiamo finalmente vederci.

Ah, ho ancora una notizia: ho conosciuto un ragazzo simpaticissimo, si chiama Marco ed è medico. Ci vediamo spesso e siamo andati a Firenze insieme, devi proprio conoscerlo!

Spero di vederti presto, saluti a tutti e un grosso bacio,

Alexandra

A letter

Dear Silvia,

I've been in Milan for two months now and still haven't managed to write to you but I really don't have much free time. Can you forgive me? I want to tell you a lot of things but I don't know where to start! I live with the Simoni family who are unbelievably kind to me; Mrs. Simoni cooks delicious meals and ... you were right, one really does eat a lot in Italy: I will have to go on a diet!

Valentina, the Simoni's daughter, and I have become good friends and we spend a lot of time together. I've already visited Milan and the area around it. I've been to the sea and on a trip to Florence, and I was lucky because the weather was always marvellous: sun and a few clouds but never any rain.

I also really enjoy working; my colleagues are nice and there is a lot I can learn.

When I was in Florence I called your sister who told me that you were planning to come for a week during the holidays in June. Is that certain? I look forward to your answer so that we can finally see each other.

Oh, there is one more piece of news: I met a very nice guy. His name is Marco and he is a doctor. We see each other often and have been to Florence together. You've got to meet him!

I look forward to seeing you soon, greetings to everybody and a big kiss.

                    Alexandra

"si" constructions

The Italian impersonal pronoun **si**, equivalent to the English **one**, takes the **verb in the third person singular**:

> *In questo ristorante **si mangia** bene.*

When **si** is followed by a singular direct object, the verb also takes the third person singular.

> *In questo ristorante **si mangia** pesce.*

If, however, it is followed by a plural direct object, the verb takes the third person plural.

> *In questo ristorante **si mangiano** ottimi dolci.*

In front of reflexive verbs, **si** is replaced by **ci** to avoid a repetition of **si**.

> *In vacanza **ci si alza** sempre tardi.*

The weather

Che tempo fa?	How is the weather?
fa bello/brutto	it is nice/bad
fa caldo/freddo	it is warm/cold
c'è il sole	it is sunny
c'è nebbia	it is foggy
c'è vento	it is windy
ci sono temporali	it is stormy
è sereno	it is bright
è nuvoloso	it is cloudy
è coperto	it is overcast
piove	it is raining
nevica	it is snowing

Exercise 1

Write the impersonal form of the verbs provided as shown in the example.

Che cosa si fa in vacanza al mare?
Si prende il sole.

1. .... in barca.   (andare)

2. .... nuovi amici.   (conoscere)

3. .... il bagno.   (fare)

4. .... molti libri.   (leggere)

5. .... delle gite.   (fare)

6. .... molto pesce. (mangiare)

Exercise 2

Complete the sentences with *si può, si deve, si vuole*.

1. In questo ristorante ....
   mangiare fino alle 23.00.

2. Non .... guidare la macchina
   senza patente.

3. Se .... dimagrire non ....
   mangiare troppo.

4. Non .... entrare al cinema
   senza biglietto.

5. Non .... sempre fare tutto
   quello che ....

6. In questa trattoria .... fumare.

Exercise 3

Write the various actions in the past tense and add the corresponding explanation. The first one has already been done for you.

prendere l'autobus	la macchina essere rotta
mettersi il cappotto	fare freddo
mangiare un hamburger	avere fame
prendere l'ombrello	piovere
non andare al cinema	essere stanco

▶

comprare dei fiori   essere il comple-
                          anno di Pia

fare una passeggiata   fare bello

bere una birra   avere sete

1. Domenica ho preso l'autobus perché
la macchina era rotta.

2. ....

3. ....

4. ....

5. ....

6. ....

7. ....

8. ....

Complete the postcard by filling in the appropriate expressions.

Exercise 4

abbiamo deciso – nuotavamo – è rimasta –
eravamo – doveva – hai visto – abbiamo
fatto – faceva – abbiamo visto

Carissimo Alberto,

come stai? Spero bene. .... che

bel mare? Io e Filippo .... molto

stanchi così .... di fare una set-

timana di vacanza in Sicilia. Il posto è

meraviglioso. Ieri .... una gita in

barca a vela perché .... bel

tempo, e mentre ....,

.... dei pesci stupendi.

▶

Purtroppo Laura .... a Roma

perché .... lavorare. E tu,

quando vai in vacanza? Vieni presto a

trovarci o almeno scrivi!

Un abbraccio,

                                                    Anna

Exercise 5

Che tempo fa in Italia?
How is the weather in these Italian cities?

1. A Torino ....

2. A Venezia ....

3. A Pisa ....

4. A Roma ....

5. A Bari ....

6. A Catania ....

7. A Cagliari ....

Match the adjectives given with the corresponding noun.	ristorante pesce viaggio fragola vestito acqua	dolce verde naturale lungo messicano fresco

Di che colore è? Can you specify the colour of these items?

1. Il latte è ....

2. Il mare è ....

3. I pomodori sono ....

4. Il sole è ....

5. Il vino è ....

6. L'erba è ....

a disposizione	at one's disposal	**mettersi a dieta**	to go on a diet
		nebbia *f*	fog
ambientarsi	to settle in	**nevicare**	to snow
assolutamente	absolutely	**nostalgia** *f*	homesickness
cerchio *m*	circle	**nuvola** *f*	cloud
cielo *m*	sky	**nuvoloso**	cloudy
coperto	overcast	**ombrello** *m*	umbrella
dare soddisfazione	to please (s.o.)	**ormai**	now
		parecchio	rather much
dimagrire	to lose weight	**partire**	to leave
dintorni *m pl*	surrounding area	**patente** *f*	driving licence *Br* / driver's license *Am*
essere fortunato	to be lucky		
guidare	to drive (car)	**pecora** *f*	sheep
imparare	to learn	**pecorella** *f*	lamb
intenzione *f*	intention	**perdonare**	to forgive
luna *f*	moon	**pioggia** *f*	rain
meraviglioso	wonderful	**piovere**	to rain

▶

presto	soon	**temporale** *m*	thunderstorm
rimanere	to stay	**trascorrere**	to spend, stay
risposta *f*	answer	**trattoria** *f*	inn,
riuscire	to succeed		restaurant
saluto *m*	greeting	**un sacco di**	a whole lot of
sereno	clear, bright	**venire a trovare**	to come for
splendido	marvellous		a visit
squisito	delightful,	**vento** *m*	wind
	exquisite	**veramente**	really
stupendo	wonderful		

The weather

Like anyone else, Italians also have their variations of proverbial weather forecast expressions. Things don't look too good when you hear the expression *cielo a pecorelle, acqua a catinelle,* as these fleecy clouds herald pouring rain.

However, you can count on a fine day to come when you hear: *rosso di sera, bel tempo si spera*. Ground mist should not cause you any heartbreak either as this will not change the sunny weather: *nebbia bassa, bel tempo lascia*. Keep your umbrella and raincoat ready when you see a halo around the moon because they say: *se la luna il cerchio fa, vento o pioggia vi sarà.*

In farmacia

Alexandra:	Buongiorno.
Farmacista:	Buongiorno, desidera?
Alexandra:	Vorrei qualcosa contro il raffreddore, per favore.
Farmacista:	Ha la febbre?
Alexandra:	No, ma sono molto raffreddata, ho il naso chiuso e anche un po' di mal di gola.
Farmacista:	Allora le do uno sciroppo e delle compresse per il mal di gola. Lo sciroppo lo prenda tre volte al giorno prima dei pasti e le pastiglie una ogni due o tre ore.
Alexandra:	Va bene.
Farmacista:	Se fra due o tre giorni i disturbi persistono o se le viene la febbre, vada dal medico perché senza ricetta non posso darle qualcosa di più forte.
Alexandra:	Sì. Ah... vorrei anche delle pastiglie per il mal di testa.
Farmacista:	Vuole provare questo medicinale omeopatico a base di sostanze naturali? È veramente efficace.
Alexandra:	Va bene, lo provo. Come lo devo prendere?
Farmacista:	Sempre a stomaco pieno.
Alexandra:	Un'ultima cosa, volevo una crema da sole.

Farmacista:	Questa è una crema con fattore protettivo 6, ma forse per la Sua pelle chiara è meglio un fattore più alto, 10 o 12. Che cosa le do?
Alexandra:	Prendo quella col fattore più alto perché mi scotto facilmente.
Farmacista:	Va bene così?
Alexandra:	Sì, è tutto grazie.
Farmacista:	28,30 euro.
Alexandra:	Ecco a Lei. Arrivederci.
Farmacista:	Arrivederci e grazie.

At the pharmacy

Alexandra:	Hello.
Pharmacist:	Hello, what would you like?
Alexandra:	I would like something for a cold, please.
Pharmacist:	Do you have a temperature?
Alexandra:	No, but I have a very bad cold; my nose is stuffed up and I have a bit of a sore throat.
Pharmacist:	In that case I'll give you syrup and some tablets for the sore throat. Take the syrup three times a day before meals and one of the tablets every two or three hours.
Alexandra:	OK.
Pharmacist:	If your symptoms continue over the next two or three days and should you develop a fever, see a doctor because I cannot give you anything stronger without a prescription.
Alexandra:	Yes, oh ... I'd like pills for my headache as well.
Pharmacist:	Do you want to try this homeopathic medicine that is based on natural substances? It is really effective.
Alexandra:	OK, I'll try it. How do I have to take it?
Pharmacist:	Always on a full stomach.
Alexandra:	One last thing, I wanted to get suntan lotion.
Pharmacist:	This is a lotion with a protection factor of 6, but maybe a higher factor would be better for your light skin, a 10 or 12. Which one do you want?

▶

Alexandra:	I'll take the one with the highest factor because I burn easily in the sun.
Pharmacist:	Is that all?
Alexandra:	Yes, that's all. Thank you.
Pharmacist:	28 euros 30.
Alexandra:	Here you are. Goodbye.
Pharmacist:	Thank you and goodbye.

Demonstrative pronouns

	singular	*plural*
masculine	**questo** libro	**questi** libri
feminine	**questa** macchina	**queste** macchine

Questo is used for persons or objects in the immediate vicinity. Before a vowel, **questo** is often apostrophized: Quest'anno.

	singular	*plural*
masculine	**quel** libro	**quei** libri
	quello specchio	**quegli** specchi
	quell'aereo	**quegli** aerei
feminine	**quella** macchina	**quelle** macchine
	quell'arancia	**quelle** arance

Quello is used with persons or objects that are further away and it is positioned in front of the noun like the definite article. **Quello** can also be used to avoid repeating a noun. Qual è il tuo cappotto? **Quello** blu.

In comparisons **questo** precedes **quello**.
Queste scarpe sono eleganti, ma **quelle** sono più comode.

The body

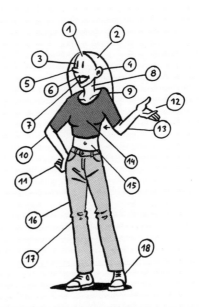

Parti del corpo

1. la testa	7. il dente	13. la schiena
2. i capelli	8. il collo	14. il petto
3. l'occhio	9. la spalla	15. la pancia
4. l'orecchio	10. il braccio	16. la gamba
5. il naso	11. la mano	17. il ginocchio
6. la bocca	12. il dito	18. il piede

Watch out for the irregular plural forms of:

il braccio *m*	le braccia *f*
il dito *m*	le dita *f*
l'orecchio *m*	le orecchie *f*
il ginocchio *m*	le ginocchia *f*

Follow the example and offer advice using the imperative.

Giovanni ha mal di schiena.

1. Vai da uno specialista. (andare da uno specialista)

2. .... (fare ginnastica)

3. .... (nuotare)

4. .... (fare un massaggio)

La signora De Rosa ha mal di testa.

1. Prenda un'aspirina. (prendere un'aspirina)

2. .... (andare a letto)

3. .... (mangiare qualcosa)

4. .... (andare dal medico)

Mariella ha il raffreddore.

1. .... (prendere un tè)

2. .... (mettersi a letto)

3. .... (non prendere freddo)

Fill in *quel, quello, quell', quella, quei, quegli,* or *quelle*.

1. Guarda! Che bella .... bicicletta verde!

2. .... libri non sono miei.

3. Vorrei vedere .... orologio.

4. Non mi piacciono le scarpe rosse, ma .... nere.

5. Vuoi davvero mangiare ....
   spaghetti?

6. Per favore dammi .... giornale.

7. Ti piace .... specchio?

Exercise 3

Complete the sentences using the correct forms of *questo* and *quello*.

1. A: Scusa, mi dai la giacca?

   B: Quale?

   A: .... marrone.

2. A: Scusi, è libero .... posto?

   B: No, ... è occupato, ma ....
   là è libero.

3. A: Vorrei vedere le scarpe col tacco
   alto che sono in vetrina.

   B: Quali? .... blu o .... nere?

   A: .... nere.

Exercise 4

Which word doesn't fit?

1. dentista – chirurgo – oculista – regista –
   ginecologo

   ....

2. discoteca – panetteria – macelleria –
   lavanderia – farmacia

   ....

3. mal di testa – fame – raffreddore – mal
   di denti – febbre

   ....

4. orecchio – naso – bocca – mano –
   occhio

   ....

5. gonna – giacca – vestito – pantaloni –
   scarpe

   ....

The following conversation takes place in the pharmacy.
You are the customer.

A: Buongiorno signora, desidera?

B: I'd like something for a headache.

....

A: Le posso dare queste gocce.

B: How many should I take?

....

A: Da venti a venticinque.

B: Thank you.

....

A: Desidera altro?

B: No, thank you. How much is that?

....

A: 6 euro.

B: Goodbye.

....

A: Arrivederci e grazie.

Exercise 5

Vocabulary

a base di	on the basis of
aspirina *f*	aspirin
bocca *f*	mouth
braccio *m*	arm
chirurgo *m*	surgeon
collo *m*	neck
contro	against, (here:) for
crema da sole *f*	suntan lotion
disturbi *m pl*	ailment, symptoms
dito *m*	finger
efficace	effective
essere raffreddato	to have a cold
facilmente	easily
farmacista *m/f*	chemist *Br* / pharmacist *Am*
fattore protettivo *m*	protection factor
febbre *f*	fever

forte	strong	**orologio** *m*	clock, watch
gamba *f*	leg	**pancia** *f*	abdomen
ginecologo *m*	gynaecologist	**pastiglia** *f*	pill, tablet
ginnastica *f*	gymnastics	**pasto** *m*	meal
ginocchio *m*	knee	**persistere**	to last, persist
goccia *f*	drop	**petto** *m*	chest
in ogni caso	in every case	**prima**	before
lavanderia *f*	laundry	**raffreddore** *m*	cold, flu
mal di gola *m*	sore throat	**schiena** *f*	back
male *m*	pain, ache	**sciroppo** *m*	syrup
massaggio *m*	massage	**scottarsi**	to burn
medicinale *m*	drug,		oneself
	medicine	**sostanza** *f*	substance
naso *m*	nose	**spalla** *f*	shoulder
occhio *m*	eye	**specialista** *m / f*	specialist
occupato	occupied	**stomaco** *m*	stomach
oculista *m/f*	ophthalmolo-	**tazza** *f*	cup
	gist	**testa** *f*	head
ogni	everybody	**vetrina** *f*	(shop)
omeopatico	homeopathic		window
orecchio *m*	ear		

The Italian health care system

Everyone who lives in Italy is covered by the national health care system and most doctors and GPs participate in this nation-wide programme. Citizens from the other EU-countries are entitled to free medical treatment as well.

Patients seeking medical advice from specialists or wishing to undergo special treatments, however, have to pay for these services themselves.

Il corso di ginnastica

Valentina:	Ciao Alessandra, che cosa stai facendo?
Alexandra:	Sto guardando gli annunci pubblicitari sul giornale. Vorrei fare un corso di ginnastica. Vuoi venire con me?
Valentina:	Io? No, la ginnastica non mi interessa, anzi, la trovo noiosa, sempre in una palestra al chiuso. Mi dispiace ma non fa per me. Perché non vai con la tua amica Laura?
Alexandra:	Sì, hai ragione, domani glielo chiedo. Ecco, guarda: »Fitness Club in linea« è qui vicino a casa nostra e sembra un posto carino. Lo conosci?
Valentina:	Di persona no, ma la mia amica Giovanna ci va ed è molto contenta.
Alexandra:	Stasera vado ad informarmi.
Alexandra:	Buonasera.
Segretaria:	Buonasera, posso aiutarla?
Alexandra:	Spero di sì, vorrei fare un corso di ginnastica.
Segretaria:	Ha già il nostro programma?
Alexandra:	No, vengo proprio per avere informazioni.
Segretaria:	Allora, questi sono i tipi di corsi che offriamo. Che cosa Le interessa?

Alexandra:	Ho pensato a qualcosa di non troppo impegnativo ed ho tempo solo alla sera.
Segretaria:	Allora Le consiglio questo corso il martedì e il giovedì dalle 19.00 alle 20.00. Il corso comincia la settimana prossima.
Alexandra:	Va bene, e quanto costa?
Segretaria:	Costa 40 euro al mese.
Alexandra:	E che cosa devo portare?
Segretaria:	Una foto per la tessera, un asciugamano e delle normali scarpe da ginnastica.
Alexandra:	Benissimo, allora a martedì.
Segretaria:	Arrivederci e buona serata.

Gymnastics classes

Valentina:	Hello Alexandra, what are you doing?
Alexandra:	I'm just looking through the ads in the newspaper. I want to take a gymnastics classes. Do you want to join me?
Valentina:	Me? Oh no, gymnastics don't interest me, on the contrary, I find it boring to be in a gym all the time. I'm sorry but that's not for me. Why don't you go with your friend Laura?
Alexandra:	Yes, you're right, I'll ask her tomorrow. Here, look! "Fitness Club in linea", it's close to our house and seems to be a nice place. Do you know it?
Valentina:	Not personally, but my friend Giovanna goes there and she's very happy.
Alexandra:	I'll go there tonight to get some information.
Alexandra:	Good evening.
Secretary:	Good evening, can I help you?
Alexandra:	I hope so; I'd like to take gymnastic classes.
Secretary:	Do you already have a programme?
Alexandra:	No, I came here to get some information.
Secretary:	Well, these are the type of classes we offer. What are you interested in?
Alexandra:	I thought of something not too demanding, and I only have time in the evening.

▶

Secretary:	Then I recommend this class on Tuesdays and Thursdays from 7 to 8. The class starts next week.
Alexandra:	OK, and how much does it cost?
Secretary:	40 euros per month.
Alexandra:	And what do I have to bring with me?
Secretary:	A photo for your pass, a towel and ordinary gym shoes.
Alexandra:	Great, see you Tuesday then.
Secretary:	Goodbye, and have a nice evening.

Personal pronouns

subject	*direct object*	*indirect object*
io	**me**	**a me**
tu	**te**	**a te**
lui	**lui**	**a lui**
lei	**lei**	**a lei**
Lei	**Lei**	**a Lei**
noi	**noi**	**a noi**
voi	**voi**	**a voi**
loro	**loro**	**a loro**
	sé	**a sé** *(reflexive)*

In Italian the stressed **subject forms** are generally omitted:
Andiamo al mare.

– They are used either without the verb (*Chi cucina?* **Io.**), or when the subject is emphasized (**Io** *prendo la macchina e* **lui** *va in bicicletta*).

Stressed **object forms** are used when the object of a sentence is emphasized:

Vi piace il caffè? **A me** *no, ma* **a lei** *sì. / Cerca proprio* **te.**

– These forms are also used after prepositions:
Vieni al corso di ginnastica **con me**?
Questi fiori sono **per te**.

▶

Some prepositions add **di** to the pronoun:

senza di noi   *without us*
sotto/sopra di loro   *below/above them*
prima/dopo di lui   *before/after him*

The object form is used:

– after **di** (than)   *Beppe è più alto **di me.***
– after **come/quando** (like)   *Guarda! Fai **come me.***
– in exclamations   ***Povero te!***

Exercise 1

Fill in the appropriate pronouns to complete the dialogues.

me - lui - loro - noi - a voi - a te - a me - lei

1. **A:** Ho visto Silvia e Carlo stamattina.

   B: Vengono anche .... a teatro?

   A: .... sì, ... no perché deve studiare.

2. **A:** Vi piace la nuova casa di Carla?

   B: A Vincenzo non piace perché è troppo moderna, ma .... sì.

3. **A:** Chi prende un tè?

   B: ......, lo beviamo proprio volentieri.

   A: E .... Elisabetta, che cosa posso fare, un caffè?

   B: Se lo fai solo per .... no, grazie.

4. **A:** E .... ha telefonato la mamma?

   B: Sì, ci ha telefonato ieri.

Fill in **con, senza, a, per, da, sotto** and the correct personal pronoun.

Exercise 2

1. Dovete assolutamente venire alla partita di calcio; .... non andiamo.

2. Attenzione Alexandra, sabato veniamo tutti a cena ....

3. E a Martina piace la pasta?
   No, ... non piace.

4. Andate a Siena con Franco? No, non andiamo ...., andiamo da soli.

5. Laura, chi abita nell'appartamento ....?

6. Sono per i signori Belli questi libri?
   Sì, sono ....

Do you remember the adjective **buono**?

Exercise 3

Buon Natale!	.... serata!
.... Pasqua!	.... fortuna!
.... compleanno!	.... vacanze!
.... viaggio!	.... Anno!

Select the appropriate sport to match the definition.

Exercise 4

sci – pallavolo – tennis – calcio – nuoto

1. Si gioca in due, con due racchette e una palla ....

2. Si pratica d'inverno con la neve. ....

3. Si pratica al mare o in piscina. ....

4. Si gioca con due squadre e una palla. ....

5. È lo sport più popolare in Italia. ....

Exercise 5

You want to enroll in an Italian class.
Translate!

A: Hello.

....

B: Buongiorno, posso aiutarla?

A: I'd like some information about the classes.

....

B: Abbiamo dei corsi intensivi di due settimane, cinque ore al giorno e dei corsi di dieci settimane, due ore due volte alla settimana.

A: Unfortunately I can only (take classes) in the evening.

....

B: Allora le consiglio un corso al lunedí e al mercoledì dalle 19.00 alle 22.00.

A: How much does the class cost?

....

B: 190 euro

A: And do I have to take a test?

....

B: Sì, se vuole anche subito.

A: No, I'll come next (prossima) week.

....

Many thanks and goodbye.

....

B: Arrivederci.

annuncio pubblicitario *m*	advertisement	**popolare**	popular
anzi	on the contrary	**povero**	poor
asciugamano *m*	towel	**praticare**	to practise, exercise
asilo nido *m*	day care/ nursery	**programma** *m*	programme
carino	kind, nice	**racchetta** *f*	(tennis) racket
consigliare	to advise	**scarpa da ginnastica** *f*	gymnastic shoes
corso *m*	course, class	**sci** *m*	skiing
impegnativo	demanding	**scuola materna** *f*	kindergarten
informarsi	to inform oneself	**scuola professionale** *f*	vocational school
intensivo	intensive	**sopra**	over, above
interessare	to interest	**sotto**	below, under(neath)
non fa per me	(that's) not for me		
normale	normal	**squadra** *f*	team
nuoto *m*	swimming	**tessera** *f*	pass, ID
palestra *f*	gym	**test** *m*	test
palla *f*	ball	**tipo** *m*	type, manner
Pasqua *f*	Easter		
piscina *f*	swimming pool		

The Italian school system

Children start school at the age of 6 with *scuola elementare* (elementary school). Most children will have spent a number of years already in the *asilo nido* (day care for 3+) and the subsequent *scuola materna* (kindergarten). After 5 years of elementary school, pupils attend another 3 years of *scuola media*. Those wishing to continue their schooling can then choose between a *liceo* (secondary school) and a more practically-oriented *scuola professionale*. Both of these school types end with the *maturità*, which constitutes the entrance qualification for university.

Test 5

1 Choose one of the two answers, then go to the square with the number of your answer.

2 Laura è più al▪ ... Gianna.

di ⇨ 25
che ⇨ 15

6 Correct! Continue:

Che tempo fa? ... bello.
Fa ⇨ 9
È ⇨ 28

7 Good! Contin▪ Mentre ... la t▪ arrivata Anna.

ho guardato ⇨ 18
guardavo ⇨ 27

11 Good! Continue:

Marco, ... le medicine!

prenda ⇨ 26
prendi ⇨ 14

12 Wrong!

Go back to number 19.

16 Great! Continue: Senza biglietto non ... entrare a teatro.

si vuole ⇨ 5
si può ⇨ 19

17 Wrong!

Go back to number 20.

21 Wrong!

Go back to number 4.

22 Correct! Continue:
... due giorni vanno in Sardegna.
Da ⇨ 3
Tra ⇨ 11

26 Wrong!

Go back to number 11.

27 Correct!

End of exercise!

Wrong!

back to
mber 22.

4 Great! Continue:

Questi vestiti sono ...

rosa ⟶ 16
rosi ⟶ 21

5 Wrong!

Go back to
number 16.

Wrong!

o back to
umber 29.

9 Correct!
Continue:

Vorrei ... giornali.

quegli ⟶ 30
quei ⟶ 20

10 Wrong!

Go back to
number 25.

Wrong!

o back to
mber 24.

14 Great! Continue:
In montagna ...
passeggiate.

si fa ⟶ 23
si fanno ⟶ 4

15 Wrong!

Go back to
number 2.

Wrong!

o back to
mber 7.

19 Well done!
Continue:
Mi piace di più viaggiare
in treno ... in aereo.
di ⟶ 12
che ⟶ 24

20 Correct!
Continue:
Da bambina ...
sempre al mare.
andavo ⟶ 29
sono andata ⟶ 17

Wrong!

o back to
mber 14.

24 Well done!
Continue:

Parto senza ...

di voi ⟶ 6
voi ⟶ 13

25 Good! Continue:
... Compleanno!

Buon ⟶ 22
Buono ⟶ 10

Wrong!

o back to
mber 6.

29 Good! Continue:

Vado al mare ...

con ti ⟶ 8
con te ⟶ 7

30 Wrong!

Go back to
number 9.

26 Un inconveniente

Valentina:	Accidenti, che cos'ha oggi questa macchina? Non vuol partire. Proprio adesso!
Alexandra:	Potrebbe mancare la benzina. Hai controllato?
Valentina:	Sì, sì, il serbatoio è pieno.
Alexandra:	Allora potrebbe essere la batteria. È accesa la spia?
Valentina:	No, mi sembra tutto a posto.
Alexandra:	Allora telefoniamo al soccorso stradale.
Valentina:	Buona idea!
Alexandra:	C'è una cabina telefonica là in fondo.
Valentina:	Ci vado io, so il numero!
Impiegato:	Pronto?
Valentina:	Buongiorno, ho un guasto al motore, potreste venire ad aiutarmi?
Impiegato:	Come si chiama?
Valentina:	Valentina Simoni.
Impiegato:	Lei è socia ACI?
Valentina:	Sì, penso di sì.
Impiegato:	Dove si trova?
Valentina:	Sono in via Larga, davanti al numero 28.
Impiegato:	Le mandiamo subito un'auto. Attenda.

Dopo pochi minuti:
Alexandra: Che velocità!!
Meccanico: Dunque, signorina, qual è il problema?
Valentina: Ma, non so, la macchina non parte.
Meccanico: Mi faccia dare un'occhiata. Dunque... ah ah!
                 Ma qui non c'è niente di rotto.
Valentina: Meno male! Ma allora perché non parte?
Meccanico: Ha dimenticato di disinserire l'antifurto,
                 ecco perché non partiva!
Valentina: Oh, che sciocca! Grazie mille, Lei è davvero
                 un angelo.

An inconvenience

Valentina: Damn it! What's wrong with this car today? It won't
                 start. And that now!
Alexandra: Maybe it's run out of petrol (gas). Did you check?
Valentina: Yeah yeah, the tank is full.
Alexandra: It could be the battery then. Is the control light on?
Valentina: No, everything seems to be fine.
Alexandra: Well, let's call the road service.
Valentina: Good idea.
Alexandra: There's a telephone booth over there.
Valentina: I'll go, I know the number.

Employee: Hello?
Valentina: Hi, my car has broken down. Could you come and
                 help?
Employee: What's your name?
Valentina: Valentina Simoni.
Employee: Are you a member of the ACI?
Valentina: Yes I think so.
Employee: Where are you?
Valentina: I am in Via Larga, in front of house number 28.
Employee: We'll send a car right away. Wait there.
After a few minutes:
Alexandra: That was fast!!
Mechanic: So, what's the problem?
Valentina: I don't know, the car won't start.

▶

Mechanic:	Let me check. Well, ... aha! There's nothing broken here.	
Valentina:	Thank goodness! But why won't it start then?	
Mechanic:	You forgot to turn off the antitheft device, that's why it won't start!	
Valentina:	How stupid of me! Thanks a million, you're an angel.	

Conditional

The conditional is used to express:

– a wish/desire
  (***Vorrei*** *un gelato alla fragola.*)

– a polite request
  (***Potrebbe*** *chiudere la finestra?*)

– a possible but by no means certain action
  (***Verrei*** *a Parigi con te, ma ho molto lavoro.*)

	guardare	*leggere*
io	*guarderei*	*leggerei*
tu	*guarderesti*	*leggeresti*
lui, lei, Lei	*guarderebbe*	*leggerebbe*
noi	*guarderemmo*	*leggeremmo*
voi	*guardereste*	*leggereste*
loro	*guarderebbero*	*leggerebbero*

	dormire	**essere**
io	*dormirei*	**sarei**
tu	*dormiresti*	**saresti**
lui, lei, Lei	*dormirebbe*	**sarebbe**
noi	*dormiremmo*	**saremmo**
voi	*dormireste*	**sareste**
loro	*dormirebbero*	**sarebbero**

▶

■ Irregular forms:

andare	→	**andrei**	dire	→	**direi**
avere	→	**avrei**	fare	→	**farei**
dovere	→	**dovrei**	stare	→	**starei**
potere	→	**potrei**	bere	→	**berrei**
vedere	→	**vedrei**	venire	→	**verrei**
sapere	→	**saprei**	volere	→	**vorrei**
dare	→	**darei**	rimanere	→	**rimarrei**

Ci

Ci could be translated with **there**, substituting an already mentioned location:

*Quando vai **a Firenze**? **Ci** vado domani.*
*Sei già stato **in Francia**? Sì, **ci** sono già stato tre volte.*

credo di sì – credo di no

When confirming or negating something in connection with the verbs *pensare, credere, dire* or *sperare* the preposition **di** is used:

– *Sandro torna oggi? **Penso di no.*** (Is Sandro coming back today? I don't think so.)
– *Paolo ha comprato il pane? **Spero di sì.***
  (Did Paolo buy bread? I hope so.)

Form the conditional of the verbs as shown in the example.
"Un sabato ideale": Che cosa fareste? – Diverse opinioni.

1. Nonna Carlotta: Io mi .... (alzare) presto e ....

(andare) subito a fare la spesa con Piera. Poi .... (pulire) un

po' la casa e .... (iniziare) a cucinare un buon pranzo per

tutta la famiglia. Al pomeriggio .... (fare) una passeggiata nel

parco con le mie amiche e poi .... (andare) al cinema. ▶

Exercise 1

2. Piera: .... (restare) in casa tutto il giorno, ...

(guardare) la televisione, ... (leggere) un po' il giornale o un

buon libro. .... (fare) un bel bagno rilassante e ....

(andare) dal parrucchiere. Non .... (cucinare) niente, però

alla sera ...... (volere) andare al ristorante.

3. Valentina e Stefano: Noi invece .... (dormire) fino alle

11.00, poi .... (fare) colazione a letto. Al pomeriggio

.... (andare) in centro o ci .... (incontrare) con i nostri

amici, oppure .... (giocare) a tennis. La sera ....

(andare) a ballare in discoteca, al "Campo verde".

Exercise 2

If you won the lottery, what would you do?

	tu	Alexandra	Piera e Luigi
fare un lungo viaggio	X	X	X
smettere di lavorare	X		X
comprare una casa	X	X	X
andare a vivere in America	X	X	
aiutare i bambini poveri	X	X	X

Express yourself more politely by rewriting the sentences using the conditional form of the underlined verbs.

Exercise 3

1. Scusi, <u>può</u> aprire la finestra?

....

2. Le <u>dispiace</u> passarmi il sale?

....

3. <u>Voglio</u> due etti di prosciutto.

....

4. Scusa, mi <u>sai</u> dire l'ora?

....

5. Mi <u>potete</u> aiutare?

....

6. Per favore, ci <u>porta</u> in camera questa valigia?

....

7. <u>Può</u> dirgli di richiamarmi?

....

Replace the locations given in the dialogues with *ci*.

Exercise 4

A: Ho deciso: domenica andiamo a Firenze.

....

B: Ma non siete stati a Firenze un mese fa?

....

A: Sì, siamo stati a Firenze per lavoro.

....

B: E perché domenica volete ritornare a Firenze?

....

A: Perché Firenze è una città molto interessante.

....

▶

B: Noi invece andiamo a Como. Perché
non venite anche voi?

....
A: Non ho voglia, sono stata a Como
anche domenica scorsa.

....
B: Ah sì? E con chi sei andata a Como?

....
A: Sono andata a Como con dei colleghi.

....

The parts of a car

a la portiera
b il volante
c il pneumatico
d il cofano
e il paraurti

f i fari
g la targa
h il sedile
i il freno a mano
l il parabrezza

Which parts belong together?	**1.** Il pieno,	**a** dei pneumatici?
	2. Mi può cambiare	**b** per favore.
	3. Può controllare la pressione	**c** il parabrezza, per favore?
	4. Il faro destro	**d** il cofano per favore?
	5. Potrebbe aprire	**e** l'olio, per favore?
	6. Mi potrebbe pulire	**f** non funziona.

Exercise 5

Vocabulary

a posto	in order, OK	**funzionare**	to function
accendere	to turn on	**guasto** *m*	breakdown
accidenti	Damn it	**ideale**	ideal
ACI	Italian motorist club	**incontrarsi**	to meet
		inconveniente *m*	inconvenience
angelo *m*	angel	**invece**	rather, on the other hand
antifurto *m*	antitheft device		
batteria *f*	battery	**meno male**	thank goodness
cabina telefonica *f*	telephone booth	**minuto** *m*	minute
campo *m*	field	**motore** *m*	engine, motor
ci	there		
cofano *m*	bonnet *Br* / (engine) hood *Am*	**occhiata** *f*	view, look
		opinione *f*	opinion
		oppure	or
		parabrezza *m*	windscreen / windshield
dare un'occhiata	to take a look		
disinserire	to switch off	**paraurti** *m*	bumper
diverso	different	**parrucchiere** *m*	hairdresser
faro *m*	headlight	**pneumatico** *m*	tyre *Br* / tire *Am*
freno *m*	brake	**polizia** *f*	police
freno a mano *m*	handbrake *Br* / emergency brake *Am*	**portiera** *f*	car door
		pressione *f*	pressure

rilassante	relaxing	**spia** *f*	control light
sciocco	stupid	**targa** *f*	number *Br* /
sedile *m*	seat		license *Am*
serbatoio *m*	petrol *Br* /gas		plate
	Am tank	**velocità** *f*	speed
soccorso	road service	**vigile del**	firefighter
stradale *m*		**fuoco** *m*	
socio *m*	member	**volante** *m*	steering
soldi *m pl*	money		wheel

Emmergency services

Italians are generally very helpful. In case of an emergency or any other problem, neighbours, friends or people just passing by will spontaneously lend a helping hand.

In case of emergency call:

113 *(Soccorso pubblico di emergenza/Polizia)*

112 *(Carabinieri)*

115 The fire brigade *(Vigili del Fuoco)*

116 ACI - Italian motorist association
(Automobile Club d'Italia)

Lezione di cucina

Alexandra:	Signora Simoni, se vuole l'aiuto ad apparecchiare la tavola.
Piera:	Grazie, Alessandra. Le posate sono nel primo cassetto a destra, i piatti e i bicchieri sono già sul tavolo. Se vuoi, però, possiamo cucinare qualcosa insieme.
Alexandra:	Oh, mi farebbe molto piacere! Io in cucina sono una frana!
Piera:	Oggi voglio preparare un dolce molto semplice ma squisito: la panna cotta. L'hai già provata?
Alexandra:	No, penso di no. Che tipo di dolce è?
Piera:	È un budino alla panna. Dunque, ci vogliono mezzo litro di latte e mezzo litro di panna, un etto di zucchero, una bustina di vanillina e dodici grammi di colla di pesce.
Alexandra:	Colla di pesce? E come si usa?

▶

Piera:	Bisogna metterla in acqua fredda per ammorbidirla e poi unirla al latte caldo.
Alexandra:	Ecco qui il latte e la panna.
Piera:	Bene, mettili in una pentola con lo zucchero e la vanillina.
Alexandra:	Devo scaldarli?
Piera:	Sì, e poi bisogna aggiungere la colla di pesce. Ma sta' attenta: non deve bollire.
Alexandra:	Quando devo spegnere il fuoco?
Piera:	Quando il latte sta per bollire ... Ecco, adesso! Ora deve raffreddare e poi bisogna metterlo in frigorifero per almeno sei ore.
Alexandra:	Già pronto?
Piera:	Sì, già pronto!
Alexandra:	Ma allora non è poi così difficile cucinare!

A cookery lesson

Alexandra:	If you want me to, Mrs. Simoni, I'll help you set the table.
Piera:	Thank you, Alexandra. The cutlery is in the first drawer on the right; the plates and glasses are already on the table. If you want to we can cook something together.
Alexandra:	Oh, I'd like that very much. I'm a total disaster in the kitchen!
Piera:	I want to make a very simple but delicious dessert today: panna cotta. Have you ever tried it?
Alexandra:	No I don't think so. What kind of dessert is it?
Piera:	It's a cream pudding. So, you need half a litre of milk, half a litre of cream, one hundred grams of sugar, one packet of vanilla sugar and twelve grams of sheet gelatine.
Alexandra:	Sheet gelatine? How do you use that?
Piera:	You have to soak it in cold water to soften it and then you add it to the warm milk.
Alexandra:	Here are the milk and sugar.
Piera:	Good, pour them into the saucepan with the sugar and the vanilla sugar.

▶

Alexandra:	Do I have to heat them?
Piera:	Yes, and you have to add the gelatine but watch it: it's not supposed to boil.
Alexandra:	When do I have to turn down the heat?
Piera:	Once the milk begins to boil ... Now, that's it! It has to cool down now and then you have to keep it in the fridge for at least six hours.
Alexandra:	That's it?
Piera:	Yes, that's it!
Alexandra:	Well, cooking isn't all that difficult after all!

If you need something

There are two ways to say "**you need**" in Italian:
ci vuole or *occorre* + noun in the singular
ci vogliono or *occorrono* + noun in the plural

– *Ci vuole* un chilo di zucchero./*Occorre* un chilo di zucchero. (You need a kilo of sugar.)
– *Ci vogliono* due litri di latte./*Occorrono* due litri di latte. (You need two litres of milk.)

Bisogna expresses the necessity of an action. It is used impersonally and accompanies a verb in the infinitive or a relative clause (*bisogna che...*):
– *Bisogna* avere pazienza. (You need/have to be patient.)
– *Bisogna* fare sport. (You need/have to play sport.)

Its meaning changes when used in the expression:
aver bisogno di = to need
– *Ho bisogno di* te. (I need you.)
– *Abbiamo bisogno di* riposo. (We need rest.)
– Marco *ha bisogno di* cambiare aria.
  (Marco needs to have a change of air.)

Prepositions defining locations

dietro	(behind)	*di fianco a*	(next to)
sopra	(on)	*dentro*	(in)
sotto	(under)		

stare per + infinitive

This construction expresses an action that one is about to begin.

Sto per *uscire.* (I'm just about to go out;
                I'm going out in a few minutes.)

Sta per *piovere.* (It will rain soon.)

Exercise 1

What do you need to set the table for six people?
Fill in the correct form: either **ci vuole/occorre** or **ci vogliono/ occorrono**.

1. una tovaglia ....
2. sei piatti ....
3. sei bicchieri ....
4. una bottiglia di vino ....
5. una candela ....
6. sei forchette ....
7. sei coltelli ....
8. sei cucchiai ....

Exercise 2

Fill in:
Ci vuole/occorre – ci vogliono/ occorrono – bisogna – aver bisogno di.

1. .... un chilo di carne.
2. .... cinque cipolle e tre peperoni.
3. .... tagliare la carne.
4. Per tagliare bene la carne il cuoco

    .... di un buon coltello.

▶

5. Poi (lui) .... una padella molto larga.

6. .... cuocere la carne per un'ora e mezza.

7. .... aggiungere sale e pepe.

Alexandra enjoys cooking, but leaves a terrible mess. She has used lots of spoons and now can't find them any more. Can you help her?

Un cucchiaio è ....
....
....
....
....
....
....

Exercise 3

Exercise 4

Wherever necessary, insert the preposition *a*, with or without the article.

1. Davanti ..... chiesa c'è il supermercato.

2. Tra ..... Nico e ..... Gina c'è Pia.

3. Di fianco ..... me c'è la mamma.

4. Simone è sempre vicino ..... mamma.

5. Di fronte ..... supermercato c'è Nina.

Exercise 5

Who is sitting where?

1. Alexandra è seduta tra Stefano e Valentina.
2. La nonna è seduta davanti a Valentina.
3. La mamma è seduta davanti a Stefano.
4. La mamma è seduta a destra del papà.

Seating plan: **A   C   E**

                B   D   F

Can you say who sits where now?

A = ...   D = ...

B = ...   E = ...

C = Alexandra   F = ...

Exercise 6

Alexandra tries to prepare a *panna cotta* all by herself, but has made a number of mistakes.
Can you help her again?

1. Ci vogliono mezzo litro di latte e mezzo litro di panna, un chilo di zucchero, 12 grammi di colla di pesce e una bustina di vanillina.

2. Bisogna ammorbidire la colla di pesce in acqua calda.

3. Bisogna bollire il latte e la panna.

4. Poi bisogna aggiungere lo zucchero, la vanillina e la colla di pesce.

5. Alla fine bisogna mettere tutto in forno per sei ore.

Arrange the hours of the day, the week days, months and seasons into their correct order.

maggio	martedì	mattina	gennaio	luglio	sera
estate	ottobre	sabato	marzo	dicembre	inverno
aprile	giovedì	settembre	lunedì	notte	pomeriggio
novembre	venerdì	autunno	febbraio	agosto	domenica
giugno	primavera	mercoledì			

Le parti del giorno.

....

I giorni della settimana.

....

....

I mesi.

....

....

....

Le stagioni.

....

aggiungere	to add	**candela** *f*	candle
ammorbidire	to soften up	**cassetto** *m*	drawer
apparecchiare	to set	**ci vuole/**	you need to
aria *f*	air	**ci vogliono**	
attento	attentive, watch out(!)	**cipolla** *f*	onion
		colla di pesce *f*	sheet gelatine
bisogna	you need to	**coltello** *m*	knife
bollire	to boil	**cotto**	cooked
budino *m*	pudding	**cucchiaio** *m*	spoon
bustina *f*	packet	**cuocere**	to cook

▶

dentro	inside, in	**raffreddare**	to cool off
di fianco a	next to	**riposo** *m*	rest
far piacere	to enjoy	**scaldare**	to warm/
forchetta *f*	fork		heat up
frana *f*	disaster,	**scontrino**	(sales) receipt
	catastrophe	**fiscale** *m*	
fuoco *m*	fire	**semplice**	simple
gelatina *f*	gelatine	**tovaglia** *f*	table cloth
grammo *m*	gramme	**unire**	to unite, add
padella *f*	saucepan	**usare**	to use
pentola *f*	pot	**vanillina** *f*	vanilla,
peperone *m*	chili pepper/		vanilla sugar
	paprika		
posata *f*	cutlery		

Sales receipts   Italian tax laws require that all shops or stores (supermarkets, small stores, hairdressers, restaurants, etc.) print out a sales receipt *(scontrino fiscale)* on payment by the customer.

Don't forget to take the sales receipt with you when you leave the premise where you shopped or paid for merchandise or a service. The tax authorities check regularly and any customer found without the sales receipt can be fined.

Un invito

Piera:	Se vuoi, Alessandra, una sera puoi invitare qualche amico a cena da noi.
Alexandra:	Ma no, non è necessario, non vorrei disturbarvi.
Piera:	Ma figurati! Nessun disturbo, anzi! Mi farebbe molto piacere conoscere qualcuno dei tuoi amici. C'è qualcuno di speciale?
Alexandra:	Speciale? No, no, sono tutti simpatici.
Piera:	Dai, Alessandra, non fare la timida. C'è qualcuno che ti viene spesso a trovare.
Alexandra:	Intende dire Marco?
Piera:	Sì, proprio lui!
Alexandra:	Mah … sì, potremmo invitarlo una sera …
Piera:	Benissimo, telefonagli subito, così organizziamo qualcosa per la prossima settimana.

Alexandra:	Pronto, Marco?
Marco:	Pronto, chi parla?

Alexandra:	Sono Alexandra. Ti telefono per chiederti se hai voglia di venire a cena da noi, una sera della prossima settimana.
Marco:	Volentieri, perché no? Quando vi andrebbe bene?
Alexandra:	Non so, venerdì forse?
Marco:	Mi dispiace, venerdì non posso. Lo sai, tutti i venerdì vado a giocare a calcio con mio fratello.
Alexandra:	Ah sì, allora facciamo sabato, va bene?
Marco:	Purtroppo sabato prossimo ho già un impegno, mi dispiace Alessandra, ma non posso proprio rimandare. Ma domenica sono libero tutto il giorno.
Alexandra:	OK, allora domenica sera. Alle otto va bene?
Marco:	Benissimo, e grazie per l'invito.

An invitation

Piera:	Alexandra, if you want you can invite some friends of yours to come for dinner one night.
Alexandra:	But that's not necessary, I don't want to trouble you.
Piera:	Oh please! We don't mind at all! I very much would like to get to know some of your friends. Is there someone special?
Alexandra:	Special? No, no, they are all nice.
Piera:	Come on, Alexandra, don't be so shy. There is someone who visits you often.
Alexandra:	Are you talking about Marco?
Piera:	Yes, that's the one.
Alexandra:	Well ... yes, we could invite him one evening ...
Piera:	Great! Call him right away and we'll organize something for next week.
Alexandra:	Hello, Marco?
Marco:	Hello, who's speaking?

Alexandra:	It's me, Alexandra. I'm calling to ask you whether you'd like to come to our house for dinner one night next week.
Marco:	Sure, why not? When would it suit you?
Alexandra:	I don't know, maybe Friday?
Marco:	I'm sorry, I can't on Friday. As you know, I play football (soccer) with my brother every Friday.
Alexandra:	Oh yes, let's make it Saturday then, OK?
Marco:	Unfortunately I already have an appointment next Saturday. I'm sorry, Alexandra, but I can't postpone that, but I'm free all day on Sunday.
Alexandra:	OK, Sunday evening then. Is eight o'clock OK?
Marco:	Great, and thank you for the invitation.

qualche, qualcuno, qualcosa

qualche = a few, some

– Ho comprato **qualche** CD per Paolo.
  (I bought a few CDs for Paolo.)

Although the term *qualche* identifies a plural, the noun it relates to is always singular.

qualcuno = someone/anyone

– **Qualcuno** ha suonato alla porta.
  (Someone rang the doorbell.)

– **Qualcuno** di voi sa suonare la chitarra?
  (Does anyone of you know how to play the guitar?)

qualcosa = something/anything

– Ho comprato **qualcosa** per te.
  (I bought something for you.)
– C'è **qualcosa** di nuovo? (Is there anything new?)
– C'è **qualcosa** da fare? (Is there anything to be done?)

When followed by an adjective it takes the preposition *di*.
When followed by an infinitive it takes the preposition *da*.

nessuno, niente/nulla

nessuno = no (one)
– *Non conosco **nessuno**.* (I know no one.)
– *Non ho comprato **nessun** libro.* (I bought no book.)

If *nessuno* precedes a noun, its ending changes like it does with the indefinite article *uno*, (*nessuna ragazza, nessun ragazzo, nessuno specchio*).

niente/nulla = nothing
– *Non ho comprato **niente (nulla)** per te.*
  (I bought nothing for you.)
– *Non c'è **niente** di nuovo.* (There is nothing new.)
– *Non c'è **niente** da fare.* (There is nothing to do.)

As with *qualcosa*, when followed by an adjective it takes the preposition *di*, and the preposition *da* with an infinitive.

Don't forget the double negative rules
(cf. Lesson 19).

ognuno, ogni

ognuno = every(one)/each one
– ***Ognuno** pensa per sé.*
  (Everyone thinks of him-/herself.)
– ***Ognuno** di voi deve parlare con il direttore.*
  (Each one of you has to speak to the headmaster.)

ogni = every(one)/each one *(+ noun)*
– ***Ogni** bambina aveva un fiore nei capelli.*
  (Each girl had a flower in her hair.)
– ***Ogni** venerdì Marco gioca a tennis.*
  (Marco plays tennis every Friday.)
– ***Ogni** volta che lo vedo, è felice.*
  (Every time I see him, he is happy.)

tutto

tutto/tutta = full/complete/entire/whole/all

– *Ho visto* **tutto** *il film*. (I saw the entire film.)

tutti/tutte = all

– **Tutti** *i miei amici sono in vacanza.*
  (All my friends are on holiday.)

– *Vanno* **tutti e tre** *al mare.* (All three go to the shore.)

Where *tutto* relates to a noun, the noun is generally accompanied by the definite article.

When relating to a number it is accompanied by **e** (*tutti/tutte* **e** *cinque*).

How do you feel today?

Mark the adjectives that define your present mood.

Noun:	*Adjective:*
depressione	❏ **depresso**
disperazione	❏ **disperato**
emozione	❏ **emozionato**
euforia	❏ **euforico**
felicità	❏ **felice**
imbarazzo	❏ **imbarazzato**
malinconia	❏ **malinconico**
rabbia	❏ **arrabbiato**
serenità	❏ **sereno**
soddisfazione	❏ **soddisfatto**
tristezza	❏ **triste**

Exercise 1

Complete the sentences with the following words.

qualche – qualcosa – tutto – tutti – tutte – ogni – nessuno – niente.

1. ..... le mattine vado al bar a bere un caffè.

2. Luigi va allo stadio ..... domenica.

3. Non parla mai con ..... .

4. Ieri sono stato ..... il giorno in casa.

5. Viene qui ..... i giorni ma non compra mai ..... .

6. ..... volta vado in ufficio in bicicletta.

7. Mi porti ..... da bere?

Exercise 2

Di or *da*? Where necessary, fill in the appropriate preposition.

1. Non ha mai niente ..... dire.

2. Stasera c'è qualcosa ..... interessante alla televisione.

3. Non ho niente ..... nuovo ..... raccontare.

4. Marina arriva sempre con qualche ..... amico.

5. Nessuno ..... voi mi può aiutare.

6. Piera sta preparando qualcosa ..... buono ..... mangiare.

Exercise 3

Fill in the correct form of *tutto:* with or without the article and the conjunction *e*.

1. La nonna ha pulito ..... casa.

2. Sono andate ..... cinque in vacanza a Otranto.

3. Mio fratello ha visitato ..... mondo.

4. Ha mangiato ..... spaghetti.

5. Ieri ho cucinato ..... giorno.

6. Sono andati via ..... due.

Write the following sentences in the negative.

1. Ieri è arrivato qualcuno dalla Spagna. ....

2. Vorrei comprare qualcosa da mangiare. ....

3. Tutti i miei amici sanno parlare inglese. ....

4. Ho letto qualche libro di Moravia. ....

5. Mi piacerebbe andare in vacanza con qualcuno di voi. ....

6. Ha qualche problema con suo marito. ....

Exercise 4

Which parts go together to form a sentence?

1. Hai voglia di venire   **a** un altro impegno.

2. Sì, mi farebbe   **b** sabato?

3. Hai tempo   **c** a cena da noi?

4. No, mi   **d** molto piacere.

5. Sabato ho già   **e** dispiace.

Exercise 5

Using the formal address "Lei", rewrite the dialogue using Mrs. Bertoli and Mrs. Gavoni as speakers.

A: Pronto?

B: Ciao Marcella, sono Cristina. Come stai?

A: Bene, grazie e tu?

B: Bene. Ti telefono perché vorremmo invitarti una sera a cena da noi.

A: Volentieri, quando?

B: Quando hai una serata libera?

A: Dunque, al martedì vado ad un corso d'inglese, ma le altre sere sono libera. ▶

Exercise 6

B: Ti andrebbe bene venerdì?

A: Sì, benissimo, a che ora?

B: Alle 8.00?

A: Benissimo, a venerdì, allora.

B: Sì, a venerdì! Ciao.

Vocabulary

dai!	come on!	**malinconia** *f*	melancholy
depressione *f*	depression	**malinconico**	melancholic
depresso	depressed	**ognuno**	every(one)
disperato	desperate	**organizzare**	to organize
disperazione *f*	despair	**qualcuno**	someone
disturbare	to disturb	**rabbia** *f*	anger
disturbo *m*	disturbance	**rimandare**	to postpone
emozionato	excited	**serenità** *f*	peacefulness, harmony
emozione *f*	excitement		
euforia *f*	euphoria	**sereno**	calm, peaceful
euforico	euphoric		
felicità *f*	happiness	**soddisfatto**	content
felice	happy	**soddisfazione** *f*	contentment satisfaction
imbarazzato	embarrassed		
imbarazzo *m*	embarrassment	**stadio** *m*	stadium
impegno *m*	appointment	**timido**	shy/timid
intendere	to intend	**triste**	sad
Ma figurati!	Oh please!	**tristezza** *f*	sadness

Invitations   Italians often invite guests for a meal. It is expected that you arrive 5 to 10 minutes later than agreed on. A gift is appropriate and expected: Flowers are always appreciated but you should keep them wrapped up. Alternatively you can bring sweets or something traditional from your home country.
Italians are usually very generous with gifts.

Valentina si sposa

Valentina: Oh Alessandra, sono così emozionata!
Alexandra: Perché? Che cosa è successo, Valentina?
Valentina: Io e Paolo ci sposeremo.
Alexandra: Vi sposerete? Quando?
Valentina: L'anno prossimo, a maggio! Daremo un
grande ricevimento. Vogliamo affittare una
villa sul lago. Abbiamo già fatto la lista degli
invitati: ci saranno circa novanta persone.
Naturalmente inviteremo anche te e la tua
famiglia.

Alexandra: Che bello! Verremo sicuramente! E i tuoi
genitori cosa dicono?
Valentina: La mamma è felicissima, il papà invece non
ha detto niente.
Alexandra: E dove andrete ad abitare?
Valentina: Non lo sappiamo ancora. Stiamo cercando
una casa in affitto, ma non è facile.

Alexandra:	Tu continuerai a studiare?
Valentina:	Sì, certamente.
Alexandra:	Andrete in viaggio di nozze?
Valentina:	Sicuramente! Ma non abbiamo ancora deciso dove. Io preferirei andare su un'isola dei Caraibi, ma Paolo non è d'accordo, preferisce restare in Europa, magari in Grecia.
Alexandra:	Avete ancora tempo per decidere.
Valentina:	Sì, ma un anno passa in fretta e ci sono così tante cose da organizzare per il matrimonio: l'abito da sposa, la chiesa, il ricevimento, i testimoni, la lista dei regali ...
Alexandra:	Santo cielo, Valentina, non iniziare adesso a stressarti!!

Valentina is getting married

Valentina:	Alexandra, I am so excited!
Alexandra:	Why? What's happened, Valentina?
Valentina:	Paolo and I are getting married.
Alexandra:	You're getting married? When?
Valentina:	Next year, in May! We'll have a big reception. We want to rent a villa by the lake. We already made a guest list: there'll be about 90 people. Of course we will also invite you and your family.
Alexandra:	How nice! We will definitely come! And what do your parents say?
Valentina:	My mother is very happy, my dad hasn't really said anything.
Alexandra:	And where will you live?
Valentina:	We don't know yet. We are looking for a flat (apartment) but it's not easy.
Alexandra:	Will you continue with your studies?
Valentina:	Yes, of course I will.
Alexandra:	Will you go on a honeymoon?
Valentina:	Sure! But we haven't decided where to go yet. I would rather go to a Caribbean island but Paolo doesn't agree with me, and wants to stay in Europe, maybe in Greece.

Alexandra:	You've got plenty of time to decide.
Valentina:	Yes, but a year goes by quickly and there are so many things to organise for the wedding: the wedding gown, the church, the reception, the witnesses, the gift list ...
Alexandra:	Good heavens, Valentina, don't get stressed already!!

Future tense

The irregularities of the future tense and its formation are similar to those of the conditional tense (cf. lesson 26).

	guardare	**leggere**
io	guard**erò**	legg**erò**
tu	guard**erai**	legg**erai**
lui, lei, Lei	guard**erà**	legg**erà**
noi	guard**eremo**	legg**eremo**
voi	guard**erete**	legg**erete**
loro	guard**eranno**	legg**eranno**

	dormire	**essere**
io	dorm**irò**	**sarò**
tu	dorm**irai**	**sarai**
lui, lei, Lei	dorm**irà**	**sarà**
noi	dorm**iremo**	**saremo**
voi	dorm**irete**	**sarete**
loro	dorm**iranno**	**saranno**

Irregular forms:

andare	→	**andrò**	dire	→	**dirò**
avere	→	**avrò**	fare	→	**farò**
dovere	→	**dovrò**	stare	→	**starò**
potere	→	**potrò**	bere	→	**berrò**
vedere	→	**vedrò**	venire	→	**verrò**
sapere	→	**saprò**	volere	→	**vorrò**
dare	→	**darò**	rimanere	→	**rimarrò**

■ Irregular forms:

andare	→	**andrò**	dire	→	**dirò**

andare   →   **andrò**   dire   →   **dirò**
avere   →   **avrò**   fare   →   **farò**
dovere   →   **dovrò**   stare   →   **starò**
potere   →   **potrò**   bere   →   **berrò**
vedere   →   **vedrò**   venire   →   **verrò**
sapere   →   **saprò**   volere   →   **vorrò**
dare   →   **darò**   rimanere →   **rimarrò**

The future tense is used to express actions and situations in the future. In spoken language the future is rarely used but replaced by the present tense, especially where actions in the immediate future are concerned:

*Quest'estate **andrò** al mare.*
*Questa sera **vado** al cinema.*

Adverbs

Adverbs modify verbs, other adverbs or adjectives.
Adverbs are formed from adjectives by adding **-mente** to the feminine form of verbs ending in **-o**:

adjective   →   *adverb*
tranquillo   →   **tranquillamente**
perfetto   →   **perfettamente**
sicuro   →   **sicuramente**

■ Exceptions:
Adjectives that end in **-e** form their adverbs by adding **-mente:**

cortese   →   **cortesemente**
recente   →   **recentemente**

Adjectives that end in **-re** and **-le** drop the **-e** before the suffix **-mente:**

facile   →   **facilmente**
regolare   →   **regolarmente**

▶

Please note:

*Marco è **tranquillo**.* (Marco is quiet.)
                    (*tranquillo* = *adjective*)

*Marco parla **tranquillamente**.* (Marco speaks quietly.)
                         (*tranquillamente* = *adverb*)

Comparative

The comparative of adverbs is formed as with the adjectives
with **più** (**più** *tranquillamente* = calmer, **più** *tardi* = later). The
absolute superlative is formed with **-issimo** and
-issimamente (*tranquill**issimamente*** = very calm;
*tard**issimo*** = very late).

Important irregular forms include:

bene (good)	**meglio** (better)	**benissimo** (very well)
male (bad)	**peggio** (worse)	**malissimo** (very bad)
poco (little)	**meno** (less)	**pochissimo** (very little)
molto (much)	**più** (more)	**moltissimo** (very much)

Rewrite this text in the future tense.

Exercise 1

L'estate scorsa Marina è andata in vacanza in Sardegna. È partita
con alcuni amici all'inizio di agosto. Sono andati fino a Genova in
macchina, poi hanno preso il traghetto per Olbia. Sono stati per
due settimane in un bell'albergo direttamente sul mare. Hanno
fatto molti bagni, preso molto sole e mangiato molto pesce. La
terza settimana l'hanno passata in barca a vela. È stata proprio
una bella vacanza!

L'estate prossima Marina . . . .
. . . .
. . . .
. . . .
. . . .
. . . .

Exercise 2

Complete the sentences with the verb in the future tense.

1. L'anno prossimo Marco .... la scuola. (finire)

2. Simona ...... al mare con me. (venire)

3. Luca e Matteo .... in vacanza insieme. (andare)

4. Purtroppo Maria .... lavorare tutto il giorno. (dovere)

5. Non so se anche Dario .... venire. (volere)

6. Teresa .... domani e .... tre giorni con noi. (arrivare / rimanere)

7. (Noi) .... alla fine di agosto. (tornare)

8. Anna e Marco .... a settembre. (sposarsi)

Exercise 3

Form the adverb from the adjectives by adding the suffix *-mente*.

Adjective	Adverb
sereno	....
gentile	....
tenero	....
difficile	....
lento	....
pigro	....
veloce	....
sincero	....
dolce	....

Adjective or adverb?
Choose the correct form.

gentile – gentilmente

1. Marco è una persona ....

2. Mi ha salutato molto ....

tenero – teneramente

3. Lo ha baciato ....

4. Questa carne è molto ....

corretto – correttamente

5. Questa frase è........

6. Ha risposto ....

silenzioso – silenziosamente

7. È uscito di casa ....

8. Questa zona non è molto ....

allegro – allegramente

9. Mio marito è sempre ....

10. Mi ha salutato ....

Exercise 4

Write the verbs in the correct tense.

1. Ieri Miriam .... alle otto. (tornare)

2. L'anno prossimo (io) .... in vacanza con i miei suoceri. (andare)

3. Da bambina (io) .... al mare con la nonna. (andare)

4. Di solito (io) .... alle 7.30. (alzarsi)

5. Dieci anni fa questa .... una città tranquilla. (essere)

6. Che cosa (tu) .... ieri sera alla TV? (vedere)

Exercise 5

7. Ieri, mentre (io) .... alla
stazione, (io) .... Andrea.
(andare – incontrare)

8. Tra dieci giorni Stefania ....
per la Francia. (partire)

9. Riccardo, ... subito qui e
.... di disturbare tua sorella!
(venire – smettere)

10. Marta non .... il tedesco.
(capire)

Exercise 6

**Arrange the
following words
into four groups.
Each group should
include four related
terms.**

dente	sposa
temporale	targa
nozze	spalla
serbatoio	pioggia
....	....
....	....
....	....
....	....
matrimonio	portiera
pancia	vento
automobile	mano
testimone	nuvola
....	....
....	....
....	....
....	....

abito *m*	dress	**lento**	slow
abito da sposa *m*	wedding gown	**lista** *f*	list
affittare	to rent	**malissimo**	very bad
affitto *m*	rent, lease	**meno**	less
allegro	happy	**moltissimo**	very much
barca a vela *f*	sail boat	**nozze** *f pl*	wedding
battesimo *m*	baptism	**peggio**	worse
bomboniera *f*	cone-shaped bag of sweets (given at weddings or baptisms)	**pigro**	lazy
		pochissimo	very little
		prima	first
		comunione *f*	communion
Caraibi *m pl*	Caribbean	**regolare**	regular
casa in affitto *f*	rented flat *Br* / apartment *Am*	**ricevimento** *m*	reception
		salutare	to greet
circa	approximately	**santo**	holy
confetto *m*	candy	**santo cielo**	good heavens
continuare	to continue		
corretto	correct, right	**Sardegna** *f*	Sardinia
cuoco *m*	cook	**silenzioso**	silent, quiet
dare un ricevimento	to have a reception	**sincero**	honest
		sposa *f*	bride
difficile	difficult	**stressarsi**	to stress (oneself)
Europa *f*	Europe	**succedere**	to happen
facile	easy	**tenero**	tender
fretta *f*	hurry	**testimone** *m/f*	witness
Genova *f*	Genoa	**traghetto** *m*	ferry
Grecia *f*	Greece	**viaggio di nozze** *m*	honeymoon
in fretta	in a hurry		
invitato *m*	guest	**villa** *f*	villa, large house
isola *f*	island		

Weddings Italian weddings are big occasions. The traditional wedding ceremony takes place in church followed by a large and opulent meal. At the end of the wedding the bride and groom hand out **bomboniere** with **confetti** as souvenirs. **Confetti** are small hard candies consisting of an almond covered with sugar icing. For the wedding they have to be white.

Bomboniere are small cones full of **confetti** and decorated with ribbons or flowers. For weddings they usually come with a little silver present. Such presents play an important role at weddings and Italians spend considerable amounts of money on them. Keeping a gift list **(liste nozze)** at a department store or with a relative is also a common custom in Italy.

By the way, **confetti** are also given out at **battesimi** (baptisms) and **prime comunioni** (communion) where they are wrapped in pink (for girls) or light blue (for boys).

Progetti

Com'è triste partire! Per Alessandra i tre mesi che ha passato in Italia sono volati. Quanti ricordi da mettere in valigia: la gita a Firenze, il fine settimana a Lerici, le serate con gli amici, la famiglia Simoni! Alessandra spera di rivedere presto le persone che ha conosciuto in Italia e soprattutto Marco... Sì, Marco è sicuramente la persona di cui sentirà di più la mancanza... Ma Alessandra ha già tanti progetti: innanzitutto in settembre tornerà in Italia per due settimane, in vacanza. Ha intenzione di andare in Sardegna, naturalmente con Marco. Ma due settimane non le bastano. I colleghi con cui ha lavorato a Milano sono proprio gentili e simpatici e le piacerebbe continuare a lavorare con loro. Ha già parlato con il suo capo e forse potrà lavorare a Milano per tutto l'inverno. Chissà cosa diranno i suoi genitori?!

Plans for the future

How sad it is to leave! The three months in Italy have just whizzed by for Alexandra! She'll be carrying lots of memories back home in her suitcase: the trip to Florence, the weekend in Lerici, the evenings spent with friends, the Simoni family! Alexandra hopes that she will soon be able to see all the people she got to know in Italy, most of all Marco ... Yes, Marco certainly is the person she will miss the most ... But Alexandra has already made many plans: First of all she is going to return to Italy for a two-week holiday in September. She intends to travel to Sardinia, with Marco, of course. However, two weeks aren't enough for her. The colleagues she worked with in Milan are very nice and she would like to continue working with them. She has already spoken with her boss and she might be able to work in Milan over the winter. Who knows what her parents will say about that?!

Relative clauses

The relative pronoun **che** can be used either as a subject or as a direct object (nominative and accusative). It is invariable relating to the *feminine* and *masculine* in the *singular* and *plural*.

– *La ragazza **che** parla è mia sorella.*
  (The girl who speaks is my sister.)
– *Il ragazzo **che** vedi è mio fratello.*
  (The boy whom you see is my brother.)

The pronoun **cui** is used with prepositions. It is invariable as well.
– *La ragazza con **cui** parli è mia sorella.*
  (The girl with whom you are speaking is my sister.)
– *Il ragazzo a **cui** ho dato il libro è mio fratello.*
  (The boy to whom I gave the book is my brother.)

The relative pronouns **che** and **cui** can be substituted by **il quale/la quale, i quali/le quali** (usually after prepositions). In this case, gender and number must agree. The article must not be omitted:
– *I ragazzi con **i quali** parli sono i miei fratelli.*
– *La ragazza con **la quale** parli è mia sorella.*
– *Le ragazze con **le quali** parli sono le mie sorelle.*

Che or ***cui***?
Fill in the correct
relative pronoun.

1. Il libro .... ho letto mi è piaciuto molto.

2. Maria è la ragazza con .... vado
   in ufficio.

3. Ho letto la lettera .... ti ha scritto
   Mario.

4. Non conosco la persona di .... parli.

5. Il ragazzo .... sta bevendo la birra
   è Paolo.

6. Questi sono i regali .... mi ha fatto
   Simona.

7. L'automobile con .... sei venuto è
   nuova.

8. Questo è il motivo per .... non sono
   venuto.

Exercise 1

Replace the relative
pronoun *cui* from
exercise 1 by using
the appropriate
form of *il quale/la
quale*.

2. ....

4. ....

7. ....

8. ....

Exercise 2

Connect the two
sentences with an
appropriate relative
pronoun.

Il ragazzo sta uscendo dalla farmacia.
Lui è Marco.
→ Il ragazzo che sta uscendo dalla
farmacia è Marco.

1. Oggi Marisa va da un'amica. L'amica
   abita davanti al mio ufficio.

   ....

2. Federica ha molti mobili antichi. Li ha
   comprati a Londra.

   ....

Exercise 3

3. Andiamo a casa di una mia collega. Lei è appena tornata dalle vacanze.

. . . .

4. Ieri ho perso l'ombrello. Tu mi hai regalato l'ombrello a Natale.

. . . .

5. Stamattina ho incontrato Marco. Mi ha invitato a cena.

. . . .

6. Alexandra prende il treno. Il treno parte alle ore 6.50.

. . . .

Exercise 4

Using the introductory phrase, form six sentences by combining each relative clause (1-6) with the appropriate statement (a-f).

Marco è il ragazzo ...

1. di cui   **a** Alexandra esce più spesso.

2. a cui   **b** Alexandra è innamorata.

3. con cui   **c** Alexandra scrive ogni giorno.

4. a cui   **d** Alexandra ha deciso di tornare a Milano.

5. di cui   **e** Alexandra pensa tutto il giorno.

6. per cui   **f** Alexandra parla sempre.

. . . .

. . . .

. . . .

. . . .

. . . .

. . . .

Form opposite pairs, as shown in the example.

chiaro	allegro	scuro	triste
presto	poco	*male*	amaro
veloce	*bene*	tanto	tardi
difficile	dolce	lento	facile

amaro	bitter	**rivedere**	to see/meet again
capo *m*	boss		
innanzitutto	first of all	**sentire la**	to miss
progetto *m*	project, plan	**mancanza di**	someone
ricordo *m*	memory, recollection	**qualcuno**	

Empty promises?

For outsiders, Italians seem to make promises they often don't keep. In reality, however, those promises are regarded rather as "good intentions". They are often made in emotional moments, such as when parting company, and they represent spontaneous expressions of good will. Occasionally, they are also born out of a sense of duty, but it is rarely possible to carry them out.

Exercise 1: **1.** Valentina è a casa con la nonna. **2.** Paolo è un amico di Valentina. **3.** No, mi dispiace, non sono Alexandra, sono Silvia. **4.** Alexandra è la ragazza bionda con la valigia. **5.** Questo non è Paolo, questo è Stefano.

Exercise 2: 1-d; 2-e; 3-a; 4-b; 5-c.

Exercise 3: **1.** Scusi, Lei è Marina Valenti? No, mi dispiace, sono Stefania De Vito. **2.** Questo è Stefano, vero? No, questo è Paolo, un amico di Valentina. **3.** Alexandra è un po' stanca per il viaggio. **4.** Alexandra è la ragazza bionda con la valigia. **5.** Stefano non è alla stazione ma a casa con la nonna.

Exercise 4: **1.** è **2.** è **3.** siamo **4.** sono **5.** è **6.** siete **7.** sono.

Exercise 5: **1.** Questa non è Valentina. **2.** La mamma non è stanca. **3.** Non siamo alla stazione. **4.** Paolo e Marco non sono a scuola. **5.** Il viaggio non è lungo. **6.** Voi non siete biondi. **7.** Stefano e Paolo non sono a casa.

Exercise 6: **1.** è **2.** la **3.** stanca **4.** viaggio **5.** benvenuta **6.** Ciao **7.** bene **8.** grazie **9.** Sei **10.** un po' **11.** Questo **12.** è **13.** questo **14.** è **15.** Piacere **16.** Piacere

Exercise 1: **1.** sta **2.** stai **3.** sto **4.** sta **5.** sta **6.** stanno **7.** state **8.** sta

Exercise 2: 1-e; 2-f; 3-b; 4-c; 5-a; 6-d.

Exercise 3: Formell: 2; 3; 5; 7. Informell: 1; 4; 6.

Exercise 4: **1.** ha **2.** ha **3.** ha **4.** hanno **5.** hai

Exercise 5: **1.** Sto bene, grazie. **2.** (Lui) è a casa con la nonna. **3.** No, questo non è Marco, questo è Paolo. **4.** Sì, sono molto stanca. **5.** No, lei non è tedesca.

Exercise 6: **1.** come **2.** sorda **3.** anni

Exercise 7: 1-c; 2-e; 3-f; 4-g; 5-d; 6-a; 7-h; 8-b.

Exercise 8: **1.** italiano **2.** inglese **3.** svizzero **4.** italiana **5.** spagnole **6.** giapponese **7.** francesi

Exercise 1: **1.** la; le porte (door) **2.** il; i letti (bed) **3.** il; i quadri (picture) **4.** la; le sedie (chair) **5.** la; le poltrone (armchair) **6.** il; i tappeti (carpet) **7.** la; le tavole (table)

Exercise 2: **1.** la; le chiavi (key) **2.** il; i bicchieri (glass)
3. la; le televisioni (TV) **4.** il; i giornali (newspaper) **5.** la; le madri
(mother) **6.** il; i padri (father)

Exercise 3: **1.** l' **2.** il **3.** l' **4.** il **5.** l' **6.** lo **7.** la **8.** l'
9. la **10.** la **11.** l' **12.** la

Exercise 4: **1.** un **2.** una **3.** una **4.** un **5.** uno **6.** uno **7.**
una **8.** un' **9.** un **10.** un' **11.** un **12.** un

Exercise 5: C'è un armadio, un letto, un tappeto, una televisione,
una poltrona, un giornale, un tavolo.
Ci sono due sedie, tre quadri, sei bicchieri.

Exercise 6: **1.** Il frigorifero è pieno. **2.** La camera di Valentina non
è grande. **3.** La casa di Simona è bella. **4.** Marco è gentile.
5. La zia di Valentina è gentile. **6.** Alexandra è tedesca e bionda.
7. La stazione è grande. **8.** Gli appartamenti sono grandi.

Lesson 4

Exercise 1: guardare; mangiare; abitare; io guardo, mangio, abito;
Carla guarda, mangia, abita; Valentina e Franco guardano, mangiano,
abitano.

Exercise 2: **1.** gioca **2.** ama **3.** parlano **4.** parlo **5.** suoni
6. lavora **7.** abita **8.** guardiamo **9.** amate **10.** lavoro

Exercise 3: **1.** fa **2.** fanno **3.** fai **4.** fa **5.** fate **6.** facciamo

Exercise 4: è; italiana; abita; Ha; è; sportiva; Parla; suona; fa;
mangia; Guarda; fa; fa; abitano; sono; gentili.

Exercise 5: Paolo è un amico di Valentina. (Lui) abita a Milano. Ha
25 anni. È sportivo. Parla italiano e non suona la chitarra. Mangia molti
dolci e guarda la televisione.

Exercise 6: tredici; trentotto; cinquantaquattro; diciannove;
ventisette; quarantasei; settantasette; novantadue; quaranta, ventitré,
ottantuno; settantadue; sessantasei; cinquantasette; novantanove;
sessantuno.

Lesson 5

Exercise 1: **1.** capire **2.** tornare **3.** finire **4.** vendere
5. sentire **6.** prendere **7.** vedere **8.** guardare **9.** lavorare
10. credere

Exercise 2: 1-e; 2-d; 3-b; 4-a; 5-c; 6-f.

Exercise 3: **1.** sentono **2.** torna **3.** preferisce **4.** guardano
5. Capisci **6.** pulisce **7.** Prendete **8.** arriva

Exercise 4: **1.** sente **2.** capite **3.** guardo **4.** preferiscono
5. dorme **6.** abitano

Exercise 5: (Tu) capisci il francese, dormi molto e guardi la tv.
Stefano e Valentina non capiscono il francese, dormono molto e non
guardano la tv. La nonna capisce il francese, non dorme molto e
guarda la tv.

Exercise 6: **1.** No, torna tardi. **2.** No, sente la musica. **3.** No, preferisce l'acqua. **4.** Sì, parla tedesco molto bene. **5.** Sì, ho fame.

Exercise 7: **1.** 894 **2.** 635 **3.** 227 **4.** 3976 **5.** 1.690.400 **6.** 1750 **7.** 3.130.000 **8.** 667.766

Lesson 6

Exercise 1: **1.** dà **2.** scegliete **3.** tengo **4.** paghiamo **5.** giocano **6.** sale **7.** dici **8.** Paghi, pago

Exercise 2: 1-b; 2-d; 3-e; 4-c; 5-a; 6-g; 7-f.

Exercise 3: Orizzontali: 4. dico 5. dicono 8. paghiamo 9. tengo 11. salgo 12. sceglie 13. salite 14. giochi
Verticali: 1. dai 2. tenete 3. scelgono 4. dà 5. diamo 6. pagate 7. giochiamo 10. date

Exercise 4: **1.** Le valigie sono leggere. **2.** I film sono interessanti. **3.** Le foto sono molto belle. **4.** Le arance sono buone. **5.** I medici sono bravi. **6.** Gli amici di Marco sono simpatici. **7.** Gli armadi sono grandi. **8.** I laghi sono vicini.

Exercise 5: 1. Preferisci acqua o vino? / Vino, grazie. / Ecco. Allora cin-cin! 2. I genitori stanno bene? / Sì grazie, sono in vacanza. / Che bello! 3. Dov'è la cucina? / La cucina è qui a destra. Hai fame? / No, grazie, non ancora.

Lesson 7

Exercise 1: **1.** Quando **2.** Che cosa **3.** Dove **4.** Quanti **5.** Perché **6.** Chi **7.** Che / Quale **8.** Come

Exercise 2: **1.** Facciamo spesso una passeggiata. **2.** Non mangio mai gli spaghetti. **3.** Marco legge sempre il giornale. **4.** Qualche volta lavoro il sabato. **5.** Viaggiamo raramente.

Exercise 3: fumo, fumi, fuma, fumiamo, fumate, fumano; chiudo, chiudi, chiude, chiudiamo, chiudete, chiudono; apro, apri, apre, apriamo, aprite, aprono.

Exercise 4: **1.** settantasette **2.** centosettantanove **3.** duemilacentocinquanta **4.** dodicimilanovecento **5.** centoventisette **6.** quindicimilaseicento

Exercise 5: **1.** la mamma, le mamme **2.** lo spagnolo, gli spagnoli **3.** l'animale, gli animali **4.** il bagno, i bagni **5.** l'aranciata, le aranciate **6.** la vacanza, le vacanze **7.** la televisione, le televisioni **8.** l'appartamento, gli appartamenti **9.** il bar, i bar **10.** la valigia, le valigie

Exercise 6: **1.** Le signore hanno due macchine. **2.** Gli appartamenti sono piccoli. **3.** I gatti stanno bene. **4.** I libri sono interessanti. **5.** Le ragazze giocano a tennis. **6.** Mangiamo sempre le pizze. **7.** Le amiche di Mara sono gentili.

Exercise 1: **1.** vanno **2.** vado **3.** va **4.** vai **5.** andiamo **6.** va **7.** andate

Exercise 2:

_	v	e	n	g	o	_	_	v
_	_	_	_	i	_	_	_	e
_	_	_	n	_	_	_	_	n
_	_	e	v	i	e	n	e	i
_	i	_	_	_	_	_	t	
v	e	n	i	a	m	o	_	e
_	_	v	e	n	g	o	n	o

Exercise 3: **1.** a, in **2.** di, a **3.** a **4.** da **5.** in **6.** a

Exercise 4: **1.** stanno **2.** guardo **3.** vengono **4.** sei **5.** andate **6.** ama **7.** hanno **8.** prende **9.** facciamo

Exercise 5: 1-e; 2-c; 3-b; 4-a; 5-d.

Exercise 6: **1.** tavolo **2.** ragazza **3.** Germania **4.** aranciata **5.** grazie

Exercise 1: mi alzo / vado / mi vesto / faccio / porto / vado / sono / lavoro / faccio / prendo / mi riposo / leggo / mangio / gioco / guardo / vado / vado / mi addormento

Exercise 2: **1.** Mario è medico e va a lavorare alle otto e un quarto. **2.** Franca è cameriera e va a lavorare alle quattro del pomeriggio. **3.** Silvia è insegnante e va a lavorare alle otto e mezza. **4.** Andrea è architetto e va a lavorare alle nove e un quarto. **5.** Francesco è cantante e va a lavorare alle dieci. **6.** Teresa è infermiera e va a lavorare alle sette meno un quarto. **7.** Sara è dentista e va a lavorare alle nove e mezza.

Exercise 3: **1.** si addormenta **2.** si svegliano **3.** ci alziamo; ci vestiamo **4.** mi chiamo **5.** vi riposate

Exercise 4: **1.** le sette meno venticinque **2.** le nove e tre **3.** le nove e un quarto **4.** mezzanotte; **5.** mezzogiorno meno venti **6.** l'una e mezza **7.** le tre e dieci **8.** mezzogiorno **9.** le otto.

Exercise 5: **1.** Alexandra non prende la metropolitana ma va in ufficio a piedi. **2.** Valentina si alza alle sette, si lava e poi fa colazione. **3.** Dopo cena la famiglia Masi guarda un film alla televisione. **4.** La nuova amica di Alexandra si chiama Laura. **5.** A mezzanotte Alexandra va a letto perché è stanca.

Exercise 1: **1.** la mia **2.** Il mio **3.** mia **4.** i miei / **1.** tuo
2. tua **3.** le tue **4.** Tuo / **1.** le nostre **2.** i nostri **3.** La nostra
4. I nostri / **1.** La vostra **2.** le vostre **3.** Il vostro **4.** le vostre

Exercise 2: **1.** i loro **2.** i suoi **3.** i suoi **4.** la loro **5.** sua
6. i loro.

Exercise 3: 1-d; 2-e; 3-f; 4-b; 5-a; 6-c.

Exercise 4: Il tuo amico Marco beve un caffè. / Tu bevi un'aranciata.
/ Paola beve un martini. / Voi bevete un tè. / Andrea e Luca bevono
una cioccolata. / Noi beviamo un cognac. / Io bevo un'acqua minerale.
/ I miei genitori bevono un cappuccino.

Exercise 5: **1.** ottantanove **2.** centoquarantasei **3.**
millecinquecentottanta **4.** centoventimila **5.** trecentosettantasei
6. cinquemilioni trecentomila **7.** duemilaseicentodieci **8.**
ventunmila

Exercise 6: **1.** letto, lampada, sedia, tavolo **2.** metropolitana,
autobus, macchina, treno **3.** zio, figlia, fratello, nonno **4.** broccoli,
insalata, zucchini, arancia

Exercise 1: voglio, posso, devo, devo, so.

Exercise 2: vuole, può, deve, deve, sa. / vogliono, possono, devono,
devono, sanno.

Exercise 3: **1.** volete, dovete **2.** Vogliono **3.** posso, devo
4. sappiamo **5.** Puoi **6.** So

Exercise 4: al, alla, al, allo / della, dell', degli / dal, dalla, dai /
nella, nel, nei / sul, sul, sulla

Exercise 5: **1.** a, in **2.** al, con i/coi **3.** di, a **4.** al, di

Exercise 6: Lunedì pomeriggio alle quattro e mezza Giovanni va dal
medico. / Martedì sera Giovanni va a teatro. / Mercoledì pomeriggio
alle sette e mezza gioca a tennis. / Giovedì sera va all'opera. / Venerdì
mattina alle undici e un quarto fa una passeggiata nel parco. / Sabato
pomeriggio all'una va a pranzo da Carla. / Domenica pomeriggio alle
quattro va alla partita di calcio.

Exercise 1: **1.** guardato **2.** leggere **3.** scritto **4.** chiudere
5. dormito **6.** aprire **7.** stato **8.** suonare **9.** preso **10.** visitare

Exercise 2: **1.** fatto **2.** sentito **3.** andati **4.** preso **5.** lavorato
6. stata **7.** arrivati **8.** chiuso

Exercise 3: **1.** ha guardato **2.** sono andato/a **3.** hai sentito
4. siete tornati/e **5.** hanno preso **6.** è venuto **7.** abbiamo aperto
8. sono arrivati/e

Exercise 4: **1.** ho risposto **2.** hai chiesto **3.** ha perso
4. ha scritto **5.** abbiamo messo

Exercise 5: Dopo colazione Alberta è andata in chiesa e Francesco
ha fatto una passeggiata in centro. All'una sono andati insieme a
pranzo dalla zia di Alberta. Al pomeriggio Francesco ha letto un libro e
Alberta ha scritto alcune lettere. Alle otto sono andati a teatro e poi a
cena in un ristorante messicano. Sono arrivati a casa alle undici e
mezzo e sono andati subito a letto.

Exercise 6: **1.** sul **2.** in **3.** nell' **4.** a **5.** di **6.** dai **7.** con
8. alla **9.** dallo **10.** del

Lesson 13

Exercise 1: arrivare, essere, andare, lavarsi, tornare, riposarsi,
costare.

Exercise 2: sono nata; si sono trasferiti; ho frequentato; ho studiato;
sono diventata; mi sono sposata; siamo andati; abbiamo comprato;
sono nate; ho lavorato

Exercise 3: Alle sette e un quarto ha fatto la doccia. / Alle sette e
mezza ha preso un caffè. / Alle otto è andata in ufficio in macchina. /
A mezzogiorno e mezzo ha mangiato in mensa. / All'una e mezza ha
fatto una passeggiata. / Alle cinque è andata in centro. / Alle sette è
tornata a casa. / Alle otto e mezza ha cenato. / Alle undici è andata a
letto. / Alle undici e un quarto si è addormentata.

Exercise 4: **1.** Quando è nato lo zio Giovanni? **2.** Quando è andata
in America? **3.** Quando hanno pranzato? **4.** Quando avete letto il
giornale?

Exercise 5: **1.** da **2.** di **3.** dal **4.** in **5.** alle

Exercise 6: 1-c; 2-a; 3-e; 4-d; 5-b.

Lesson 14

Exercise 1: del; del; della; del; dei; delle; dell'; dello; delle; degli.

Exercise 2: **1.** gli **2.** mi **3.** mi **4.** le **5.** ti **6.** vi **7.** ci **8.** gli

Exercise 3: **1.** gli **2.** ne **3.** ne **4.** Le **5.** le **6.** gli

Exercise 4: **1.** Mi piacciono **2.** mi piace **3.** Mi piace **4.** Mi piace
5. mi piacciono **6.** Mi piace

Exercise 5: 1-d; 2-a; 3-c; 4-e; 5-b.

Lesson 15

Exercise 1: **1.** Lo **2.** Le **3.** vi **4.** ti **5.** mi **6.** ci

Exercise 2: **1.** la **2.** le **3.** lo **4.** li **5.** lo **6.** la

Exercise 3: **1.** lo **2.** le **3.** li **4.** gli **5.** La **6.** Le **7.** Gli
8. le

Exercise 4: **1.** I nonni vanno a vedere un film al cinema. **2.** Nadia non ha tempo di suonare il pianoforte. **3.** Preferiscono mangiare in pizzeria. **4.** Aiuto i miei genitori a pulire l'appartamento. **5.** Nicola non ha voglia di andare a scuola.

Lesson 16

Exercise 1: **1.** chiudi **2.** scrivete **3.** porta **4.** racconta **5.** dormi **6.** telefoni **7.** vieni **8.** da' / dai **9.** dica **10.** abbiate **11.** vai / va' **12.** fai / fa'

Exercise 2: **1.** Faccia **2.** fumi **3.** Mangi **4.** Prenda **5.** Dorma **6.** beva **7.** Vada **8.** mangi

Exercise 3: Business: 1, 3, 4, 6. Private: 2, 5.

Exercise 4: **1.** È accanto alla banca. **2.** È vicino alla chiesa, dietro alla pizzeria. **3.** È vicino al parcheggio, dietro al supermercato. **4.** È accanto alla pizzeria, vicino alla farmacia. **5.** È vicino alla farmacia. **6.** È tra la banca e il supermercato.

Exercise 5: **1.** Il cinema è in fondo alla strada. **2.** Il ristorante è di fronte alla scuola. **3.** La casa di Luca è dietro alla chiesa. **4.** La panetteria è accanto al negozio di abbigliamento. **5.** La farmacia è tra il supermercato e la banca.

Exercise 6: 1-f; 2-c; 3-a; 4-b; 5-d; 6-e.

Lesson 17

Exercise 1: **1.** eccola **2.** Eccoli **3.** eccola **4.** eccolo **5.** Eccomi **6.** Eccoci **7.** Eccole

Exercise 2: **1.** La mangio. **2.** Lo devo comprare./Devo comprarlo. **3.** Che cosa le regali? **4.** La vuoi anche tu? **5.** Gli piace molto la musica jazz. **6.** È meglio prenderlo. **7.** Anche Alessandra li mangia. **8.** Gli piace giocare a tennis.

Exercise 3: **1.** te lo regala **2.** non glieli porta **3.** se li lava sempre **4.** Te li porta **5.** te la scrivo **6.** te le do

Exercise 4: **1.** Piero gliela racconta. **2.** Il signor Cattaneo gliela scrive. **3.** Andrea glielo chiede. **4.** La mamma glielo insegna. **5.** Glielo presento.

Exercise 5: Buongiorno! Un biglietto per Bologna, per favore. / Di seconda classe. / Scusi, sa a che ora parte il prossimo treno? / Molte grazie. Arrivederci.

Lesson 18

Exercise 1: **1.** Lavala! **2.** Non lavarla con l'acqua calda! **3.** Tagliala! **4.** Mettila in un'insalatiera! **5.** Condiscila con olio, aceto, pepe e sale. **6.** Assaggiala! **7.** Portala in tavola! **8.** Mangiala!

Exercise 2:   **1.** La lavi!   **2.** Non la lavi con l'acqua calda!   **3.** La tagli!   **4.** La metta in un'insalatiera!   **5.** La condisca con olio, aceto, pepe e sale.   **6.** L'assaggi!   **7.** La porti in tavola!   **8.** La mangi!

Exercise 3:   **1.** Bevilo! – Lo beva!; Provalo! – Lo provi!; Assaggialo! – Lo assaggi!; Compralo! – Lo compri!; Pagalo! – Lo paghi; Prendilo! – Lo prenda!; Guardalo! – Lo guardi!;   **2.** Provale! – Le provi!; Comprale! – Le compri!; Pagale! – Le paghi; Prendile! – Le prenda!; Guardale! – Le guardi!;   **3.** Mangiali! – Li mangi!; Provali! – Li provi!; Assaggiali! – Li assaggi!; Comprali! – Li compri!; Pagali! – Li paghi; Prendili! – Li prenda!; Guardali! – Li guardi!;   **4.** Compralo! – Lo compri!; Pagalo! – Lo paghi; Prendilo! – Lo prenda!; Guardalo! – Lo guardi!; Leggilo! – Lo legga!

Exercise 4:   **1.** la apra   **2.** mangiala   **3.** fumala   **4.** non comprarla   **5.** la chiuda   **6.** leggila

Exercise 5:   **1.** Portala in officina!   **2.** Scrivile una lettera!   **3.** Compralo!   **4.** Puliscilo!   **5.** Regalale un mazzo di fiori.

Exercise 6:   **1.** fammi   **2.** dammi   **3.** dammi   **4.** Dimmi   **5.** Dammi   **6.** dammi

Exercise 7:   1-h; 2-f; 3-d; 4-e; 5-a; 6-b; 7-c; 8-g.

Lesson 19

Exercise 1:   **1.** parlando   **2.** dando   **3.** dicendo   **4.** vedendo   **5.** pulendo   **6.** incontrando   **7.** venendo

Exercise 2:   **1.** Piera si sta vestendo in camera sua.   **2.** Zia Carla sta partendo per le vacanze.   **3.** Stiamo andando a fare la spesa al supermercato all'angolo.   **4.** Sta facendo i compiti.   **5.** Stanno telefonando a Carla per dirle di venire più tardi.   **6.** Stai ascoltando le notizie alla radio.

Exercise 3:   **1.** le sto telefonando adesso   **2.** si sta alzando adesso   **3.** le sto scrivendo adesso   **4.** lo stiamo bevendo adesso   **5.** sta uscendo adesso   **6.** lo sto preparando adesso

Exercise 4:   **1.** non va   **2.** –   **3.** non voglio   **4.** non ha invitato   **5.** –   **6.** Non sono   **7.** –   **8.** Non vuole

Exercise 5:   **1.** di   **2.** a – in   **3.** di   **4.** di – all'   **5.** di – al   **6.** di   **7.** di   **8.** a – alle

Exercise 6:   1-e; 2-d; 3-b; 4-a; 5-c.

Lesson 20

Exercise 1:   **1.** Sì, l'ho già letto.   **2.** L'ho sentita stamattina.   **3.** No, non l'ho ancora fatta.   **4.** Le ho comprate al mercato.   **5.** Sì, l'ho già vista.   **6.** Sì, li ho già provati.   **7.** Li ho conosciuti a Firenze.

Exercise 2:   **1.** o   **2.** o   **3.** a   **4.** o   **5.** o   **6.** a   **7.** a   **8.** a   **9.** a   **10.** a   **11.** a

Exercise 3: Ieri Alexandra si è svegliata alle 9.00. Alle 10.00 ha fatto una passeggiata con Piera. Alle 12.30 ha pranzato in casa. Alle 14.00 ha guardato la tv. Alle 19.00 è venuto Marco e l'ha portata a cena al ristorante „Le tre noci". A mezzanotte è andata a letto.

Exercise 4: **1.** la **2.** Gli **3.** te la **4.** li **5.** l' **6.** ti **7.** lo **8.** la **9.** gli **10.** le

Exercise 5: Ieri Roberto si è alzato presto. Ha fatto colazione in un bar e poi è andato in ufficio. Alle 11.00 gli ha telefonato Cristina e gli ha chiesto di andare a pranzo insieme. Così si sono incontrati alle 12.30 al ristorante „Al Mulino" e hanno mangiato una bella insalata. Poi Roberto è tornato in ufficio. Alle 18.00 è uscito ed è andato a casa di Mariella. Loro hanno chiacchierato un po' e poi sono andati al cinema. Dopo il cinema sono andati in un bar e a mezzanotte sono tornati a casa.

Exercise 6: Studia; pulisci; non ascoltare; fa' / fai; porta; leggi; va' / vai; non fumare; ascolta.

Exercise 7: dove abita? / Dov'è nata? / Quanti figli ha? / Lavora? / A che ora si alza la mattina? / A che ora comincia a lavorare? / Dove mangia a mezzogiorno? / A che ora finisce di lavorare?

Exercise 8: Francesca Rinaldi è nata a Foggia il 7 ottobre 1958. Dal 1964 al 1972 ha frequentato la scuola elementare e media a Foggia e dal 1973 al 1978 il liceo a Bari. Nel 1979 ha sposato Fabrizio De Santi. Dal 1980 al 1986 ha lavorato come impiegata alle poste di Bari. Nel 1986 è nata sua figlia Cristina. Dal 1990 al 1995 ha lavorato ancora come impiegata alle poste di Bari e nel 1995 è nato suo figlio Luca.

Lesson 21

Exercise 1: andavo; accompagnava; restava; tornava; doveva; andavamo; era; facevamo; andavamo; era; giocavamo; telefonavamo; raccontavamo

Exercise 2: **1.** mangiava **2.** tornava – ha incontrato **3.** usciva **4.** aveva **5.** aspettava – è svenuta **6.** guardavo – è arrivato **7.** piaceva

Exercise 3: **1.** Ieri, mentre dormivo, ha suonato il telefono **2.** Ieri, mentre bevevo il caffè, è arrivata la mia collega. **3.** Ieri, mentre facevo la maglia, è entrato un gatto. **4.** Ieri, mentre lavoravo, il mio collega ha fumato una sigaretta.

Exercise 4: **1.** dal **2.** durante **3.** da **4.** per **5.** Mentre **6.** A – Alle **7.** Tra

Exercise 5: 1-b; 2-c; 3-a; 4-c.

Lesson 22

Exercise 1: **1.** Il cappotto è più elegante della giacca. **2.** L'aereo è più comodo del treno. **3.** La lambada è più moderna del valzer. **4.** I pantaloni sono più pratici della gonna. **5.** L'inglese è più facile dell'italiano.

Exercise 2:   **1.** Mi piace di più andare a piedi che andare in macchina.   **2.** Mi piace di più la mia bicicletta della tua.   **3.** Mi piace di più Venezia di Bologna.   **4.** Mi piace di più suonare il pianoforte che andare a un concerto.   **5.** Mi piace di più il cappuccino del tè.

Exercise 3:   **1.** Qual è il vino più buono della Germania?   **2.** Qual è la montagna più alta del mondo?   **3.** Qual è il film più bello dell'anno?   **4.** Qual è il ristorante peggiore della città?   **5.** Qual è il vestito più bello del negozio?

Exercise 4:   bello specchio / bei quadri / begli armadi / bella casa / bell'ufficio / belle poltrone

Lesson 23

Exercise 1:   **1.** si va   **2.** si conoscono   **3.** si fa   **4.** si leggono   **5.** si fanno   **6.** si mangia

Exercise 2:   **1.** si può   **2.** si deve   **3.** si vuole, si deve   **4.** si può   **5.** si può, si vuole   **6.** si può

Exercise 3:   **2.** Mi sono messo/a il cappotto perché faceva freddo.   **3.** Ho mangiato un hamburger perché avevo fame.   **4.** Ho preso l'ombrello perché pioveva.   **5.** Non sono andato/a al cinema perché ero stanco/a.   **6.** Ho comprato dei fiori perché era il compleanno di Pia.   **7.** Ho fatto una passeggiata perché faceva bello.   **8.** Ho bevuto una birra perché avevo sete.

Exercise 4:   Hai visto / eravamo / abbiamo deciso / abbiamo fatto / faceva / nuotavamo / abbiamo visto / è rimasta / doveva.

Exercise 5:   **1.** A Torino è sereno, c'è il sole, fa bello.   **2.** A Venezia c'è il sole, è nuvoloso.   **3.** A Pisa è nuvoloso, è coperto.   **4.** A Roma è coperto, è nuvoloso.   **5.** A Bari piove.   **6.** A Catania piove.   **7.** A Cagliari ci sono temporali.

Exercise 6:   ristorante messicano; pesce fresco; viaggio lungo; fragola dolce; vestito verde; acqua naturale.

Exercise 7:   **1.** bianco   **2.** blu   **3.** rossi   **4.** giallo   **5.** bianco, rosso   **6.** verde

Lesson 24

Exercise 1:   **2.** Fai / Fa' ginnastica   **3.** Nuota   **4.** Fai / Fa' un massaggio /   **2.** Vada a letto   **3.** Mangi qualcosa   **4.** Vada dal medico /   **1.** Prendi un tè   **2.** Mettiti a letto   **3.** Non prendere freddo

Exercise 2:   **1.** quella   **2.** Quei   **3.** quell'   **4.** quelle   **5.** quegli   **6.** quel   **7.** quello

Exercise 3:   **1.** Quella   **2.** questo, questo, quello   **3.** Quelle, quelle, Quelle

Exercise 4:   **1.** regista   **2.** discoteca   **3.** fame   **4.** mano   **5.** scarpe

Exercise 5:   Vorrei qualcosa contro il mal di testa. / Quante ne devo prendere? / Grazie. / No, grazie. Quanto fa? / Arrivederci.

Exercise 1:   **1.** loro; Lei; lui   **2.** a me   **3.** Noi; a te; me   **4.** a voi

Exercise 2:   **1.** senza di voi   **2.** da te   **3.** a lei   **4.** con lui
5. sotto di te   **6.** per loro

Exercise 3:   Buona serata! Buona Pasqua! Buona fortuna! Buon compleanno! Buone vacanze! Buon viaggio! Buon Anno!

Exercise 4:   **1.** tennis   **2.** sci   **3.** nuoto   **4.** pallavolo   **5.** calcio

Exercise 5:   Buongiorno. / Vorrei avere alcune informazioni sui corsi. / Purtroppo posso solo la sera. / Quanto costa il corso? / E devo fare un test? / No, vengo la settimana prossima. Molte grazie e arrivederci.

Exercise 1:   **1.** alzerei; andrei; pulirei; inizierei; farei; andrei   **2.** resterei; guarderei; leggerei; farei; andrei; cucinerei; vorrei   **3.** dormiremmo, faremmo, andremmo, incontreremmo, giocheremmo, andremmo

Exercise 2:   Tu: Faresti un lungo viaggio. Smetteresti di lavorare. Compreresti una casa. Andresti a vivere in America. Aiuteresti i bambini poveri. /   Alexandra: Farebbe un lungo viaggio. Comprerebbe una casa. Andrebbe a vivere in America. Aiuterebbe i bambini poveri. / Piera e Luigi: Farebbero un lungo viaggio. Smetterebbero di lavorare. Comprerebbero una casa. Aiuterebbero i bambini poveri.

Exercise 3:   **1.** potrebbe   **2.** dispiacerebbe   **3.** Vorrei   **4.** sapresti
5. potreste   **6.** porterebbe   **7.** Potrebbe

Exercise 4:   A: Ho deciso: domenica andiamo a Firenze. B: Ma non ci siete stati un mese fa? A: Sì, ci siamo stati per lavoro. B: E perché domenica ci volete ritornare? A: Perché Firenze è una città molto interessante. B: Noi invece andiamo a Como. Perché non venite anche voi? A: Non ho voglia, ci sono stata anche domenica scorsa. B: Ah sì? E con chi ci sei andata? A: Ci sono andata con dei colleghi.

Exercise 5:   1-b; 2-e; 3-a; 4-f; 5-d; 6-c.

Exercise 1:   **1.** ci vuole/occorre   **2.** ci vogliono/occorrono
3. ci vogliono/occorrono   **4.** ci vuole/occorre   **5.** ci vuole/occorre
6. ci vogliono/occorrono   **7.** ci vogliono/occorrono
8. ci vogliono/occorrono

Exercise 2:   **1.** Ci vuole/Occorre   **2.** Ci vogliono/Occorrono
3. Bisogna   **4.** ha bisogno di   **5.** ha bisogno di   **6.** bisogna
7. bisogna

Exercise 3:   Un cucchiaio è sotto la sedia / sulla sedia / accanto ai piatti / nella tazza / dietro la bottiglia / sul forno

Exercise 4:   **1.** alla   **2.** –; –   **3.** a   **4.** alla   **5.** al

Exercise 5:   A = Valentina B = nonna C = Alexandra D = papà
E = Stefano F = mamma.

Exercise 6: **1.** Non ci vuole un chilo di zucchero ma un etto. **2.** Bisogna ammorbidire la colla di pesce in acqua fredda. **3.** Non bisogna bollire il latte e la panna. **4.** Giusto. **5.** Alla fine non bisogna mettere tutto in forno ma in frigorifero per sei ore.

Exercise 7: mattino, pomeriggio, sera, notte / lunedì, martedì, mercoledì, giovedì, venerdì, sabato, domenica / gennaio, fabbraio, marzo, aprile, maggio, giugno, luglio, agosto, settembre, ottobre, novembre, dicembre / primavera, estate, autunno, inverno.

Lesson 28

Exercise 1: **1.** tutte **2.** ogni **3.** nessuno **4.** tutto **5.** tutti, niente **6.** qualche **7.** qualcosa

Exercise 2: **1.** da **2.** di **3.** di, da **4.** – **5.** di **6.** di, da

Exercise 3: **1.** tutta la **2.** tutte e **3.** tutto il **4.** tutti gli **5.** tutto il **6.** tutti e

Exercise 4: **1.** Ieri non è arrivato nessuno dalla Spagna. **2.** Non vorrei comprare niente da mangiare. **3.** Nessuno dei miei amici sa parlare inglese. **4.** Non ho letto nessun libro di Moravia. **5.** Non mi piacerebbe andare in vacanza con nessuno di voi. **6.** Non ha nessun problema con suo marito.

Exercise 5: 1-c; 2-d; 3-b; 4-e; 5-a.

Exercise 6: A: Pronto? B: Buongiorno, signora Bertoli, sono la signora Gavoni. Come sta? A: Bene, grazie, e Lei? B: Bene. Le telefono perché vorremmo invitarLa una sera a cena da noi. A: Volentieri, quando?
B: Quando ha una serata libera? A: Dunque, al martedì vado ad un corso d'inglese, ma le altre sere sono libera. B: Le andrebbe bene venerdì? A: Sì, benissimo, a che ora? B: Alle 8.00? A: Benissimo, a venerdì, allora. B: Sì a venerdì! Arrivederci.

Lesson 29

Exercise 1: andrà; Partirà; Andranno; prenderanno; Staranno; Faranno; prenderanno; mangeranno; passeranno; Sarà.

Exercise 2: **1.** finirà **2.** verrà **3.** andranno **4.** dovrà **5.** vorrà **6.** arriverà, rimarrà **7.** torneremo **8.** si sposeranno

Exercise 3: serenamente; gentilmente; teneramente; difficilmente; lentamente; pigramente; velocemente; sinceramente, dolcemente.

Exercise 4: **1.** gentile **2.** gentilmente **3.** teneramente **4.** tenera **5.** corretta **6.** correttamente **7.** silenziosamente **8.** silenziosa **9.** allegro **10.** allegramente

Exercise 5: **1.** è tornata **2.** andrò **3.** andavo **4.** mi alzo **5.** era **6.** hai visto **7.** andavo, ho incontrato **8.** partirà **9.** vieni, smetti **10.** capisce

Exercise 6: **1.** dente, spalla, pancia, mano **2.** temporale, pioggia, vento, nuvola **3.** nozze, sposa, matrimonio, testimone **4.** serbatoio, targa, automobile, portiera

Exercise 1:   **1.** che   **2.** cui   **3.** che   **4.** cui   **5.** che   **6.** che
7. cui   **8.** cui

Exercise 2:   **2.** la quale   **4.** della quale   **7.** la quale   **8.** il quale

Exercise 3:   **1.** Oggi Marisa va da un'amica che abita davanti al mio ufficio.   **2.** Federica ha molti mobili antichi che ha comprato a Londra.
3. Andiamo a casa di una mia collega che è appena tornata dalle vacanze.   **4.** Ieri ho perso l'ombrello che tu mi hai regalato a Natale.
5. Stamattina ho incontrato Marco che mi ha invitato a cena.   **6.** Alexandra prende il treno che parte alle ore 6.50.

Exercise 4:   1-b; 2-c; 3-a; 4-e; 5-f; 6-d.

Exercise 5:   chiaro – scuro; presto – tardi; veloce – lento; difficile – facile; allegro – triste; poco – tanto; bene – male; dolce – amaro.

Vocabulary

Here is a list of all of the vocabulary that you have encountered throughout the book.

A

a base di	on the basis of
a buon mercato	cheap
a casa	at home
a causa di	because of
a dire la verità	to be honest, tell the truth
a disposizione	at one's disposal
a notte	per night
a piedi	on foot
a più tardi	see you later
a posto	in order, OK
a presto	see you soon
a proposito	by the way
a righe	striped
abbastanza	enough, pretty much
abbigliamento *m*	clothing
abbronzato	tanned
abitare	to live
abito da sposa *m*	wedding dress
accanto a	besides
accendere	to turn on
accessorio *m*	accessory
accidenti	Damn it!
accompagnare	to accompany
accostare	to pull over
aceto *m*	vinegar
ACI	Italian motorist club
acqua *f*	water
acqua minerale naturale *f*	non-carbonated mineral water
addormentarsi	to fall asleep
adesso	now
aereo *m*	aeroplane *Br* / airplane *Am*
affascinante	fascinating
affittare	to rent
affitto *m*	rent, lease
aggiungere	to add
agosto *m*	August
aiutare	to help
aiuto *m*	help

albicocca *f*	apricot
alcuni	a few
alfabeto *m*	alphabet
all'aperto	outdoors
alla salute	to your health
alla stazione	at the station
allegro	happy
allora	so, then
almeno	at least
alto	high
altrettanto	to you too
altrimenti	otherwise
altro	others
alzarsi	to get up
amare	to love
amaro	bitter
ambientarsi	to settle in
ambiente *m*	atmosphere
America *f*	America
americano	American
amicizia *f*	friendship
amico *m*	friend (male)
ammorbidire	to soften up
anch'io	me too
anche	also
ancora	still, yet
andare	to go, drive
andare via	to leave
andata e ritorno	return *Br* / round-trip *Am* ticket
andiamo	let's go
angelo *m*	angel
angolo *m*	corner
angora *f*	angora wool
animale *m*	animal
anni trenta	thirties
anno *m*	year
annoiarsi	to be bored
annuncio pubblicitario *m*	advertisement
antico	old, antique
antifurto *m*	antitheft device
antipatico	unpleasant
anzi	on the contrary

apparecchiare	to set
appetito *m*	appetite
appuntamento *m*	appointment
aprile *m*	April
aprire	to open
arancia *f*	orange
architetto *m*	architect
argentino *m*	Argentinian
aria *f*	air
arrabbiato	angry, upset
arrivare	to arrive
arrivederci	goodbye
arrosto *m*	roast
asciugamano *m*	towel
ascoltare	to listen, hear
asilo nido *m*	day care/nursery
asparago *m*	asparagus
aspettare	to wait
aspirina *f*	aspirin
assaggiare	to taste, try
assolutamente	absolutely
attendere	to wait
attento	attentive, attention
attenzione *f*	attention, care
attimo *m*	moment
attore *m* / attrice *f*	actor (*male/female*)
augurio *m*	wish
austriaco *m*	Austrian
autobus *m*	bus
autunno *m*	autumn *Br* / fall *Am*
avanti	come in
avere	to have
avere voglia	to want to do
avventura *f*	adventure
azzurro	blue

B

bacione *m*	big kiss
baffi *m pl*	moustache
balcone *m*	balcony
ballare	to dance
bambino *m*	child
bambola *f*	doll
banana *f*	banana
banca *f*	bank
bar *m*	(coffee) bar
barca *f*	boat, ship
barca a vela *f*	sail boat
basso	low
bastare	to suffice, be enough
batteria *f*	battery

battesimo *m*	baptism
beige	beige
bene	good, fine
benissimo	excellent
benvenuto	welcome
benzina *f*	petrol, gasoline
benzinaio *m*	attendant (at a petrol *Br* / gas *Am* station)
bere	to drink
bianco	white
bibita *f*	drink
biblioteca *f*	library
bicicletta *f*	bicycle
biglietto *m*	ticket
biondo	blond
birra *f*	beer
birreria *f*	pub, bar
biscotto *m*	biscuit *Br* / cookie *Am*
bisogna	you need to
blu	blue
bocca *f*	mouth
bollire	to boil
bomboniera *f*	box of sweets (given at weddings, baptism, etc.)
borsa *f*	bag
bottiglia *f*	bottle
braccio *m*	arm
bravo	good
broccolo *m*	broccoli
bruciare	to burn
brutto	ugly
budino *m*	pudding
buonanotte	good night
buonasera	good evening
buongiorno	good day, hello
buono	good
bustina *f*	packet

C

cabina telefonica *f*	telephone booth
caffè *m*	coffee
calcio *m*	football *Br* / soccer *Am*
caldo	warm
cambiare	to change, switch
camera doppia *f*	double room
camera matrimoniale *f*	room with a double bed
camera singola *f*	single room
cameriera *f*	waitress

cameriere *m*	waiter
camicetta *f*	blouse
camicia *f*	shirt
camminare	to walk, go on foot
camoscio *m*	suede
campionario *m*	sample catalogue
campo *m*	field
canale *m*	channel
candela *f*	candle
cane *m*	dog
cantante *m/f*	singer
cantare	to sing
caotico	chaotic
capello *m*	hair
capire	to understand
capo *m*	boss
cappotto *m*	coat
cappuccino *m*	coffee (with frothy milk)
Caraibi *m pl*	Caribbean
caramella *f*	sweets *Br* / hard candy *Am*
carino	kind, nice
carne *f*	meat
caro	dear
carota *f*	carrot
carte *f pl*	cards
cartolina *f*	postcard
casa *f*	house, flat *Br* / apartment *Am*
casa in affitto *f*	rental flat *Br* / apartment *Am*
casalinga *f*	housewife
cassetto *m*	drawer
cattivo	nasty, mean, bad
cellulare *m*	mobile *Br* / wireless *Am* phone
cena *f*	dinner
cenare	to eat dinner
centro *m*	centre
cercare di	to try
cerchio *m*	circle
cerotto *m*	plasters/band-aids
certamente	certain(ly)
certo	certainly, sure
cestino *m*	basket/punnet
che	which/who/that
Che bello!	How nice!
che cosa	what
Che fortuna!	Lucky you!
Che ora è?	What time is it?

Che sorpresa!	What a surprise!
chi	who
chiacchierare	to chat
chiamarsi	to call
chiaro	bright
chiedere	to ask
chiesa *f*	church
chilo *m*	kilo(gramme)
chirurgo *m*	surgeon
chissà	who knows
chitarra *f*	guitar
chiudere	to close
chiuso	closed
ci	there
ci vediamo	we'll see each other
ci vuole/ci vogliono	you need to
ciao	hello, goodbye
cielo *m*	sky
ciliegia *f*	cherry
cin-cin	cheers
cinema *m*	cinema
cinese	Chinese
cioccolata *f*	hot chocolate
cipolla *f*	onion
circa	approximately
città *f*	city, town
classe *f*	class
classico	classic(al)
cofano *m*	bonnet *Br* / (engine) hood *Am*
cognata *f*	sister-in-law
cognato *m*	brother-in-law
cognome *m*	surname
colazione *f*	breakfast
colla di pesce *f*	sheet gelati
collega *m /f*	colleague
collezione *f*	collection
collo *m*	neck
colore *m*	colour
coltello *m*	knife
come	how
Come stai/sta?	How are you? (informal/formal)
cominciare	to start
commedia *f*	comedy
commissione *f*	errand
comodo	comfortable
compito *m*	homework
compleanno *m*	birthday
comprare	to buy

comprendere	to consist of, understand
compreso	inclusive
comunale	municipal
con	with
con me	with me
concerto *m*	concert
condire	to prepare (salad)
confermare	to confirm
confetto *m*	candy
conoscere	to know, get to know
conoscersi	to get to know one another
consigliare	to advise
consiglio *m*	advice
contadino *m*	farmer
contento	happy,
continuare	to drive on/continue
conto *m*	bill *Br* / check *Am* (in restaurant)
contro	against, for
controllare	to control
coperto	overcast
corretto	correct, right
corso *m*	course, class
corto	short
cosa *f*	cause, matter
così	so
costare	to cost
costoso	expensive
costume da bagno *m*	bathing suit
cotto	cooked
credere	to believe
crema da sole *f*	suntan lotion
cucchiaio *m*	spoon
cucinare / cuocere	to cook
cugino *m*	cousin
cuoco *m*	cook

D

d'accordo	agreed
da queste parti	in this area
da solo	alone
da tre anni	since three years
Dai!	Come on!
dal... al...	from...to...
dare	to give
dare (al cinema)	to show, (in the cinema)
dare soddisfazione	to please (someone)

dare un ricevimento	to have a reception
dare un'occhiata	to take a look
data *f*	date
data di nascita *f*	date of birth
davanti a	before
decidere (di)	to decide
decorare	to decorate
dente *m*	tooth
dentifricio *m*	toothpaste
dentista *m*/*f*	dentist
dentro	inside, in
depressione *f*	depression
depresso	depressed
desiderare	to wish, desire
d'estate	in the summer
d'inverno	in the winter
di	from
di buon'umore	in a good mood
di corsa	in a hurry
di fianco a	next to
di fronte a	opposite
di nascosto	secretly
di persona	personally
di sicuro	certainly
di solito	normally
diario *m*	diary
dicembre *m*	December
dieta *f*	diet
dietro a	behind
difficile	difficult
dimagrire	to lose weight
dimenticare	to forget
dintorni *m pl*	surrounding area
dipingere	to paint
dire	to say
direttamente	directly
direttore *m*	director
discoteca *f*	disco, nightclub
disinserire	to switch off
disordine *m*	disorder
disperato	desperate
disperazione *f*	despair
disponibile	available
disturbare	to disturb
disturbi *m pl*	ailment, symptoms
disturbo *m*	disturbance
dito *m*	finger
ditta *f*	company
diventare	to become
diverso	different
divertente	funny, amusing

Vocabulary

divertirsi	to have fun, enjoy
divieto di sosta	no parking
dizionario *m*	dictionary
doccia *f*	shower
dolce *m*	sweets *Br* /candy *Am*
dolcissimo	very sweet
domani	tomorrow
domenica *f*	Sunday
dopo	after(wards)
dormire	to sleep
dottore *m*	GP *Br* / doctor *Am*
dove	where
dovere	to have to, must
dritto	straight ahead
dunque	well then
durante	during

E

e	and
e così via	and so on
ecco	here/there is
eccoci	here we are
eccola	here she is
economia *f*	economics
ed	and
edicola *f*	newsstand
efficace	effective
elegante	elegant
emigrare	to emigrate
emozionato	excited
emozione *f*	excitement
entrare	to enter
erba *f*	grass
esame *m*	exam, test
espresso *m*	espresso
essere	to be
essere fortunato	to be lucky
essere in ritardo	to be late
essere raffreddato	to have a cold
estate *f*	summer
etto *m*	100 grammes
euforia *f*	euphoria
euforico	euphoric
Europa *f*	Europe

F

fa freddo	it is cold
fa caldo	it is warm
facile	easy
facilmente	easily
fame *f*	hunger

famiglia *f*	family
famoso *f*	famous
fare	to do
far bene	to do good
far piacere	to enjoy
fare amicizia	to make friends
fare attenzione	to pay attention, watch out
fare il pieno	to fill up
fare la doccia	to take a shower
fare la maglia	to knit
fare la spesa	to go shopping
fare le vacanze	to spend a holiday *Br* / go on vacation *Am*
fare quattro salti	to go for a dance
fare un giro per negozi	to go for a stroll through the city
farmacia *f*	chemist's *Br* / pharmacy *Am*
farmacista *m* /*f*	chemist *Br* / pharmacist *Am*
faro *m*	headlight
faticoso	exhausting
fattore protettivo *m*	protection factor (of sunscreen)
fattoria *f*	farm
favola *f*	story
favore *m*	favour
febbraio *m*	February
febbre *f*	fever
felice	happy, content
felicità *f*	happiness
ferie *f pl*	holidays
festa *f*	holiday, feast
festeggiare	to celebrate
fidanzato	engaged
fidanzato *m*	fiancé
figlia *f*	daughter
figlio *m*	son
film *m*	film, movie
finalmente	at last, finally
fine *f*	end
finestra *f*	window
finire	to end
fino a	until
fiore *m*	flower
focaccia *f*	flat bread
forchetta *f*	fork
forno *m*	oven
forse	maybe
forte	strong

fortuna *f*	fortune
foto *f*	photo
fotografia *f*	photo
fra	between
fragola *f*	strawberry
frana *f*	disaster, catastrophe
francese	French
francobollo *m*	postage stamp
fratello *m*	brother
freno *m*	brake
freno a mano *m*	hand brake
frequentare	to visit
fresco	fresh
fretta *f*	hurry
frutta *f*	fruit
fruttivendolo *m*	fruit vendor
fumare	to smoke
funzionare	to function
fuoco *m*	fire

G

galleria *f*	gallery
gamba *f*	leg
gatto *m*	cat
gelatina *f*	gelatine
gelato misto *m*	mixed ice cream
gemello *m*	twin
genere *m*	kind, genre
genitori *m pl*	parents
gennaio *m*	January
Genova *f*	Genoa
gentile	nice, friendly
gettone *m*	telephone
già	already
giacca *f*	jacket
giallo	yellow
giapponese	Japanese
giardino *m*	garden
ginecologo *m*	gynaecologist
ginnastica *f*	gymnastics
ginocchio *m*	knee
giocare	to play
giocare a pallavolo	to play volleyball
giocare a tennis	to play tennis
giornata *f*	day
giorno *m*	day
giovane	young
giovedì *m*	Thursday
giovinezza *f*	youth
girare	to turn
giro *m*	stroll, tour

gita *f*	trip
giugno *m*	June
giusto	correct, right
goccia *f*	drop
golf *m*	golf
gonna *f*	skirt
grammo *m*	gram
grazie	thank you
grazie mille	many thanks
Grecia *f*	Greece
grigio	grey
grissino *m*	breadstick
gruppo *m*	group
guadagnare	to earn
guardare	to look
guasto *m*	breakdown
guerra *f*	war
guidare	to drive (car)
gusto *m*	taste

H

ha 83 anni	he/she is 83 years old
hai proprio ragione	you are absolutely right

I

ideale	ideal
ieri	yesterday
il tempo vola	time flies
imbarazzato	embarrassed
imbarazzo *m*	embarrassment
imparare	to learn
impegnativo	demanding
impegno *m*	appointment
impiegata *f*	employee
in fretta	in a hurry
in mezzo a	in the middle of
in montagna	in the mountains
in ogni caso	in every case
in questi giorni	these days
in tinta unita	uni-coloured
incontrare	to meet
incontrarsi	to meet
inconveniente *m*	inconvenience
infermiera *f*	nurse
informarsi	to inform oneself
informazione *f*	information
inglese	English
iniziare	to start
inizio *m*	start, beginning
innamorato (di)	in love (with)
innanzitutto	first of all

Vocabulary

insalata *f*	salad, lettuce
insegnante *m / f*	teacher
insieme	together
intendere	to intend
intensivo	intensive
intenzione *f*	intention
interessante	interesting
interessare	to interest
interesse *m*	interest
inutile	useless
invalido *m*	disabled person
invece	rather, on the other hand
inverno *m*	winter
invitare	to invite
invitato *m*	guest
invito *m*	invitation
isola *f*	island
italiano	Italian

L

l'altro ieri	day before yesterday
là	there
lago *m*	lake
lampada *f*	lamp
lana *f*	wool
lasagne *f pl*	lasagne
lasciare	to leave (behind)
latte *m*	milk
lattina *f*	can
lavanderia *f*	laundry
lavare	to wash
lavarsi	to wash oneself
lavorare	to work
lavorare come	to work as
leggere	to read
lento	slow
lettera *f*	letter
lezione *f*	lesson
lì	there
libero	free
libertà *f*	freedom
libreria *f*	bookshop
libro *m*	book
liceo *m*	secondary school (high school)
lingua *f*	language
lista *f*	list
litigare	to quarrel
litro *m*	litre
lo stesso	anyway, nevertheless

locale *m*	restaurant, bar
luglio *m*	July
luna *f*	moon
lunedì *m*	Monday
lungo	long
luogo *m*	place
luogo di nascita *m*	place of birth

M

ma	but
Ma figurati!	Oh please!
macchina *f*	car
macchina da scrivere *f*	typewriter
macchina da corsa *f*	racing car
macellaio *m*	butcher
macelleria *f*	butcher's
magari	maybe
maggio *m*	May
maglia *f*	knitting
maglione *m*	pullover *Br* / sweater *Am*
mai	never
mal di gola *m*	sore throat
male	bad
male *m*	pain, ache
malinconia *f*	melancholy
malinconico	melancholic
malissimo	very bad
mamma *f*	mother, mum
mancare	to lack, miss
mancia *f*	tip
mandare	to send
mangiare	to eat
mangiare di gusto	to enjoy eating
mano *f*	hand
mare *m*	sea
marito *m*	husband
marmellata *f*	jam
marrone	brown
martedì *m*	Tuesday
marzo *m*	March
massaggio *m*	massage
matita *f*	pencil
matrimonio *m*	wedding
mattina *f* / mattino *m*	(early) morning
maturità *f*	secondary school exam
maturo	ripe
mazzo *m*	bouquet (flowers)
media	(here:) half a litre of beer
medicina *f*	medicine, drugs

medicinale *m*	medicine, drugs	naso *m*	nose
medico *m*	doctor	Natale *m*	Christmas
meglio	better	natura *f*	nature
melanzana *f*	aubergine *Br* / eggplant *Am*	naturalmente	naturally
		ne	some, any, of (something)
meno	less		
meno male	thank goodness	neanche	not even
mensa *f*	cafeteria	nebbia *f*	fog
mentre	while	necessario	necessary
meraviglioso	wonderful	negozio *m*	shop, store
mercato *m*	market	nemmeno	not even
mercoledì *m*	Wednesday	neppure	not even
mese m	month	nero	black
messaggio *m*	message	nervoso	nervous
messicano	Mexican	nessuno	no one
metropolitana *f*	subway	nevicare	to snow
mettere	to put	niente	nothing
mettersi a dieta	to go on a diet	niente di speciale	nothing special
mezz'ora	half hour	nipote *m* / *f*	grandchild, niece, nephew
mezzanotte *f*	midnight		
mezzo	half	no	no
mezzogiorno *m*	midday	noce *f*	nut
mi dispiace	I am sorry	noioso	boring
militare *m*	soldier	nome *m*	name
minestrone *m*	minestrone, vegetable soup	non	not
		non ancora	not yet
minuto *m*	minute	non c'è male	not bad
mio	my, mine	non fa per me	(that's) not for me
miracolo *m*	miracle	non importa	it doesn't matter, it's not important, that's OK
moda *f*	fashion		
modello *m*	model		
moderno	modern	non lo so	I don't know
moglie *f*	wife	non nessuno	no one
moltissimo	very much	non vedo l'ora	I can hardly wait
molto	much, plenty	nonna *f*	grandmother
momento *m*	moment	nonni *m pl*	grandparents
mondo m	world	nonno *m*	grandfather
montagna *f*	mountain	normale	normal
morire	to die	nostalgia *f*	homesickness
motore *m*	engine, motor	notizia *f*	news
movimentato	(here:) exciting	notte *f*	night
mulino *m*	mill	novembre *m*	November
museo *m*	museum	nozze *f pl*	wedding
musica *f*	music	nulla	nothing
musica lirica *f*	opera music	numero *m*	number
muso *m*	snout, mouth,	nuotare	to swim
		nuoto *m*	swimming
N		nuovo	new
nascere	to be born	nuvola *f*	cloud
nascita *f*	birth	nuvoloso	cloudy
nascondersi	to hide (oneself)		

Vocabulary

O

o	or
occhiali da sole *m pl*	sunglasses
occhiata *f*	view, look
occhio *m*	eye
occupato	occupied
oculista *m / f*	ophthalmologist
officina *f*	repair shop
offrire	to offer
oggi	today
ogni	everybody
ognuno	every(one)
olio *m*	oil
oltre a	except
ombrello *m*	umbrella
omeopatico	homeopathic
onomastico *m*	name day
opera *f*	opera
opinione *f*	opinion
oppure	or
ora	now
ora *f*	hour
ora di punta *f*	rush hour
orario *m*	schedule
orario di apertura *m*	opening hours
orecchio *m*	ear
organizzare	to organize
ormai	now
orologio *m*	clock, watch
ospedale *m*	hospital
ottimo	excellent
ottobre *m*	October

P

pacco *m*	package
padella *f*	saucepan
paese *m*	village, country(side)
pagare	to pay
palestra *f*	gym
palla *f*	ball
pancia *f*	abdomen
pane *m*	bread
panetteria *f*	bakery
panna *f*	cream
pantaloni *m pl*	trousers *Br* / pants *Am*
papà *m*	father
parabrezza *m*	windscreen *Br* / windshield *Am*
paraurti *m*	bumper
parcheggiare	to park

parcheggio *m*	parking space
parco *m*	park
parecchio	rather much
parlare	to speak
parrucchiere *m*	hairdresser
partire	to leave
partita *f*	match, game
Pasqua *f*	Easter
passaporto *m*	passport
passare	to go by (time), to connect with
passare a prendere	to pick up, collect
passeggiata *f*	walk
pasta *f*	pasta
pasticceria *f*	pastry shop
pastiglia *f*	pill, tablet
pasto *m*	meal
patata *f*	potato
patente *f*	driving licence *Br* / driver's license *Am*
paura *f*	fear
pausa *f*	break, pause
pazienza *f*	patience
pecora *f*	sheep
pecorella *f*	lamb
pediatra *m / f*	pediatrician
peggio	worse
pelle *f*	leather
pendolare *m*	commuter
pensare	to think
pensionato *m*	retiree/senior citizen
pensione *f*	guesthouse
pentola *f*	pot
pepe *m*	pepper
peperone *m*	paprica
per cena	for dinner
per favore	please
per il viaggio	because of the journey
per questo	therefore
perché	why, because
perdere	to lose, miss
perdonare	to forgive
perfetto	perfect
pericoloso	dangerous
periodo *m*	time, period
permesso	May I?
però	but
persistere	to last, persist
persona *f*	person
pesante	heavy
pescatore *m*	fisherman

pesce *m*	fish
petto *m*	chest
piacere	to like, enjoy, pleasure to meet you
pianoforte *m*	piano
piatto *m*	plate, dish
piazza *f*	square
piccolo	small
pigro	lazy
pioggia *f*	rain
piombo *m*	lead
piovere	to rain
piscina *f*	swimming pool
pisello *m*	pea
più	more
più veloce	quicker, faster
piuttosto	rather
pizza *f*	pizza
pneumatico *m*	tyre *Br* / tire *Am*
pochissimo	very little
poco	a little
polizia *f*	police
pomeriggio *m*	afternoon
pomodoro *m*	tomato
ponte *m*	bridge
popolare	popular
porcellino *m*	piglet
portare	to bring
portare fuori	to take out
portiera *f*	car door
posata *f*	silverware
posta *f*	post *Br* / mail *Am*
posto *m*	position, place
potere	to be able / allowed to
povero	poor
poverino	poor thing
pranzare	to eat lunch
pranzo *m*	lunch
praticare	to practise, exercise,
pratico	practical
precedente	previous
preferire	to prefer
preferito	favourite
prego	you're welcome, my pleasure, please
prendere	to take
prendere il sole	to lie in the sun
prenotare	to book, reserve
preparare	to prepare
presentare	to present, introduce

pressione *f*	pressure
presto	soon
prete *m*	priest
prezzo *m*	price
prima	before
prima colazione *f*	breakfast
prima comunione *f*	first communion
primavera *f*	spring (time)
primo *m*	(here:) first course
problema *m*	problem
professore *m*	professor
progetto *m*	project, plan
programma *m*	program
proibire	to forbid, prohibit
promettere	to promise
pronto	ready, hello (on the phone)
proprio	straight, exact
prosciutto *m*	ham
prossimo	next
protestare	to protest
provare	to try (out)
pulire	to clean
puntuale	on time
pure	if you want
purtroppo	unfortunately

Q

quaderno *m*	exercise book
qualche	some
qualche volta	sometimes
qualcosa	something
qualcuno	someone
quale	which
quando	when, if
quanto	how much
Quant'è?	How much is it?
Quanto Le devo?	How much do I owe you?
quartiere *m*	neighbourhood
questo/questa	this
qui	here
qui vicino	nearby

R

rabbia *f*	anger
racchetta *f*	(tennis) racket
raccontare	to tell, narrate
radio *f*	radio
raffreddare	to cool off
raffreddore *m*	cold, flu

Vocabulary

ragazza *f*	girl	sapere	to know
ragazzo *m*	boy, young man	saporito	tasty
raramente	seldom	Sardegna *f*	Sardinia
regalare	to give (as a present)	sbagliare	to err, be mistaken
regalo *m*	gift, present	sbagliare strada	to get lost
regista *m* / *f*	(film) director	scala *f*	stair
regolare	regular	scaldare	to warm/heat up
restare	to stay	scappare	to flee, run away
ricamare	to stitch, embroider	scarpa *f*	shoe
ricco	rich	scarpa da	gymnastics shoes
ricetta *f*	recipe	ginnastica *f*	
ricevimento *m*	reception	scegliere	to choose, select
richiamare	to call back	scena *f*	scene
riconoscere	to recognize	scherzare	to joke
ricordo *m*	memory, recollection	schiena *f*	back
ridotto	discounted	sci *m*	skiing
	admission ticket	sciare	to go skiing
rilassante	relaxing	sciocco	stupid
rimandare	to postpone	sciroppo *m*	syrup
rimanere	to stay	sconto *m*	reduction
ringraziare	to thank	scontrino fiscale *m*	sales receipt
rionale	local	scoppiare	to burst, break out
ripetere	to repeat	scoppia la guerra	the war breaks out
riposarsi	to rest	scorso	past
riposo *m*	rest	scottarsi	to burn oneself
rispondere	to answer	scozzese	Scottish
risposta *f*	answer	scritta *f*	inscription
ristorante *m*	restaurant	scrivania *f*	desk
ritardo *m*	delay	scrivere	to write
riunione *f*	meeting	scrivere a	to write with a
riuscire	to succeed	macchina	typewriter
rivedere	to see/meet again	scriversi	to write
romantico	romantic	scuola *f*	school
rosa	pink	scuola elementare *f*	elementary school
rosso	red	scuola materna *f*	kindergarten
rotto	broken	scuola media *f*	middle school
		scuola	vocational school
S		professionale *f*	
sabato *m*	Saturday	scuro	dark
salare	to salt	scusa	excuse me
sale *m*	salt	scusi	excuse me
salire	to go/come up	secondo *m*	second, second course
salti	dance	secondo me	to my mind
saltimbocca alla	Roman style veal cutlet	sedile *m*	seat
romana *f*		segretaria *f*	secretary
salutare	to greet	seguire	to follow
salute *f*	to your health	semaforo *m*	traffic lights
saluto *m*	greeting	sembrare	to seem
sano	healthy	semplice	simple
santo	holy	sentire	to hear, feel
santo cielo	good heavens	sentire la mancanza	to miss someone

di qualcuno	
senz'altro	definitely
senza	without
senza piombo	unleaded
sera *f*	evening
serata *f*	evening
serbatoio *m*	petrol *Br* / gas *Am* tank
serenità *f*	comfort, harmony
sereno	clear, bright, calm, peaceful
servire	to serve
seta *f*	silk
sete *f*	thirst
settembre *m*	September
settimana *f*	week
severo	strict
sfilata di moda *f*	fashion show
si	one
sì	yes
sicuramente	certain
sicuro	certain(ly), sure
sigaretta *f*	cigarette
signora *f*	woman, lady
silenzioso	silent, quiet
simpatico	likeable
sincero	honest
smettere	to stop
soccorso stradale *m*	road service
socio *m*	member
soddisfatto	content
soddisfazione *f*	contentment, satisfaction
soldi *m pl*	money
solo	only, alone
sopra	over, above
soprattutto	above all
sordo	deaf, hard of hearing
sorella *f*	sister
sorpresa *f*	surprise
sostanza *f*	substance
sotto	below, under(neath)
sottovoce	quietly
spagnolo	Spanish, Spaniard
spalla *f*	shoulder
specchio *m*	mirror
speciale	special
specialista *m* / *f*	specialist
spegnere	to arrange, agree
sperare	to hope
spesa *f*	shopping

spesso	often
spettacolo *m*	show, presentation
spia *f*	control light
spiaggia *f*	beach
spiegare	to explain
splendido	marvellous
sport *m*	sport
sportivo	sporty, athletic
sposa *f*	bride
sposare/sposarsi	to marry
squadra *f*	team
squisito	delightful, exquisite
stadio *m*	stadium
stanco	tired
stanco morto	dead tired
stanza *f*	room
stare	to stay, remain
stasera	tonight
statua *f*	statue
stazione *f*	train station
stesso	the same
stoffa *f*	fabric
stomaco *m*	stomach
storia *f*	history
strada *f*	street
strano	strange, unusual
strega *f*	witch
stressarsi	to stress (oneself)
studiare	to study, learn
stupendo	wonderful
subito	immediately
succedere	to happen
succo di frutta *m*	fruit juice
sul lago	at the lake
sul mare	by the sea
sull'angolo	at the corner
suocera *f*	mother-in-law
suocero *m*	father-in-law
suonare	to play (an instrument), to ring
supermercato *m*	supermarket
superstizioso	superstitious
supplemento *m*	surcharge
svedese	Swedish, Swede
sveglia *f*	alarm clock
svegliarsi	to wake up
svenire	to faint
svizzero	Swiss

T

tacco *m*	heel

Vocabulary

tagliare	to cut
tagliatelle *f pl*	tagliatelle pasta
tardi	late
targa *f*	number *Br* / licence *Am* plate
tavola *f*	dinner table
taxi *m*	taxi
tazza *f*	cup
teatro *m*	theatre
tedesco	German
telecomando *m*	remote control
telefonare	to call, phone
telefonata *f*	telephone call
telefonino *m*	mobile *Br* / wireless *Am* phone
telefono *m*	telephone
televisore *m*	TV set
tempo *m*	time, weather
tempo libero *m*	free time, leisure time
temporale *m*	thunderstorm
tenere	to hold
tenero	tender
terra *f*	earth
terrazza *f*	terrace
tessera *f*	pass, ID
test *m*	test
testa *f*	head
testimone *m* / *f*	witness
ti telefono	I'll call you
tifoso *m*	football *Br* / soccer *Am* fan
timido	timid
tipo *m*	type, manner
toccare	to touch
tornare	to return
torta *f*	layered cake
tovaglia *f*	table cloth
tra	between, in
tradurre	to translate
traffico *m*	traffic
traghetto *m*	ferry
tram *m*	tram
tranquillo	calm, quiet
trascorrere	to spend, stay
trasferirsi	to move
trattoria *f*	inn, restaurant
triste	sad
tristezza *f*	sadness
troppo	too much
trovare	to find
trovarsi	to be, feel

tutto	all, whole
tutto bene	everything's OK
tutto il giorno	the whole day
tv *f*	TV, to watch TV

U

uffa	phew
ufficio *m*	office
ufficio postale *m*	post office
ultimo	last
umore *m*	mood
un po'	a little
un po' di	a little (+noun)
un sacco di	a whole lot of
unire	to unite, add
università *f*	university
uomo *m*	human being, man
uovo *m*	egg
usare	to use
uscire	to go out
uso *m*	use
utile	useful

V

va bene	OK
vacanza *f*	vacation, holiday
valigia *f*	suitcase
vanillina *f*	vanilla, vanilla sugar
vasetto *m*	glass
vecchio	old
vedere	to watch, see
vedersi	to see (each other)
veloce	fast, quick
velocemente	quickly
velocità *f*	speed
vendere	to sell
venerdì *m*	Friday
venire	to come
venire a trovare	to come for a visit
vento *m*	wind
veramente	really
verde	green
verdura *f*	vegetable
verità *f*	truth
vero	true
vestirsi	to get dressed
vestito *m*	dress
vestito da	dressed up as
vetrina *f*	(shop) window
viaggiare	to travel, journey
viaggio *m*	journey

viaggio di nozze *m*	honeymoon
vicino	near (by)
vicino a	near
vigile *m*	traffic police
vigile del fuoco *m*	fire fighter
villa *f*	villa
vino *m*	wine
viola	violet
visitare	to visit
vista *f*	view
vita *f*	life
vitello *m*	veal
vivere	to live
volante *m*	steering wheel
volare	to fly
volentieri	gladly, like to
volere	to want
volta *f*	time
vorrei	I would like to
vostro	your

Z

zoo *m*	zoo
zucchero *m*	sugar
zucchino *m*	courgette *Br* / zucchini *Am*